# DOGME IN PRACTICE

## CLASSROOM REFECTIONS BY FELLOW TEACHERS

SCOTT THORNBURY

LUKE MEDDINGS

INTERNATIONAL
TEACHER DEVELOPMENT
INSTITUTE (iTDi)

Publisher's Cataloging-in-Publication Data

Names: Thornbury, Scott, 1950-, author. | Meddings, Luke, 1965-, author.

Title: Dogme in practice : reflections from fellow teachers around the world / Scott Thornbury; Luke Meddings.

Description: Includes bibliographical references. | Sheridan, WY: International Teacher Development Institute, 2025.

Identifiers: LCCN: 2025904929 | ISBN: 979-8-9880892-5-4 (hardcover) | 979-8-9880892-4-7 (paperback) | 979-8-9880892-6-1 (ebook)

Subjects: LCSH English language--Study and teaching--Foreign speakers. | Language and languages--Study and teaching. |BISAC LANGUAGE STUDY / English as a Second Language | EDUCATION / Teaching / Methods & Strategies | EDUCATION / Professional Development

Classification: LCC PE1128.A2 .T46 2025 | DDC 428.0071/05--dc23

ISBNs:
Paperback: 979-8-9880892-4-7
Hardcover: 979-8-9880892-5-4
Ebook: 979-8-9880892-6-1

Print and ebook formatting by Jerry Talandis Jr.
Cover design by *Getcovers*.
Paper airplane icon made by *Eight Black Dots* from www.flaticon.com

❀ Created with Vellum

# CONTENTS

# PREFACE
## THE JOURNEY SO FAR

 As I write this, Dogme ELT turns 25. That is, if you date its birthday from my article 'A Dogma for ELT' that appeared in February 2000. Or if you date it from the formation, a month later, of the Yahoo-hosted discussion forum, called *Dogme ELT*, with the by-line: *For a pedagogy of bare essentials*, and its enigmatic epigraph from Samuel Beckett's *Endgame*:

CLOVE: What is there to keep me here?
HAMM: The dialogue.

Of course, it's misleading to suggest that the principles behind Dogme were born then. In fact, initial forum posts identified a long tradition of materials-light and learner-centred pedagogies dating back to Socrates! But giving the pedagogy a name somehow validated it.

Since those first tentative steps, interest in Dogme grew rapidly. Key milestones included a rowdy panel discussion at the IATEFL conference in Brighton in 2003, the publication of our book *Teaching Unplugged* in

2009, and the first conference dedicated entirely to Dogme, held at Oxford House School in Barcelona in May 2011.

In subsequent years postings about Dogme on the Yahoo group started to tail off, suggesting that interest in Dogme might have peaked.

But it seems it hadn't. In 2018 and 2019 I ran intensive workshops in Moscow and Kiev for teachers whose understanding and commitment to Dogme principles had me struggling to keep up. The pandemic forced subsequent workshops online: in 2020 iTDi hosted what was to become the first of a series.

25 years on, it seems there's a whole new generation of teachers who are keen to embrace Dogme – as this collection of lesson accounts so persuasively demonstrates. The dialogue continues.

Revisiting my 'story' from the start of *Teaching Unplugged* reminds me that the book marked the start of a new chapter, and a new challenge, in my ELT career.

I'd been a teacher, journalist and school manager, but I hadn't done much teacher training. The enthusiastic response to our book meant I had to learn fast.

I did learn, partly by trial and error, and partly from the colleagues who participated in training days and short courses around the world.

What did I have to offer educators with years more experience than me? The power of an idea which resonated. How should I train? It needed to be true to Dogme, using a blend of framework planning and improvisation.

Training in new contexts naturally prompted deeper reflection, as trainee enthusiasms and concerns fed back into my own understanding of the approach.

I realised that teachers around the world were constrained by the same test-driven education models, and I saw how radical the idea of unplugging is in practice.

I learned that technology in the classroom is neither friend nor foe, and that it's all about how we use it. Active use makes so much sense – working up from classroom interests and language needs, finding stimulus, using online tools to capture and collate student texts. But just delivering top-down digital material takes us back where we started: not enough room for the learners and their language.

Now when I train I think in terms of 'learning space'. How can we find it, and how can we use it? Coursebooks remain crammed with content, while assessment is more corporate and atomised than ever. Students and teachers still need room to breathe and grow, and unplugging is one way to create it.

# INTRODUCTION
## SCOTT THORNBURY & LUKE MEDDINGS

As is now fairly well known, Dogme ELT was inspired by the 'back to basics' philosophy of the Dogme 95 film movement. When Lars von Trier, one of the co-founders of that movement, was asked by a colleague what Dogme was all about, he responded, 'It's to give you and me our joyful filmmaking back.'[1] The same might be said of the Dogme ELT movement: 'It's to give us our joyful teaching back.'

Indeed, the original online Dogme discussion list (which started in 2000 and continued for ten years until the list service was terminated) includes many posts that report a revived interest in, and enjoyment of, teaching – not just by teachers but also by learners. For example, a teacher in Italy wrote:

> I'm buzzing at the moment 'cos I've been lucky enough to hit on a couple of new groups who seem to have invented Dogme them-selves, and the things we're coming up with together are stunning me into a state of 'I've never loved teaching so much before – but is this

---

1.  Kelly, R. (2000). *The name of this book is Dogme 95*. Faber and Faber, p. 156.

really teaching?!'. Well, it certainly seems to be *learning* – enthusiastically and really joyfully – for all of us.

What is it, then, that takes the joy *out* of teaching and of learning? There are, of course, a multitude of factors, many of them institutional, and beyond the remit of individual teachers to change. All teachers work within constraints, to a greater or lesser degree, and most of us do not have the freedom to design our own curricula, write our own tests, or choose our own resources, let alone select our students, regulate class size or negotiate our wages and working hours.

We do have some freedom, though, in terms of how we interact with our learners, how we structure and monitor classroom activities, and how we confer a degree of agency and autonomy on our learners. This is where Dogme comes in.

From the start, Dogme placed interaction at the heart of things, consistent with Dick Allwright's argument that 'the importance of interaction is not simply that it creates learning opportunities, it is that it constitutes learning itself.'[2] To this end, and analogous with the Dogme 95 film movement's rejection of high-tech, big-budget production values, Dogme ELT started life as a metaphorical broom, sweeping aside anything in the classroom ecology that might inhibit or impoverish interaction. This ecological 'clutter' included not only the coursebook, with its endlessly reproduced menu of grammar 'McNuggets', but also intrusive and distracting technological aids, inauthentic and primarily form-focused language practice activities, prolonged sequences of teacher-led display questions, and texts and tasks that only superficially engaged the learners. Freeing the classroom space in this way – it was argued – maximised learning opportunities by 1. allowing learners more say in choosing lesson content and in initiating and controlling the classroom discourse; 2. increasing the time spent actually using language; 3. enhancing the class-

---

2.   Allwright, R. L. (1984). The importance of interaction in classroom language learning. *Applied Linguistics*, 5(2), 156–171.

room dynamic through processes of socialization; 4. orienting the curriculum towards the learners' needs and interests; and, ultimately, 5. boosting motivation, engagement, and – yes – the joy of learning.

Although Dogme was never intended to be a 'method', in the sense of a prescribed set of classroom procedures allied to a theory of learning, it did – and still does – have the potential of changing the way teachers teach, and, ultimately, of exerting pressure for curriculum reform. As Leo van Lier argued,

> Curriculum innovation … can only come about through a funda-mental change in the way educators and students interact with one another […] Reform thus occurs from the bottom up, one pedagogical action at a time.[3]

This is the thinking that underlies the first 'maxim' of Dogme teaching, i.e. that Dogme is about teaching that is *conversation-driven*. (It's worth noting that conversation can be spoken, written, and even visual – think of the variety of audio, texts, and images we share every day on messaging services). The way that teachers and students interact with one another through spoken or written communication is the foundation on which language development is constructed and on which curriculum reform is expedited – 'one pedagogical action at a time.'

The second maxim, that Dogme is about teaching that is *materials-light*, follows from the first: it does not need a great deal of kindling to light a conversational fire. Indeed, there is a long history of accounts of highly interactive teaching occurring in minimally resourced situations: see for example, those by Sylvia Ashton-Warner[4] and John Wade.[5]

The third pillar of Dogme practice, that 'Dogme is about teaching that

---

3.   van Lier, L. (1996). *Interaction in the language curriculum: Awareness, autonomy & authenticity*. Longman, p. 158.
4.   Warner, S.A. (1963/1980) *Teacher*. Virago.
5.   Wade, E.J. (1992) *Teaching without textbooks*. CIS Educational.

focuses on *emergent language'*, is the pedagogical crunch. That is to say, the success or not of Dogme as a viable pedagogical option depends on the willingness and capacity of the interlocutors (and not just the teacher) to shift attention from content to linguistic code and back again. Initially conceived as a way of implementing Mike Long's notion of 'focus-on-form' during or immediately after a communicative task,[6] the attentional shift involved in dealing with emergent language has, more recently, been validated through research into what Seedhouse and Walsh term 'classroom interactive competence' (CIC):

> CIC entails teachers being able to *shape* learner contributions by scaffolding, paraphrasing, re-iterating, and so on. Essentially, through shaping the discourse, a teacher is helping learners to say what they mean by using the most appropriate language to do so.[7]

The term 'emergent language' has now firmly established itself in teachers' discourse: witness the publication of the very Dogme-friendly resource book *Working with Emergent Language.*[8] Meanwhile, developments in second language acquisition (SLA) theory and research, particularly in what is called usage-based learning, which foregrounds the experiential, embodied, and social aspects of language learning over the purely cognitive, have provided further support to Dogme's foundational principles, especially the claim that 'learning is a social and *dialogic* process, where knowledge is co-constructed rather than "transmitted" or "imported" from teacher/coursebook to the learner'.[9]

6.   Long, M. H. (1991). Focus on form: A design feature in language teaching methodology. In K. de Bot, R. Ginsberg, & C. Kramsch (Eds.), *Foreign language research in cross-cultural perspective* (pp. 39–52). John Benjamins.
7.   Seedhouse, P., & Walsh, S. (2013). Learning a second language through classroom interaction. In P. Seedhouse, S. Walsh, & C. Jenks (Eds.), *Conceptualising 'learning' in applied linguistics.* Palgrave Macmillan, p. 141.
8.   Chinn, R., & Norrington-Davie, D. (2023). *Working with emergent language.* Pavilion ELT.
9.   Meddings, L., & Thornbury, S. (2009). *Teaching unplugged: Dogme in ELT.* Delta Publishing, p. 8.

Initially ignored or dismissed by the educational establishment, Dogme (or Teaching Unplugged) is increasingly referenced in methodology texts, especially since the 2009 publication of *Teaching Unplugged: Dogme in ELT*.[10] Mentions include Jane Spiro's *Changing Methodologies in TESOL* (Edinburgh University Press, 2013), the latest edition of Richards and Rodgers' *Approaches and Methods in Language Teaching* (Cambridge 2014), the 2015 edition of Jeremy Harmer's *The Practice of English Language Teaching* (Pearson), and (no surprise!) Scott Thornbury's 30 *Language Teaching Methods* (Cambridge 2017). And, more recently still, the authors *of English Language Teaching: Now and How It Could Be* (Geoff Jordan and Mike Long[11]) devote a section to Dogme in their final chapter, titled 'Signs of struggle: Towards an alternative organization of ELT.' In this segment, they quote Scott's contention that 'Dogme, now two decades old, has experienced a renaissance, partly as a response to the increasing commodification of ELT, including the all-pervasive grammar syllabus and the alienation effect created by the precipitate shift into online teaching.'[12] In the face of threats of this kind, including the increasing use of AI as a machine-generated source of language learning content and instruction, Dogme – with its emphasis on human interaction and organic, socially situated teaching and learning opportunities – seems to offer a kind of solution.

Despite this acceptance and the renewed interest in Dogme, the fact remains that there are few descriptions of how Dogme actually manifests itself in classroom practice. 'Yes, but what is a Dogme lesson actually like?' is a question that comes up again and again in workshops and online seminars.

Hence this book: it is designed to answer that question. Especially since the demise of the online discussion group, we have always wanted to provide an alternative platform for teachers to share how – and why –

10. Ibid.
11. Jordan, G., & Long, M. (2023). *English language teaching: Now and how it could be.* Cambridge Scholars.
12. Jordan & Long, op. cit. p. 267

they are implementing the Dogme principles in their classes. So, we have invited a worldwide array of practitioners to do exactly that: to tell us how you 'do' Dogme. The only conditions were that the lesson descriptions should situate the lesson in its local context, describe its process and outcomes, and explicitly state how the lesson enshrines Dogme principles.

What has transpired is a fascinating collection of first-person accounts from a wide range of learning contexts (young learners, online, university, one-to-one, etc) and 30 different countries (with the UK, Japan, Spain, and Brazil leading the way), but all – often ingeniously – faithful to the Dogme philosophy, whether Dogme-light or Dogme-heavy. All share an enthusiasm for teaching and for putting the learners at the heart of the process. And for retrieving the joy of teaching and learning. To quote from another post on the discontinued discussion list, a teacher in China wrote:

> I think if you tried to pin down what dogme is from my teaching alone, you'd leave thinking it isn't much of anything at all (and I still don't feel I've succeeded in adapting dogme to fit my school). But Dogme goes beyond just teaching for me, and evidently other members of the list too. The real meaning of dogme for me is that where before the things I loved about teaching were methods, techniques, and approaches, now the thing I love about it is people.

We hope you feel as inspired in reading this amazingly rich resource as we have been in compiling and commenting on it.

Thanks,

Scott and Luke

# 1

# SCAFFOLDING THE UNDER-30 BUCKET LIST
## BRUNO ALBUQUERQUE

### BRAZIL | ADULTS | A1

This was a small class of only two A1, Brazilian students, friends and workmates, who decided they needed English lessons to progress in their careers here in Brazil and, in the future, abroad. They were in their early twenties and work in an architecture office. We had been studying together for two months, meeting weekly for 45 minutes. The students were often encouraged to do extra activities between classes, such as working in the coursebook, watching TV shows in English and writing down interesting words, and communicating through a messaging app for conversation practice.

I acted as teacher, course designer, and manager all together as a one-teacher school/company. I began teaching private students shortly after taking the CELTA, and now after DELTA, I feel more confident to experiment in class and have adopted a more flexible, back-to-the-roots approach to ELT. I feel that my initial qualification gave me the necessary tools for the craft and that the diploma taught me to use those tools to make it an art. This is where Dogme ELT comes in.

I always began the classes with a chat, asking them what they did on the weekend and their plans for the week ahead. We usually had a light conversation to set the tone and "flip the switch" from Portuguese to English. This time, they told me that together they had ticked one of the items from their "before-30 bucket list". I could not let that slide.

The students explained that the bucket list was made up of things you had to do before you turned 30. I mentioned that it was unfortunate I was 32 and must have missed out on many of the items. I asked them to write down their top 5 items from their list and prepare to share them. I told them that, for that moment, I wasn't going to participate in the interaction in order to focus on my notes. After a minute, they were done with their notes and ready to share.

I asked them to share their lists and write down their friend's list to comment on it later. I thought that taking notes would foster more active and intensive listening and be an interesting way of developing listening and note-taking skills. The students shared their lists, negotiated meaning, and used the language they had at hand to talk about their bucket lists.

At some point, one of them asked, "Teacher, I like visit all capitals in Brazil?", clearly hinting at whether I would like to talk about my plans or desires for the future. I replied, "Try, 'I'd like to visit all the capitals in Brazil'". She rephrased and kept going.

Both students were then using "I'd like to..." or "I would like to talk about my bucket list." After they were done, I gave them feedback based on my notes. Mostly, I praised their use of these structures and attempts at some more interesting vocabulary such as "do an extreme sport", "go on a cruise", and "ride an off-road motorcycle". They were excited with each other's lists so I asked them to report what their friend had on their list. The idea was to allow them another shot at using the emergent language we looked into during the first feedback phase and work on fluency, as the message had already been conveyed.

Students then reported what their friends shared and I wrote their information on the board. I commented and asked some follow-up questions to expand the conversation in a scaffolded way to try and get more emergent language from them. After this wrap-up moment, I told them I had five items on my list that I would talk about for a minute or so and that they should take notes the same way they did before. I got my cellphone, set it on voice recorder, and talked into it like a microphone while students listened and took their notes.

When I was done, students checked their answers in pairs and then I sent them the audio file in our message app so they could listen to it again and check their answers. After checking, students asked me a couple of questions about my list, I answered them and we had a final feedback session before the end of the lesson.

The students seemed to enjoy these spur-of-the-moment lessons the most. It's not that they didn't enjoy our coursebook-based lessons, but they seemed much more "into it" when the lesson happened more organically as this one did. The students were eager to share their bucket lists and were also excited to learn about mine. They learned how to talk about their dreams and aspirations with language deeply connected to their immediate needs and that naturally emerged in the given context. There was work on vocabulary, grammar, speaking, listening, and note-taking skills in a well-rounded, skills-integrated lesson and all of that happened naturally because I did not shy away from improvising based on student input and my experience as a teacher.

This kind of teaching and learning experience fosters more learner and teacher agency. Learners feel that the teaching is done taking their needs and wants into account as well as who they are into account. Dogme ELT and this level of reactive teaching deeply values students' and teachers' contributions in class, creating a more democratic and less authoritarian space for learning to take place. It also deals with language from a holistic perspective, focusing on learning the language at the point of need through a conversational manner. I believe this is the kind of teaching that would make Paulo Freire and bell hooks proud.

A NOTE FROM SCOTT:

> *In his book on classroom interaction, Steve Walsh writes: "The role of the teacher is central to co-constructing a dialogue in which learning opportunities are maximised through the use of specific interactional strategies to scaffold, shape and clarify learner contributions."*[1]

> *Bruno's lesson is a good example of how this is done. But it's worth revisiting the original literature about scaffolding, and noticing that it's not just about 'tidying up' emergent language: there is a strong motivational and affective element involved too.*

> *These are what Wood, Bruner, and Ross considered to be the elements of scaffolding: "recruiting interest in the task; simplifying the task; maintaining pursuit of the goal; marking critical features and discrepancies between what has been produced and the ideal solution; controlling frustration during problem-solving; demonstrating an idealized version of the act to be performed."*[2]

> *On this last point, Bruno's use of his phone to record an 'idealized version' of the task is inspired.*

---

1. Walsh, S. (2006) *Investigating classroom discourse*. Routledge.
2. Wood, D., Bruner, J. S., & Ross, G. (1976). The role of tutoring in problem solving. *Journal of Child Psychology and Psychiatry*, 17(2), 89–100.

2

# A RAINY DAY IN JEDDAH
## ZARAFSHAN ASLAM, SYEDA

## SAUDI ARABIA | ADULTS | A1 – A2

I led a session for foundation year students at the English Language Institute of King Abdulaziz University, located in Jeddah, Kingdom of Saudi Arabia. The attendees were young women in their late teens. The course was designed for beginners, aligning with the A1 CEFR level, and catered to a diverse group of 30 students with mostly lower levels of proficiency. English, not being their subject of choice, was a requisite for them to fulfill their academic requirements and contribute to their GPA. On this particular day, the classroom was unusually quiet with only half of the enrolled students present—15 in total.

The reduced number of attendees created a more intimate setting, allowing for a personalized teaching approach. Despite their initial lack of enthusiasm for the subject, the smaller class size provided an opportunity to engage the students more deeply and address individual learning needs. This particular session became an unexpected chance to spark an interest in the English language through interactive and student-centered teaching methods. The day's unique circumstances paved the way for an enriching educational experience for both the students and myself.

At the time, the English Language Institute (ELI) operated on a modular system, with each module spanning 5 to 6 weeks. We were using the New Headway Plus series, special edition. Adhering to a weekly pacing guide was crucial, as student assessments were based on this schedule. The class began at 8:00 AM in early October. Typically, Jeddah experiences a predominantly summer climate with little to no rain. Yet, on this day, the sky was overcast from the early hours with thunder and lightning preceding the rain, which likely contributed to the low attendance. In this region, residents can have apprehension about rain due to past flooding incidents. Understandably, the students showed little interest in the lesson and wished for the class to be dismissed. However, seizing the moment, I decided to introduce Dogme teaching, assuring them that we would not have a 'textbook lesson' and wouldn't even open our textbooks, which lifted their spirits.

Having been a teacher and mentor for some time, I relish experimentation. However, the strict pacing schedule often limited such opportunities. This situation presented a perfect chance to try something new.

I invited the students to share words that described the weather, their emotions, or their thoughts about the day. As they spoke, I wrote their words on the board, and soon we had a rich vocabulary chart. Admittedly, the words varied, describing the weather, emotions, and even food and drinks.

> Afraid, loud, rain, thunder, bed, coffee, hot drinks, blanket, jacket, lightening, shower, dark, bright, happy, scared, ice cream, walk, watch TV, listen to music, read a book, go home

With a student-generated vocabulary list at hand, I divided the class into three groups of five. Their task was to create sentences using these words, reflecting their personal truths. The results were a mix of fragmented phrases and some well-constructed sentences appropriate for their level.

I like to eat ice cream in the rain.
I am afraid of thunder
We want to listen to music.
I want to stay in my blanket.
We want to go home.
I like to drink coffee now
I like walking in the rain
It is so dark
We are wearing jackets
It is not bright
We can hear thunder

Instead of having them read their sentences aloud to the class, I circulated the room to review their work. Remembering my promise that they wouldn't need to open their bags or textbooks, I distributed A4 sheets and pencils to each group.

Thirty minutes later, I introduced a new activity. I gave each group sticky notes of different colors and instructed them to write one word from their sentences on each note. After placing their notes on the wall, they stepped back, allowing other groups to rearrange the words into coherent sentences. This competitive element spurred enthusiasm and participation, even among the less active students. It was interesting to note that the kind of sentences that came out of this activity were sometimes different from the original sentences. Once completed, each group presented their sentences, and we collectively evaluated their grammatical accuracy. The group with the most correct sentences earned a point.

After the activity, the students returned to their seats. I prompted them to describe the day's lesson in a single word. The responses were overwhelmingly positive: 'interesting,' 'fun,' 'good,' 'happy,' 'nice,' 'lovely.' Aiming at fluency, I then asked them to express their current feelings, and solely for the purpose of differentiation I added that they could do so using simple words, phrases, or sentences. This activity aimed to help them distinguish between descriptive words for objects, weather, and emotions. At the same time, I got some very positive responses reflecting their engagement with the Dogme approach on this rainy day in Jeddah. We concluded the lesson there, and the students left with positive sentiments, while I felt a sense of accomplishment for trying something new.

Reflecting on the day, I realized it was the first time I conducted a class without a lesson plan, textbooks, or materials—aside from plain A4 sheets, sticky notes, and pencils. Notably, I hadn't written any lesson objectives on the board at the start, as I typically would. The language used was entirely student-generated, with minimal guidance from me. Although we began without explicit lesson objectives as we normally do, by the end, I could confidently state that my students had learned to:

- Use accurate words to describe the weather.
- Use appropriate words to describe feelings.
- Create meaningful sentences using these words to articulate feelings, describe objects, and depict weather conditions.

This approach marked a departure from my usual structured lessons, yet it proved to be an enriching experience for both the students and myself.

A NOTE FROM LUKE:

> This lesson exhibits an impressive fluidity in terms of strategies and outcomes.
>
> Zarafshan reflects at the end on a personal 'first', having taught a lesson without a plan, and where the language was wholly generated by the students.
>
> Her flexibility in seizing the opportunity – at a moment when students were anxious about the weather and asking to go home –

is an object lesson in personal development: it's only by experimenting that we learn new things.

Then there are the outcomes. Tasked to share words describing the weather or their feelings about it, the students – and this always happens, because human thought is liquid and overflows – came up with words around the target areas and more: weather and emotions for sure, but also clothing, food, and activities.

The teacher embraces this and has the students create sentences with these words. But what happens next is magical: Zarafshan has the students deconstruct their own sentences and make new ones – 'sometimes different from the original' ones. Here is language, like thought, flowing into new shapes.

# 3

# TEETH
## BRAD BARKER

### JAPAN | ADULTS | B1 – C2

This group of 12 were 2nd, 3rd, and 4th-year university students enrolled in the elective course English Communication 1 at Rikkyo University in Tokyo, Japan. The majority were from Japan, but there was one regular student from China. There were also three "special international students" studying abroad for a semester or year at the university. These class members were from China, Canada, and the United States. English proficiencies ranged from approximately CEFR B1 to a first-language English speaker. Students' majors and interests were wide-ranging. Classroom culture was centered on lively communication and intercultural exchange.

For the elective course English Communication 1, the class met twice a week during a 14-week spring semester in 2023. This was a dream-like class to teach. Although there were challenges, such as working with a wide range of language proficiencies, students were motivated, cooperative, and had chosen to be there. I was fortunate to find myself teaching a course that allows for a high degree of teacher agency and the option to not choose a coursebook. This amount of freedom has been quite rare during my teaching career as a whole. Much of my past teaching has been within relatively tightly controlled courses with required coursebooks.

I would suggest that using a general language coursebook would not be the best way to hold this particular group's attention. To give students greater control of the course, I decided to implement a process syllabus (also known as a negotiated syllabus; e.g., see Breen & Littlejohn, 2000[1]). Basically all of my classroom decisions were inspired by Dogme ELT.

Due to the course guidelines and syllabus, some aspects of the course could not be changed, such as the type of assessment (discussion tests) and weighted grades, however, there was a lot of room for teacher and student agency. Many aspects of the course emerged through negotiation. The university guidelines stated that the main course objective was to develop students' abilities to "produce and respond to language on everyday social topics." In the first few lessons, six main topics were decided after negotiation with students: Social Media, Age, Sustainability, Culture, Beauty, and Rights.

Students were starting the new topic of Beauty. At this point in week 10 of the semester, all I had to do was instruct students to begin discussing Beauty in small groups. I asked them what questions and ideas they had about the topic and directed them to a shared Google Doc in which all students could add notes, pictures or memes. The Google Doc was entitled Beauty, but was blank, to begin with.

After about twenty minutes of student discussion, I sat down next to one of the groups.[2]

**Teacher**: So, what ideas have you talked about so far for Beauty?
**Student 1**: [softly] Teeth.
**T**: Say it again.

---

1.   Breen, M. P., & Littlejohn, A. (Eds.). (2000). *Classroom decision-making: Negotiation and process syllabus in practice*. Cambridge University Press.
2.   Transcribed with permission from students and Rikkyo University.

**S1**: Teeth.

**T**: Teeth! [students laugh] Nice! Okay, tell me more about teeth.

**S2**: Maybe Americans and some other cultures care about teeth, but maybe Japanese, not so much.

**T**: Really? So, you're saying that Japanese people don't care about their teeth?

**S2**: Compared to other countries.

**T**: That's really interesting. This is something that I would have never thought about to discuss, but I like it. Can you talk more about that? Why is that the case? Because I think it's somewhat true.

**S2**: Eh?

**S1**: Costs a lot.

**T**: It costs a lot. To do what? What…toothpaste? [students laugh]

**S1**: Whitening.

**T**: Whitening. Okay, yeah. So there's whitening toothpaste but there's also whitening treatments. […] I don't even know, but it can be very expensive. What else? [pause] What do you call the things that you put on your teeth to make them straight?

**S1**: Ah, *kyousei*.

**S2**: *Kyousei* in Japanese.

**T**: Does anybody know what that is in English? How do you say it in Japanese? *Kyousei*?

**S2**: *Kyousei*.

**T**: *Kyousei*. What would that be in English? [students check a dictionary]

**S1**: [slowly sounding the word out] Orthodontics.

**T**: True. That's true, but that's the high-level word. Most people don't use that.

**S2**: Ah, braces.

**T**: Braces! Braces. That's the one! Did you have braces?

The discussion of teeth continued for about 30 more minutes in this lesson and also into the following lesson as groups exchanged ideas with other groups. Students and I added pages of emergent language, discussion questions, and memes as we discussed teeth and other beauty-related topics such as tattoos, plastic surgery, traditional clothing, beauty standards, lookism, fast fashion, cosmetics, and men with long hair.

Teeth-related emergent language included: tooth whitening, orthodontics, orthodontist, braces, *ohaguro* (the historic Japanese practice of blackening teeth with a mixture of iron and vinegar), *yaeba* (literally "double tooth," referring to a fang-like snaggletooth that may be considered a sign of natural beauty or youthfulness in Japan), straight teeth, snaggletooth, gums, and tooth decay.

Teeth are such a simple, interesting, and obvious topic of discussion—but it only became apparent to me after it had emerged naturally in class. I never would have thought of it while planning a lesson or course.

Isn't it strange that some Americans seem obsessed with unnaturally white, straight teeth? How fascinating is it that historically, Japanese society embraced *ohaguro*—the blackening of teeth—as a symbol of beauty and status, or that *yaeba* is sometimes seen as a sign of natural beauty and youthfulness in modern Japan?[3]

I did not ask students to reflect on this specific activity and topic, but I did ask what they liked about the course through a Google Forms questionnaire. One comment in particular presents a good summary of the general feeling among students: "I liked the people and freedom of discussion we had in this class, no topic was off limits and we were able to talk about things that would never be in a textbook."

Students are experts at introducing topics that they and their peers are interested in talking about. In many cases, introducing vocabulary when there is a communicative need for it seems superior to pre-planning it. I'm reluctant to use emergent vocabulary as a chance to go into teacher mode and teach. There's no need to derail a good discussion. I think that in some contexts, it may be more beneficial when students and the teacher simply record emergent language in a shared Google Doc or

3.   Poon, R. X. M. (2018). The perfect smile – Part 4. *British Dental Journal*, 225(8), 743–746.

incorporate it immediately into the classroom discussion. Maybe simply drawing attention to certain language features by underlining or using bold text is enough focus on form. If only every course could be like this one!

A NOTE FROM SCOTT:

*"No topic was off limits and we were able to talk about things that would never be in a textbook," reported one student after Brad's classes.*

*This 'Dogmetic' sense of freedom is enhanced when – as in this instance – the learners are able to choose the topics of the program themselves. Of course, not every class has the freedom to do this. But even when topics are pre-selected, e.g. because they are in the coursebook, Brad's approach to developing them seems perfectly viable, i.e. asking the learners – even before they open the course-book, and working in small groups – to brainstorm ideas and questions on to a blank Google document (It could, of course, be a blank whiteboard – but the blankness is important!)*

*This document can then become the repository for all the topic-related products that are generated over subsequent lessons, e.g. class surveys, interviews, anecdotes, news stories, poems, and so on.*

*One advantage of this topic-driven approach is that the vocabulary generated is likely to be frequently recycled, ensuring its memorability.*

# 4

# DOGME IN CRITICAL THINKING: WORKING WITH EMERGENT BELIEFS

PETER BRERETON

## JAPAN | ADULTS | B1 – B2

This class consisted of 18 students who were five weeks into their first semester at a Japanese university. Their English level was around CEFR B1-B2 and they came to university with a broadly similar background of going through the Japanese school system, some with brief periods of study abroad. This Academic Reading and Writing course was part of a mandatory first-year English for Academic Purposes (EAP) program which aims to equip students with the necessary academic skills to tackle an undergraduate education in English. As the name suggests, the course had a heavy emphasis on academic reading and writing but also on developing students' logical reasoning and critical thinking skills.

My teaching philosophy has long been closely aligned with Dogme principles, particularly in prioritising student-generated content and emergent language. Until recently, I always tended to interpret "emergent language" as referring primarily to vocabulary (and, to a lesser extent, to grammatical structures). However, as this case demonstrates, it is also possible to apply these principles to emergent ideas and beliefs. In this lesson, I chose to work predominantly with student-generated beliefs as I believed this would provide us with authentic responses that we could exploit for critical analysis and discussion.

With students sitting in groups of three, the lesson began with one word written on the board: xenophobia. Students immediately began discussing the meaning, and I encouraged them to check with other groups if they were unsure. We quickly went over the pronunciation, the meaning of "a phobia", and I elicited/explained a few similar types of phobia (e.g. Islamo-, trans-, homo-). I asked them to discuss why I might have written this on the board, though no one seemed to know the answer at this stage. I then displayed a Guardian headline on the projector screen:

Joe Biden

## Biden calls Japan and India xenophobic: 'They don't want immigrants'

US president says 'immigrants are what makes us strong' and criticizes countries, plus China and Russia, over migration policy

I asked students if they agreed with Joe Biden's assessment of Japan[1]. This prompted some immediate small-group discussions, which I monitored closely, taking copious notes. Note-taking, for me, is a necessity in any conversation-driven lesson; keeping track of the emerging threads helps me to weave them together in a more meaningful way. It quickly became apparent from the discussions that many students had reacted instinctively to the headline, shaking their heads or saying "no". In a way, I was pleased to see this as it gave us an obvious emerging thread to examine and exploit for further development.

I paused the conversation after a few minutes and asked students to reflect on their responses, specifically asking them to consider their reasons for their opinions. At the same time I noted two of their reactions on the board:

- "No, I disagree" / Shaking heads
- It's because we're an island

Drawing students' attention to the top line, I explained that this had been the most common reaction I had noticed. I wondered aloud how so many of them were able to dismiss Biden's view so quickly, especially given that none of them seemed to have read Biden's full comments. As such, I asked them to reflect in their groups on where this disagreement may have stemmed from. This led to a wider group discussion which I summarised on the board as:

---

1.  Associated Press. (2024, May 2). Biden calls Japan and India xenophobic: 'They don't want immigrants'. *The Guardian*.

| | |
|---|---|
| • "No, I disagree" / Shaking heads | • Attack on a strong belief -> Makes us defensive? |
| • It's because we're an island | • Strong beliefs (often) connected to our identity |
| | • Emotional responses (from the heart) |
| | • Not based on evidence/logical reasoning (from the head) |

I chided students gently at this stage, reminding them that as university students they are expected to be aware of their biases, to consider issues with an open mind, to examine the evidence, and not to rush to conclusions. At this point, I noticed a few sheepish faces and, as two students later commented, "I realize I tend to have very biased opinions about things" and "I should not answer just based on my emotion without sufficient knowledge about the topic." I then directed attention back to the second of the initial responses ("It's because we're an island"). After establishing that this speaker likely agreed that Japan is xenophobic, I asked whether this was a valid reason for xenophobia. Students were able to conclude that it was an attempt to defend or "justify" (a word I fed into the discussion) xenophobia. I elaborated on this by suggesting this is also an emotional response: although the speaker acknowledged there may be xenophobia in Japan, they were more focused on defending its existence than in critically considering the issue.

As it felt like we'd exhausted this thread of the discussion, I suggested we return to Biden's comments and projected the contextualised quote[2] in the article onto the screen:

> At a hotel fundraiser where the donor audience was largely Asian American, Biden said the upcoming US election was about "freedom, America and democracy" and that the nation's economy was thriving "because of you and many others".

---

2.   Ibid.

"Why? Because we welcome immigrants," Biden said. "Look, think about it. Why is China stalling so badly economically? Why is Japan having trouble? Why is Russia? Why is India? Because they're xeno-phobic. They don't want immigrants."

I proposed that we break down his comments about Japan to help us better evaluate his argument. Highlighting Biden's quote "Why is Japan having [economic] trouble?", I explained that he assumes that the Japanese economy is struggling. I wondered aloud whether the Japanese Prime Minister might agree. I then asked students to work together to identify other assumptions that Biden made. Although this was challeng-ing, it led to the following questions on the board:

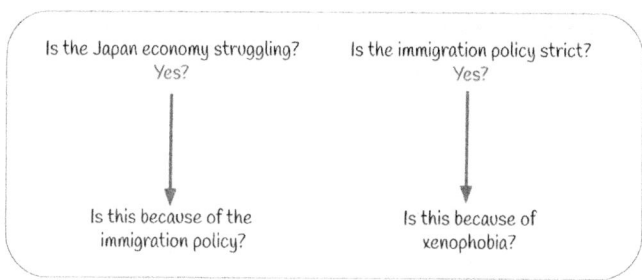

Is the Japan economy struggling?
Yes?

Is this because of the immigration policy?

Is the immigration policy strict?
Yes?

Is this because of xenophobia?

We were now in a better position to consider Biden's claims more objec-tively and, in small groups, I asked students to consider their opinions. During this discussion, students' responses seemed more nuanced and more considered, and there was clearly more acknowledgment of the validity of Biden's claims. When students subsequently shared their ideas with the whole class, some interesting insights included:

- The economic situation is likely caused by more than just the immigration policy. I elaborated that this sounds like a single-cause fallacy.
- "Strict" is quite subjective. One student volunteered that the immigration policy was "comparatively" strict.

- Some students concluded the discussion by stating simply "I don't know". I praised this response: it is unrealistic and unhelpful for students to believe they always have to have an opinion, and it shows great awareness to admit ignorance or uncertainty. I suggested simply adding "yet" to show an intention to learn.

The final stage of this lesson involved students sharing their reflections in small groups on if/how their ideas had evolved since the beginning of the class, and what their main takeaways from the lesson would be. Students were also asked to write a brief response to the question "Did you find today's discussion interesting?", from which the student voices in this article are taken. For me, the act of preparing and writing this article has been a very reflective process in itself: I spent a great deal of time discussing this lesson with peers, looking over my lesson notes, and taking additional notes to help me better understand the lesson's structure and flow.

Driven primarily by emerging student content, this lesson had at its core the main course aim of developing critical thinking skills. It was validating to read student comments that this lesson was meaningful for them and introduced these new university students to valuable lessons about thinking, such as recognising the instinct to react emotionally, analysing reasons and assumptions that underpin beliefs, and identifying logical fallacies (which we revisited and expanded upon in subsequent lessons). One student testimony concisely summarised the views of many when she wrote: "I have often felt pressured by the thinking that I always have to make an answer quickly, even though I do not have any proof or support. I always have a mind that I must respond to the question. It seems simple but I was so relieved when you said, "It is okay to say I don't know yet."

A note from Scott:

> *The notion of student-generated, or emergent, beliefs is a sugges-*
> *tive one, and resonates with the original Dogme 'mission state-*
> *ment', as posted on the opening page of the (now discontinued)*
> *online discussion group: "We are looking for ways of exploiting*
> *the learning opportunities offered by the raw material of the class-*
> *room, that is the language that emerges from the needs, interests,*
> *concerns and desires of the people in the room".*
>
> *What is perhaps missing from that list is 'beliefs', perhaps out of a*
> *concern for its association with religious or political beliefs. But –*
> *and especially in a class that focuses on critical thinking – there is*
> *no reason for learners not to share their beliefs, and to hold these*
> *up for critical inspection.*
>
> *Indeed, Paulo Freire[3] – who is the acknowledged originator of crit-*
> *ical pedagogy – developed a pedagogy not hugely different from*
> *Peter's approach in this lesson. In Freire's 'culture circles',*
> *designed both to teach literacy but also to develop a 'critical*
> *consciousness', he would start with just a single word or image,*
> *which would trigger a 'dialogic' discussion, mediated by a coor-*
> *dinator.*
>
> *In Freire's words: 'Whoever enters into dialogue does so with*
> *someone about something; and that something ought to constitute*
> *the new content of our proposed education.'*

---

3.  Freire, P. (1993) *Education for critical consciousness*. Continuum.

# 5

# GETTING STUDENTS INTO THE ZONE

## ALEXANDRA JANE BURKE

## JAPAN | ADULTS | B1

In Japan, I have been researching hard-to-engage students in language classrooms for many years. In all classes, there are students with energy levels and the ability to sustain concentration consistent with having learning differences but few are ever identified. This is not unusual, as currently, only 1.79% of Japanese people declare any disability status to their university, even with the protection of laws. The most common difficulties are with reading and writing, affecting nearly 10-20% of the population. But some have an extra hurdle, focusing for long periods, and getting ideas out of their head and into assignments.

There is a temptation to "dumb down" classwork because these students can sometimes "fail" at lower-level tasks, but the opposite is what they actually need. Typical rewards have no impact but challenge, interest and time pressure are what activate these students. I didn't reach this conclusion alone. During every course design or revision, I rely on three great thinkers, whose works span nearly a century, but all understood how imperative "relevance" is to student engagement.

1. 1916 – John Dewey:[1] utility, interest, experience, and integration.
2. 1975 – Pricilla Vail:[2] "These students are not looking for the easy way out of education but the right way in."
3. 2012 – William Dodson, MD: Most people have an importance-based nervous system responding to rules and priorities. However, people with ADHD have an interest-based nervous system responding to interest, challenge, novelty, and urgency.

If interest is the foundation, engagement with English tasks, and connection to the class follows. I learned about Vail and Dodson from Edward Hallowell and John Ratey (both doctors with ADHD) who explain that people with ADHD live in the world of "Now" or "Not now".[3] So for teachers, creating "positive" urgency can overcome problems with deadlines and homework.

This class included 38 first-year Japanese university students, who took required English classes. They were non-English majors meaning most had a history of only experiencing a grammar/translation-focused, university entrance preparation approach widely used at most high schools in Japan. Most had few positive opportunities for face-to-face interaction with a first-language English-speaking instructor, much less using English to communicate or make a solo presentation. The students in this class ranged from High A1 to B1 on the CEFR scale.

The goal of the course was to compare differences in the cultures and economies of countries around the world and Japan. Students had a lower-level textbook exploring daily life activities, biographies, and inter-

---

1.   Dewey, J. (1916). *Democracy and education: An introduction to the philosophy of education.* The Free Press.
2.   Vail, P. (2022, April 26). *Smart kids with school problems,* quoted by Ed Hallowell on his "Wonderful World of Different" podcast with Victoria Waller.
3.   Hallowell, E. M., & Ratey, J. J. (2021). *ADHD 2.0: New science and essential strategies for thriving with distraction—from childhood through adulthood.* Ballantine Books.

views. Of course, students were free to draw on information from the Internet.

In this course, students were graded based on five presentations over the year, each one using more and more student-generated materials. Having created and refined this course, these presentations were designed for students to enjoy the process, feel a sense of personal control of content, and gain confidence in using English.

Academically, studying Economics was one of the main focuses of this class, however, it can certainly be a dry subject at the best of times. So I wanted to use Dogme to get my students "into the zone". The Dogme approach allowed me to give complete control to the students and I could support their emergent language needs in real time. Experiencing agency and autonomy through English was important because, until that point, textbooks and teachers had controlled every word they had seen or heard in a classroom. I wanted students to choose what was personally interesting to them.

At the beginning of the course, I set out the following tasks:

1. Showing and telling me about a photograph they had taken (One-minute speaking task).
2. A one-to-one country report to me (Students speak 90% of the time).
3. Student-to-student briefing of their country (Speaking notes and data comparisons).
4. A biographical poster presentation of a meaningful individual, using a timeline, the global influence of the person, and the impact on the student.
5. A small group poster session, with students comparing three countries with Japan (Figure 1).

To give context, I showed them student samples and then gave them my samples below. Students were initially shocked because the posters had many icons and images, but few words (Dodson's challenge).

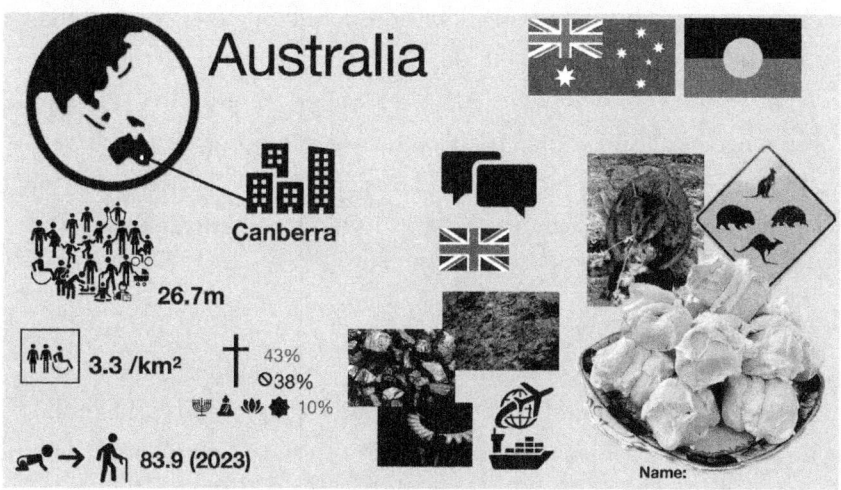

Figure 1. Group poster session comparing 3 countries with Japan

One of the activities that benefitted the most from the Dogme approach was students choosing the vocabulary that would become the basis of their discussions and presentations (Dewey's "utility and interest").

For vocabulary acquisition, students first needed to choose appropriate vocabulary, then learn how to pronounce it and use it correctly in sentences. Their textbook offered core demographic vocabulary such as population, life expectancy, and exports. They searched for words that were country-specific through online research. Whenever possible, I encouraged them to put their keywords on the board. I used syllable breakdown to help students transition from Japanese syllable patterns to a typical English syllable pattern. I also put key questions on the board with gap fills for everyone's specific content. I demonstrated word and sentence-level fluency. First, they practiced connected speech by listening to the end and beginning sounds of words in the sentence. Then they practiced building their fluency and speed.

As their personal vocabulary lists grew, they realized they needed a system to make these new words their own. From reading prior research, I knew that making paper-based word cards would get a lukewarm reception from about 60% of students. I was prepared for this! I showed them a free, online flashcard app called *Quizlet*.[4] They could make their own word cards, vocabulary quizzes, individual word games, and even play an exciting, live in-class game on their phones or computers, using shared vocabulary lists built by previous students. Their eyes opened wide when they heard the voices of other Japanese students and university staff as voice actors.

A student said, "Now we need an exports set." I asked, "What words should we put in it?" After creating the set, I opened the "add card" feature and asked, "Would anyone like to be a voice actor?". Then the magic happened. Just like that, English came alive. Students recorded the Japanese and I recorded the English while tapping the syllables on the desk. They opened the new card set and Dewey's "utility" was engaged. They listened and practiced the new words for a few minutes: "experience". Then we played a Quizlet Live match where students anonymously competed to match words and meanings, first as individuals and then as teams (Dodson's "urgency").

They could do their second and third challenges, with relative ease, due to using a study system that suited them because they had agency in the process. Finally, in their last challenge, they made posters with all the economic terms reduced to globally recognizable icons. Students could interact and maintain eye contact during rather complex discussions more easily than when relying on a script. One student commented, "I didn't think it would be possible to do an English project with only pictures and numbers, but it worked!" (Vail's "right way in').

The focus on emergent language in Dogme underpins the success of this course every year. Students should be encouraged to use the correct

---

4.  https://quizlet.com/

English term for what they want to say, even if something like "intrinsic semiconductors" seems hard to say. If I can push the right buttons for ADHD students or other marginalized students, then everyone can soar on the energy these academically enigmatic students generate.

A NOTE FROM SCOTT:

*Whether your learners have special needs or not, or whether you even subscribe to Dogme or not, Alexandra's lesson embodies a key principle when it comes to engaging learners in collaborative text construction: Start with the words.*

*The beauty of a topic-based vocabulary brainstorm is that (a) it allows all the learners to contribute to the task, regardless of their ability, especially where they have the means (and the permission) to access words through (print or online) dictionaries; (b) the cognitive work involved in thinking of words and then searching for them and sharing them helps entrench the words in memory, especially if aided with tools like Quizlet; and (c) the words help activate and organize mental 'schemata', i.e. the thought structures that form the basis of texts and graphics.*

*In Alexandra's case, the topics were represented graphically. Still, I can easily imagine how these graphics could be transformed into (spoken) texts. The words that inspired them can be retrieved and reactivated, by the simple device of having students ask and answer questions about the posters in pairs, small groups, as a 'gallery walk', or as a whole-class activity.*

# 6

# A LOVE STORY
## JAMIE CLAYTON

## VIETNAM I ADULTS I A2 – B2

This was a class of pre-intermediate adults studying a general English course twice a week. All students were Vietnamese, ranging in age from 16 to 50.

It was an evening class, after work for most of the students and I quickly realised they didn't want to study predetermined grammar points and turn pages of a coursebook. They wanted to talk and find out about each other. It was probably one of the first classes I had where I realised how teaching outside the coursebook could really boost motivation and student productivity.

A feature of the class was a class blog where students did written homework, which often involved responding to videos, as well as writing reflections and stories.

At the time, I was really getting into alternative teaching methodologies in the run-up to doing the Cambridge Delta. While keenly exploring such alternatives, I was fortunate to be given this wonderful group of students to work with. It seemed the perfect opportunity to push myself as a teacher and experiment with Dogme, a concept that was becoming a major influence in my professional development at the time.

Viet (45ish, male) wrote a tender, heartfelt story on the class blog about a long-lost love. The story was so good I had to find a way of using it in class. Here it is:

> Thirty years ago,we had group 3 people.Mr Tan ,Miss Trinh and me.We were the best friend since we were classmates in hight school.We usually watch movie,go out to eat together.So,mr Tân and I love her together. I thought she know it. But mr Tân and I never talk about that. I want to tell her that I loved her but didn't know how to start.I decided every Sunday morning I sent her the rose by post office.but I don't write my name. she is very happy about that, but she didn't know who gave her flowers.Until once day,I discovered Mr Tan and her going out together without me. Mr Tân and her loved each other because she thought Mr Tân who gave her the flowers every Sunday morning.

Wanting to use this text with the class, I prepared the lesson with the same thinking as a dictation – that getting the students to notice the differences between their text and my version may lead to a positive restructuring of their own language. To do this, I re-wrote Viet's story in my own words. I didn't change the content, just upgraded and corrected the language.

First, students read Viet's version and decided on a title, settling on the delightful 'One Way Love'. Then there was time for the class to ask Viet questions about his story. These two reading activities provoked some of the most fully engaged student discussions I've ever seen.

Once this stage had settled down, I gave students my version of the text and asked them to read and compare it with Viet's, trying to find differences between them and explain why I had changed those parts in my reformulated version.

After feedback, I then gave students a gapped version of the rewritten text to complete. The gaps focused on the differences between mine and Viet's text.

For feedback, students came to the board to write the missing words from the gapped version in the order of the story. They then turned over their papers and tried to retell the story using this list of language that was now on the board.

After these noticing and re-telling activities, students then wrote a similar romantic story using the same language on the board.

Firstly, it's important to say this lesson wasn't perfect. Engagement levels were through the roof, but in analysing the reformulated story, I gave students too many different language features to deal with. The focus on form stage of the lesson was just too broad in scope.

This failure reminded me of an important issue with Dogme teaching and using learner language as the syllabus: Learner output is unruly, and I find things can get out of control quickly, in terms of emergent language. Before you know it there are 15 phrases containing a fantastic range of different forms on the board.

This lesson left me with more questions than I had before: How much language should we try and teach in one lesson? When does a wide focus of language in a single lesson become unhelpfully broad for students? Is it better to go 'wide but shallow or deep and narrow' when it comes to studying language structures in class? (Thanks to Mark Jones for these terms).

Without permitting a wide range of language structures to come up in the classroom, communication can get stifled – 'we're not studying that today so you don't need to know it now', says the teacher. This must be so frustrating for students. On the other side, is being overwhelmed with too much language even more frustrating?

Wherever the sweet spot is between a 'wide and shallow' or 'deep and narrow' approach to language study in the classroom, the overwhelming positive from this lesson was simply how incredibly stimulating the content was. Getting that level of engagement can be the hardest part of using coursebooks, but it is something that Dogme can far better provide. Once we have students wholeheartedly participating, teaching language should become a lot easier.

This group was one of the most important classes I have ever taught for my own development as a teacher. I proposed that we abandon the coursebook early in the course, and the students agreed. I usually took some material to class: a topic idea, or some student-produced text with an activity sequence, though I often never used it. Something else would come up in the initial stages of the lesson and we would explore in that direction instead. I think, more than anything, these supplementary materials were a safety net to manage the nervous excitement of using a Dogme approach. It was truly thrilling at times.

Even though, teaching EAP courses now, I am not able to employ such a radical teaching approach, the experiences I had as a teacher with that group were profoundly influential in how I continue to approach the classroom many years later. My love for Dogme remains.

A note from Luke:

> This is a wonderfully multi-layered account of a lesson, its place in the story of a particular class, and its role in the arc of one teacher's personal development. The questions Jamie asks about the challenges and rewards of working with emergent language are ones that all teachers working with Dogme will encounter.
>
> The 'wide but shallow, or deep and narrow' framework he mentions is a helpful binary rubric (one of several in this book).

*Perhaps it's only by going wide but shallow, allowing the conversation to take its course, that one can then meaningfully go deep and narrow, focusing in on emergent language. And selecting the most worthwhile language to highlight and explore is a skill that takes time to develop.*

*At its heart is a text written by a student which, in its poignant economy, is worthy of a novella. Aptly titled 'One Way Love' by classmates, Jamie's treatment of the story is anything but one-way – the text is interrogated by the students, rewritten by the teacher, and upcycled by the class (folding in some of the new language) into new stories.*

# 7

# GRAMMAR AT THE POINT OF NEED FOR EXAM PREPARATION

## FERNANDA CWIERTNIA

## BRAZIL | ADULT | C1 – C2

This was a 1:1 online writing session with a Brazilian student, who is also an English teacher, preparing to take the Cambridge C2 Proficiency exam. At the start of the course, the student's level was C1, having already passed the Cambridge C1 Advanced exam. Each week, the student was assigned a writing task, to be submitted 72 hours before the session. This timeline allowed me to review and mark the work in advance, providing feedback so the student could reflect on my comments and come to class ready to discuss how to improve her writing. My goal in giving feedback ahead of time was to create a gap to be bridged during our class.

From 2012 to 2020, I taught 1:1 general English and exam preparation lessons at a language institute, where teachers were trained to use coursebooks. However, our manager encouraged us to set the textbook aside whenever students were communicating effectively, which is when I first experienced Dogme moments in my general English lessons. In contrast, in C1 exam preparation lessons, I was unable to teach reactively. It wasn't until I began preparing for the Cambridge C2 Proficiency exam myself that my perspective on language started to shift. After passing the exam, Dogme moments gradually became a part of my exam preparation lessons.

Simply following exam preparation coursebooks from cover to cover never felt right. I had somewhat done that myself when preparing for the Cambridge C2 Proficiency exam. Although I succeeded in the exam, I never truly felt confident in my approach. I disliked the idea of telling my students things like, "This is the answer because it's a strong collocation," or "Here's a template for your writing paper." Providing the correct answer or offering a formula for writing wasn't my concept of development, let alone proficiency. This is when I began to move away from relying on coursebooks. While I still needed exam-like exercises to be central to my lessons, I eventually shifted the dynamics. I encouraged students to complete homework and writing assignments "at home" and used class time to focus on extrapolating from mistakes.

So, 72 hours before the online writing class in question, my student submitted her writing for correction. 24 hours before the class, she received detailed feedback. I used a color code to highlight errors in grammar, vocabulary, punctuation, and register. The text contained several problems to address, but, for this chapter, I selected an excerpt that demonstrates how I responded to a grammar mistake without explicitly teaching grammar. The sentence was:

> Last but not least, as if it hadn't been for the usage of leaflets in the last campaigns, the city would not still be dirty, thereby making it appalling for tourists.

Using my color code, I highlighted:

> As if
> Would not still

In the feedback report sent to the student before class, she was not told how to correct the mistake; instead, the problem was only highlighted to encourage her to discover for herself what was wrong and how it could be revised.

In the first 10 minutes of the session, I asked the student how she felt about her writing and whether the feedback had met her expectations. I also wanted to know if she was surprised by the corrections. During this time, she explained her reasoning behind the inaccuracies.

We addressed one inaccuracy at a time. As the student explained her thought process, I paused screen sharing and noted what she said:

> Using leaflets in the last campaigns caused the cities to be dirty, and this is appalling for tourists.

Once the student finished her explanation, I resumed screen sharing and asked if the sentence I had written reflected her intended meaning. She confirmed it did. I then asked her to identify the key ideas in my sentence and connect them to what she had written in her piece. She pointed out:

> *Using leaflets in the last campaigns* → as if it hadn't *been for the usage of leaflets in the last campaigns*
> *[caused] the cities to be dirty* → the city would not still be dirty
> *this is appalling for tourists.* → thereby making it appalling for tourists

As an advanced student, she was able to easily match the key ideas. We then proceeded to compare her sentence with mine:

> Last but not least, as if it hadn't been for the usage of leaflets in the last campaigns, the city would not still be dirty, thereby making it appalling for tourists.

> Last but not least, using leaflets in the last campaigns caused the cities to be dirty, and this is appalling for tourists.

I asked the student to identify where in the second sentence we conveyed the same meaning as "as if." She couldn't find it. That was when she realized that what she had actually meant was:

> Last but not least, if it hadn't been for the usage of leaflets in the last campaigns…

Next, I asked her to compare the two sentences again and point out where in my sentence I conveyed "the city would not still be dirty." This proved more challenging, and the student needed additional time. To help her, I used Google to find two images: one of a dirty city and one of a clean city. I then asked, "If it hadn't been for the use of leaflets in the last campaign, which image would best represent the result here?" She selected the image of the dirty city. I then asked her to reconsider her sentence ("the city would not still be dirty") and decide if it accurately reflected the image she had chosen. The student realized that what she had meant was "the city would still be dirty," not "the city would not still be dirty."

To encourage the student, I asked if she could rephrase her corrected sentence, "Last but not least, if it hadn't been for the use of leaflets in the last campaigns, the city would still be dirty…" using alternatives like "thanks to" and "but for." This allowed us to explore different forms of disguised conditionals.

In this lesson, we addressed several grammar points that would typically be covered in separate lessons, depending on the approach. Students preparing for the C2 Proficiency exam usually know most grammar rules and perform well in gap-fill exercises. The challenge lies in seeing the language they've already studied in action. This approach makes the lesson more meaningful by ensuring that grammar is relevant and addressed at the point of need, respecting their own pace. While getting the message across is sufficient for real-life tasks, students aiming for proficiency need to focus on accuracy.

After the lesson, the student expressed a strong motivation to revisit the grammar points covered in class and apply them to her next writing assignment. This approach ensured that each lesson built on the previous one. Despite the lack of linearity in the way grammar was approached, it helped the student feel a sense of direction and progress.

A NOTE FROM SCOTT:

> *This lesson adopts a 'flipped' model of instruction, whereby writing tasks are completed and feedback given in advance of the lesson, maximizing the time available in the actual lesson for the kind of detailed analysis of errors (or, better, non-standard forms) as described by Fernanda in this account.*

> *I can imagine the same, essentially reactive, approach being adopted for a larger class, where extracts from students' homework, anonymised and with errors highlighted, are distributed to the class who work in small groups in order to correct them.*

> *In this way, the first Dogme principle, i.e. that lessons be based around the texts that the learners themselves produce, is nicely fulfilled.*

# 8

# AN OFF-GRID LESSON LIGHTS UP THE ROOM

## HASSAN DAJANI

## EGYPT | TEENS | A1

In my English Club sessions in this poor 1700-family Giza village – with about 8-9 grades 3-7 Pre A1 English learners, the students wanted to go to the board and write words that they knew. The girls took the lead over boys with their timid passion for always excelling, and outnumbering the boys in each English Club session.

The students were very excited to be learning English in a relaxed class setting. They were under the impression that there were no summative tests or assessments to worry about. Feeling laid back in a way encouraged them to be themselves and do what they long wished to do in a classroom – go to the board and write!

According to Dogme ELT teachings, language learning occurs within an 'emergent syllabus', which comes from the learners themselves – not from outside factors like course books or curricula. So in a way, progressive education comes out from learners' discourse autonomy and empowerment. I believe that students in this underrepresented population don't just want to improve their English reading and writing skills, but their listening comprehension and speaking as well.

I started by asking all students to write their names in English on the right side of the board, as well as any words that came to their mind. After spending some time at the board learning letters, colours, and numbers 1-10, groups were formed to play word races as many times as possible in the allotted time in class.

My intention was to teach the given (vowel sounds) syllabus for grades 7-8, and 3-4 Pre A1 English learners. But, then I thought maybe I can extract some English language from the students if I challenge them to a 'word race' game as an ice-breaker!

I divided the class into two groups of 4, and I challenged them to write down on the board as many correct English words as they could think of. The output was astounding. Students wrote down their names in English, which was a leap. They also proceeded to write as many words from their word bank as they possibly could remember, and even sentences emerged. These students are passionate about writing, but definitely not speaking!

The whole class was spent writing on the board – I tried to do some pair work but it didn't last long – the learners just wanted to go to the board, and produce language for all to see. The only time these young students sat down at their desks was to draw and colour, and even this exercise they did independently on their own, only sharing colour markers with their colleagues.

Many words and even sentences relevant to students' learning were written on the board. These students have a reserve of learned language that they passionately want to produce for everyone to see, including their peers as competition. I gave them some corrective feedback on third person singular in simple present tense, like putting third person '-s' and the article "a" in the "she eat cow" phrase, and finishing this question, "How old?"

In another session, the students did the same 'word race', only to be interrupted twice by electricity shutdowns. In this minimal resource mode, I asked them to say 1-10 out loud in the dark – with some classroom management interruptions in L1 from the students. I went around the class choosing volunteers who wished to recall the numbers. Most of them struggled with pronunciation: For example, saying the number '6' as 'Sikes" rather than 'Six', was a challenge. It was rectified by drilling the numbers and letting each student repeat.

Several students produced sentence structures that were correct. For the first time, Menna, grade 7, actually produced real emergent written text in her three-minute 'word race' turn. "How old are you?", "She eats an apple.", "What's your name?" Third and seventh graders – in one English club setting capture – produced authentic English language. Wow, that's my Dogme moment.

One lesson learned is that these young students need to do more aural and pair work in these sessions. Scott Thornbury, in his March 2021 Dogme ELT Course, wisely alluded, "When you see it written down in detail like this, you may think the whole process is complex. It's not. There are only three basic steps:

1. Set up a situation where students talk about relevant topics that are important to them.
2. Write down what they want to say.

3. Use what is written to teach them about various aspects of the language."

My challenge with this young English Club setting was getting the students to talk. The reading and writing were comfortably doable by the students, but it is the productive act of speaking and comprehending that will constitute future sessions.

A note from Luke:

*Student language sometimes emerges naturally: perhaps that's a classic 'dogme moment', where conversation becomes irresistible. But we can also create the conditions for language to emerge. This is what happens in Hassan's lesson, where students are induced through a simple word race game to use all the English language resources at their disposal.*

*Where Hassan notes that: 'These students have a reserve of learned language that they passionately wanted to produce for everyone to see,' he speaks in a way for all learners. As he notes, summative testing is one thing that stands in the way. And as he also notes, Dogme is part of a progressive tradition that challenges this, privileging 'learners' discourse autonomy and empowerment'.*

*I'm often asked how (and even if ) Dogme works with beginners. This lesson shows emphatically that it can – not only with beginners but with disenfranchised beginners, in their early teens, in a low-resource classroom where there are power cuts. The electricity on the grid may fail us, but empowerment is a powerful thing and creates its own energy.*

# 9

# DOGME AS PART OF MY DELTA JOURNEY

## MARÍA JOSÉ DEARMAS

## URUGUAY | YOUNG LEARNERS | A1 – B1

I decided to use Dogme as part of my Experimental Practice (EP) for my DELTA Module 2. I made this choice in order to use the Dogme approach more fully; even though I deliver materials-free lessons which is one of Dogme's principles, I was sure I was not taking full advantage of the approach.

This lesson involved a group made up of 23 students (13 girls and 10 boys). It was a monolingual group as they were all from Uruguay, and therefore, native Spanish speakers. They were all 11 years old and had been studying English for five years in a bilingual private school.

Our school follows the International Baccalaureate (IB) program. This is an internationally recognized education program that aims to develop students' intellectual, personal, emotional, and social skills. Therefore, the lessons are generally planned taking into consideration the importance of developing critical thinking and transdisciplinary learning. It also promotes active learning and develops students' confidence to make connections between what they learn at school and what they learn in the real world. We do not use any specific course book as we prepare the lessons based on our students' needs and a specific syllabus prepared by the school based on the CEFR descriptors to help learners reach an A2 or B1 level of English.

As part of my tutor's advice, I knew I had to reduce my teacher talking time, exploit the whiteboard more, and most importantly, promote a more student-centered environment — aspects I could develop while promoting emergent language and active learning.

Before delivering the Dogme lesson, learners had read a book called "Smart Research Strategies" which had given them input on how to do research. I had asked them to work in pairs on some reading comprehension questions to discuss the most relevant information and to better understand how they would have to carry out research. As a follow-up, I thought it would be a good idea to discuss what they had understood about the text, leading learners to use L2 more naturally and spontaneously.

I asked learners if they remembered the name of the book they had read for the previous class and encouraged them to think of facts they would like to mention about it. Then, I gave them 5 minutes to note down some relevant information taken from the book. While they were working on this, I monitored and provided help when necessary. Then I encouraged them to take 10 minutes to discuss in pairs what they had written down, complement each other's ideas, and help each other to add information or clarify meaning. To continue developing the discussion, I encouraged learners to work in groups of four for about 15 minutes while I continued monitoring students' work and providing help when necessary. This is when the magic began...

During the following 20 minutes, I used the whiteboard to write down emergent language and other language points, and we analysed the meaning, form, and pronunciation of possible emergent language. Although students were not explicitly instructed to take notes from the whiteboard, many of them did so voluntarily. In the future, I would encourage them to take pictures or transcribe key points to ensure retention. Participation was generally well-distributed as I monitored closely, prompting quieter students to contribute and ensuring that roles were rotated during group discussions. Students supported each other in refining their ideas, which helped balance engagement across the class.

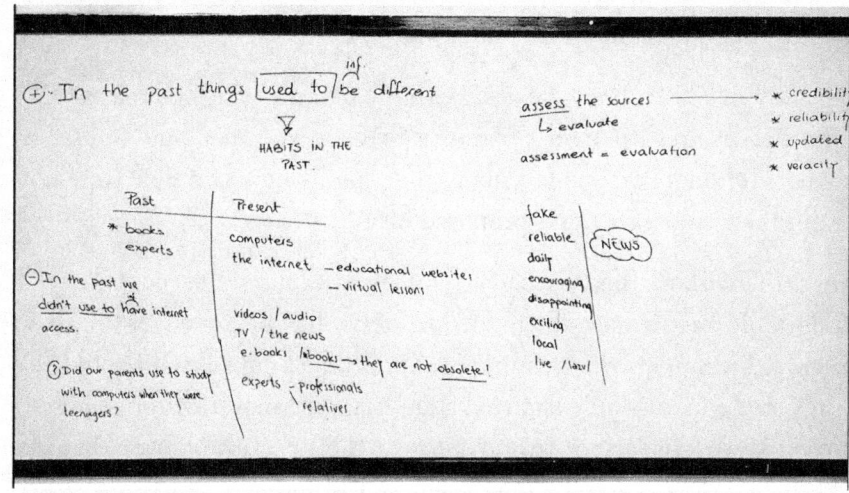

Finally, I gave them another 10 minutes to organise and rehearse their presentations based on the analysis on the whiteboard, so that everybody could participate during the group presentation to the whole class.

All in all, I believe it was a very engaging lesson even though it was not an easy topic for young learners to discuss. My learners could actively participate, and I did not feel the need to intervene other than to organise the discussion and identify key language structures and lexis to work on. Having a flexible lesson plan allowed me and my students to exploit the topic according to their interests, therefore becoming a more memorable lesson. I was able to analyse both language structures and lexis at a more spontaneous pace, and despite the lack of a written guided discovery task, learners proved their understanding of meaning, form, and use of "used to" which was identified as the main structure of the lesson. Concept-checking questions helped narrow the meaning of different adjectives used to describe the noun "news".

To reinforce the language that emerged in the lesson, I assigned a follow-up task where students had to write a short research-based paragraph incorporating some of the structures and vocabulary discussed. This ensured that the learning extended beyond the class discussion and provided an opportunity for further practice.

I am convinced that being flexible with my planning allowed me to feel more at ease and helped me to cater to my learners´ needs and interests. Learners felt motivated to talk about the topic, even when they were not the ones who spontaneously proposed it.

I am sure I will use this approach again soon because I felt much more comfortable and relaxed due to the fact of not having to deliver such a structured lesson in which timing could become a constraint. I could also see my students´ attitude changed a lot. Even the most disruptive learners were more attentive and engaged. This was also proven thanks to the feedback form I asked them to complete after delivering the lesson. I had some noisy and disruptive students and their attitude and feedback were both positive or within the parameters expected.

| Name: Alfonso | Strongly agree | Agree | Disagree | Strongly disagree | Not applicable |
|---|---|---|---|---|---|
| The lesson was relevant to my needs. | | ✓ | | | |
| Materials provided / used were helpful. | | ✓ | | | |
| The lesson was well organised. | | | ✓ | | |
| We could ask questions. | | | ✓ | | |
| Information was clear. | | ✓ | | | |
| The teacher was supportive all the time. | | ✓ | | | |
| The lesson held my attention. | | ✓ | | | |
| I enjoyed the lesson. | | ✓ | | | |

A NOTE FROM SCOTT:

*In the Introduction we mentioned the 'Dogme renaissance', refer-ring to the renewed interest teachers are showing in Dogme world-wide. One contributing factor to this renaissance, I would argue, is the way that Dogme has been enlisted to inspire 'Experimental Practice' lessons, such as the type María José describes in her account.*

*In fact, I can't count the number of times that – at conferences around the world – teachers have come up to me and told me that they 'did Dogme' for their experimental practice assignment. And, in response to the question, "How did it go?", they are unani-mously positive. So, it's great to be able to include the description of one such lesson here – especially one that includes the sentence: "This is when the magic began!"*

*Of course, it does raise the question as to whether a Dogme lesson is simply a one-off, experimental option. When does it stop being experimental and become a regular fixture in teachers' practice? That's why I'm encouraged by María José's takeaways from this experiment and her conviction that she will keep 'doing Dogme'. And she has the students' endorsement too!*

# 10

# THE PERFECT SCHOOL
## JACQUELINE DOUGLAS

## UK I ADULTS I B1

The learners were at B1 level, ranging from ages 18 to over 40, and were a mix of six language backgrounds. Students were following a general English course at a private language school in Cambridge, and I was with them for six weeks teaching a three-hour class Monday to Friday.

What drove me was a wish to put the learner, and the language they need and want to express themselves, at the heart of my teaching – naturally, Dogme was in harmony with that. I found myself on Day 1 telling the students that we were going to do something different. They would choose both the topics and how much or how little we used their course-book. They chose the lowest percentage of coursebook time from the options I offered, 30-40%, and there followed weeks of fruitful lessons that were theirs rather than mine.

Among several lessons drawn from Teaching Unplugged that have stayed with me, this account discusses "The Perfect School".

**The Perfect School (Teaching Unplugged, p.46)**[1]

1. *Set it Up*: introduce the concept of brainstorming by putting a word on the board ("school") and having students call out words that come to mind. The teacher talks about or asks questions about some of the words.
2. *Let it Run*: Make groups, and assign a scribe to note down ideas. Have students brainstorm a target of 5 ideas for The Perfect School. The teacher gives feedback as students are working.
3. *Round it Off*: Groups present their ideas in front of the class. Students vote on the top three ideas.
4. *Follow-up*: Pairs of students draft a letter to the head of the school asking if any ideas can be implemented. The teacher gives ongoing feedback, then the letter is sent.

To introduce the theme of positive features of a school in a meaningful way, I began the lesson by asking why they chose our school and, listening with care to responses, dealing with emergent language. For example 'for work' became 'through work' and 'because of work'.

I then brought in the idea of 'the perfect school' and they took their time brainstorming, moving on to record group ideas on mini whiteboards:

---

1. Meddings, L., & Thornbury, S. (2009). *Teaching unplugged: Dogme in English language teaching*. Delta Publishing.

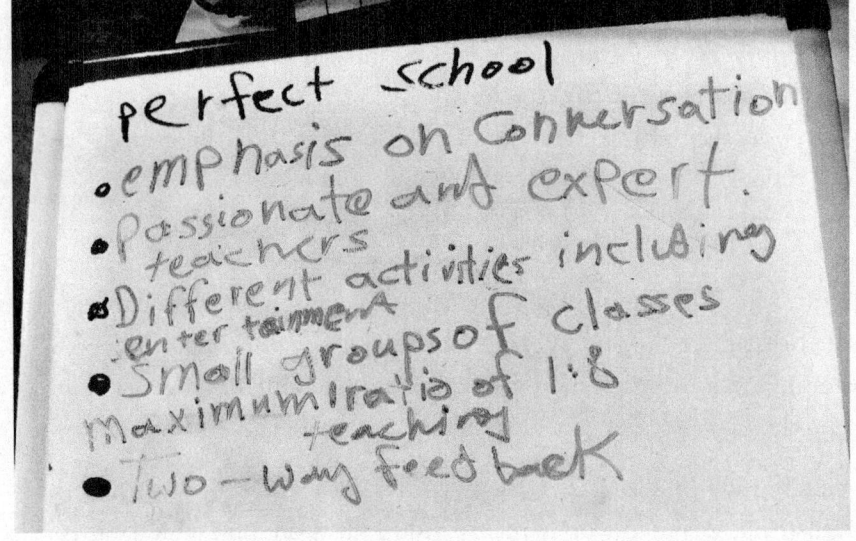

You can see in the images above 'two-way feedback', 'teaching ratio', and 'complimentary' which are upgrades resulting from my monitoring. After a walk around the classroom in which each group looked at all the ideas, students then wrote individual letters to the school principal.

After the activity, I asked the students to reflect on this and other lessons, and responses included comments such as the following:

- **Student 1**: "The face-to-face feedback, review, is more important than exams and no structure focus in the book, you understand the book is a guide, your style is change my English."

- **Student 2:** "If I speak English more in this class maybe I can improve my English more, because when I communicate with other people in English I have to speak, now it's not shy because I always talk with my friend in this class. If I don't remember the vocabulary I always check my book then when I talk I use the vocabulary."
- **Student 3**: "It's more interesting for you when you speak what you live."
- **Student 4**: "I want to have time at the class to speak a lot, like for half an hour, Methodology is better because I need to express myself. It's difficult for you because you have more job to do but for us it's perfect."

In terms of my own reflection, I ended this lesson as so many with that class, buzzing and knowing that I needed to be full of energy and present-minded. At times, I had to fight inertia among students who wrote half heartedly in their lexical notebooks. Additionally, I had to be disciplined to stay with the emergent language and devise an impromptu practice task to help highlight its importance and aid student retention.

Student-written letters are what lent this Dogme lesson its authenticity, ie communication was real, particularly since I decided to pass them on to the head of school. This was rare, something I had never done before, and as far as I'm aware, was a first at the school. Nevertheless, he was instantly keen, and he visited us the next day to give responses.

The principal stood with their letters in his hand and gave individual feedback as he went one by one through the whole pile, making eye contact with each student as he did this.

There had been a mix of surprised and excited reactions when I said I'd invite him, and when he was with us, he had their full attention, faces turned up from start to finish.

This memory of the yellow letters is something that will stay with me for a long time, a special memory in my teaching and one that I have referred to in the training room when encouraging trainee teachers to try dogme.

Ultimately, I saw my efforts repaid in student motivation, enhanced output, and increased self-expression. These positive results affirmed my desire to deliver lessons in this way and kept me putting learner language at the centre of my teaching.

In addition to the samples shown on the mini whiteboards above, here is a sample from the letters students wrote to the Principal:

Cambridge 2019

Dear Frank,
I am writing to suggest the ways to make Bell a perfect School.
1. I think it would be a good idea to give each student his own workbook. I think that the idea of delivering so many photocopies is not comfortable and it's probably more expensive.
2. Small groups of classes. Maximum teaching ratio of 1:8
3. To continue with emphasis on conversation method.
4. All students should have experience of 1-to-1 classes
5. Studying through activities like watching films and movies as learning methods
I hope that these suggestions will be useful for you.

Yours sincerely,
Luis

A NOTE FROM SCOTT:

*How gratifying it is to find an account of a lesson idea that we included in Teaching Unplugged! Writers of cookbooks must get a similar buzz when readers send them photos of how their cake turned out.*

*And there's the added interest of seeing how the original recipe was adapted to the new context.*

*The use of the mini-whiteboards, for example, is a nice touch, as is the fact that the principal responded – in person – to the students' letters, thereby providing a sense of closure to a sustained communicative event, rare to the point of being non-existent in most classroom writing tasks.*

# 11

# TEACHING ABOUT JACKIE ROBINSON IN JAPAN
## JEREMIAH DUTCH

### JAPAN I ADULTS I C1 – C2

Several years ago, I taught what was meant to be a short, fun CLIL (Content and Language Integrated Learning) class with English as the language of instruction, for the general public. It was three 90-minute classes for a few nights over one semester. There were nine students enrolled, mostly older men and one young woman. The course was a part of the Extension Program at Yokohama City University. It was entitled, From Jackie Robinson to Ichiro: Major League Baseball from the End of WWII to the Present.

Covering the entire history of Major League Baseball (MLB) would be too much, and to my mind baseball didn't become very interesting until the 1940s. After Babe Ruth revolutionized the game with his home runs in the 1920s, there was little change in the sport except for stadium lighting and the All-Star Game, but following the war, baseball saw integration, relocation, expansion, cookie-cutter stadiums, Astroturf, the designated hitter, free agency, collusion, strikes, steroids and more.

I wanted to begin with the famous quote by French-born American historian Jaques Barzun, "Whoever wants to know the heart and mind of

America had better learn baseball, the rules and realities of the game." But I wondered if my students really wanted to know the heart and mind of America through baseball. I was advised to make the course more Japan-centric.

Conversations about America often consisted of my students asking me what Americans thought of Japan and Japanese people. More than a few had asked what Americans thought of Ichiro, probably the most famous Japanese person in America at the time. "They think he's a terrific baseball player," was my typical answer.

So, I was sure to mention Japanese players in the Majors in my course plan, including the little-known pitcher Masanori Murakami, who played for San Francisco briefly in the 1960s as the first Japanese in the Majors, the much more successful hurler Hideo Nomo, and of course the first regular Japanese position player in the Majors and bona fide superstar, Ichiro. The plan was to provide some background history about the league that the national hero played in.

I did not intend for the class to be as Dogme as it became; I wanted to have some fun trivia questions with prizes and introduce some video clips of famous moments in baseball history, using mainly Ken Burns' documentary series, *Baseball*, as the primary source. I began the class with a guest speaker who gave a brief talk on Jackie Robinson, who was the first modern African-American Major Leaguer, and from there I intended to move forward in baseball history, but the students threw me a curveball.

First, nine students were less than I expected, creating a potentially cozier teaching environment, but the atmosphere was cold, at least at first. The students all arrived early and sat silently watching (judging?) me as I set up the classroom with materials, mostly coffee table books on baseball to peruse before the class began. Also, they did not seem particularly impressed by the video for John Fogerty's baseball theme song *Centerfield*, which I showed.

Second, I underestimated their knowledge of MLB history. One of my students was an executive for the Japanese Baseball Hall of Fame, a man who had met the legendary Stan Musial personally. Another second guessed my knowledge of Jackie Robinson. "Yes, Robinson played some third base, but he was mostly a second baseman," I explained. Even the youngest among them was a former Washington Nationals season ticket holder.

More importantly, however, instead of moving forward, we were moving backward. Rather than discussing Major League Baseball after integration, they were more interested in why it was segregated in the first place. The emergent language became follow-up questions and instead of me quizzing the students, they were grilling me.

> Why were African Americans not allowed to play?
>
> Why was there discrimination against African Americans?
>
> Why is discrimination a part of American history?

It was becoming improvisational teaching, what Underhill and Maley (2012) call "the dark matter of teaching, that may make up the bulk of lessons, but cannot be scripted or planned."[1] In this case, the subject was dark too. It was as if prejudice and bigotry, sad parts of human nature, were unknown concepts. I wasn't sure if my students were being obtuse or not, but suddenly the theme of the course became very serious. They were not easy or comfortable questions, but I didn't avoid answering them – nor did I become defensive. The students were asking the questions they wanted to ask, instead of what I had planned, and maybe learning something about American history along the way. I always make my students feel like they can ask me any question, but that night I was being tested.

---

1.   Underhill, A., & Maley, A. (2012). Expect the unexpected. *English Teaching Professional*, (82), 4–7.

At last, we moved on to the relocation and expansion of MLB teams and such lighter topics as the designated hitter. Ultimately, I think I won them over, and the class was a success. Yes, the lengthy discussion of segregation put me behind in my course plan, and I was forced to skip over some other aspects, but I learned a lot from that class.

There were a lot of takeaways from that course. In terms of Dogme ELT, one take-away was that sometimes you must jettison what you like to cover and the materials and technology you would like to use in favor of what students would like to learn, or need to learn, and how they would like to learn it. I have tried to remember this in my classes since then.

A NOTE FROM SCOTT:

*Jeremiah's absorbing narrative deals with a teaching context – content-based instruction – that is rarely mentioned in discussions of Dogme, but in fact shares many Dogme characteristics, not least the primary focus on meaning.*

*That is to say, the organizing principle of the programme is the content of the course itself, and its related materials, rather than a preselected list of linguistic items, as in most language teaching situations. But this does not always mean that content-based instruction (CBI), or its most recent manifestation, CLIL, is neces-sarily learner-centred.*

*In fact CBI/CLIL can be just as 'transmissive' in its approach as traditional grammar teaching. So, why I liked Jeremiah's account is that it shows that this need not be the case: that a responsive teacher of content adapts the instruction according to what the students already know, and to their own interests and experiences.*

# 12

# HAVE YOU EVER BEEN BITTEN BY A SHARK?

## JENNY GALLIGAN

### SPAIN | TEENS | A2 – B1

This was a group of young A2 Spanish adolescents, ranging in age from 12-14 years old. The 8 students were coming to private language classes as a supplement to the English classes they received in school. The learners showed great motivation whenever they were tasked with generating their own language, as opposed to learning lists of vocabulary from the coursebook.

The overall aim of the course was to provide learners with a base that could enable them to take the Cambridge B1 PET exam in the next academic year. A coursebook was used, but this did not tend to capture learners' attention. I tried to branch out when possible into coursebook-free classes.

Having read about Dogme for my TESOL Diploma, I started to experiment with it with this group as I continued with my studies. As we neared the summer holidays, learners began to discuss their plans and I decided to capitalise on this. Due to the age, level, and maturity of the students, I decided to use a scaffolded approach, first focusing on lexis and then incorporating sentence structures.

In the previous lesson, learners had been talking in L1 before class began about their summer plans and were curious about my own plans. Therefore, I decided to dedicate the next lesson to this topic, using whatever language they wanted. We started the lesson with a game of charades depicting some typical (go to the beach) and more unusual (get stung by a jellyfish) summer activities. With this adolescent group, I found this initial 'hook' of a game to be productive in boosting their language production in the next stage.

I then asked learners to brainstorm some summer activities – either ones they had done in the past, would do in the coming summer months, or would like to do. This involved some translation support from L1 to English. They then shared their ideas with a partner, and then as a class we shared the ideas. They came up with ideas such as 'go camping', 'go stargazing', 'go sailing' and 'be bitten by a shark' (!). Whilst the last example is a little outlandish, the learners were motivated by the ridiculousness of it. With this group, given their age and level, this stage was key in ensuring communication later on, as well as helping them to feel comfortable.

Learners then created a survey to interview their classmates about summer activities they had done in the past. I gave them the initial chunk 'Have you ever...' and asked them to write as many questions as they could in 10 minutes. Learners were free to add new ideas if they occurred to them during this writing process. Learners wrote questions such as:

> Have you ever gone fishing?
> Have you ever gone stargazing?
> Have you ever been to an outdoor concert?

Learners then took part in a 'speed dating' activity, where they interviewed classmates using their own questions. They were encouraged to ask natural follow-up questions (something that this group of learners struggled with!). Following this was a short time for learners to report back and for us to focus on form, which was mostly concerned with irregular past participles learners had struggled with.

After this, I asked them to choose one classmate who they had interviewed and write a few sentences about what they learned about this person. Student A wrote:

> This person has been on a catamaran with her family, hasn't been bitten by a shark and has been to an outdoor concert in Seville.

Student B wrote:

> This person has been camping, but they haven't been on a cruise.

These sentences were then used as the basis of a 'quiz' style activity. The sentences were read out to a partner, who had to guess which classmate the sentences were about. Once learners had completed this with one partner, they swapped and repeated with two more partners, but this time without the support of their written sentences.

Learners flourished in the brainstorming activity, coming up with far more ideas than I would have been able to myself. The sharing of these ideas led to rich, varied surveys. Fairly key to the lesson's success was the gamification of the final stage, something that the teenage learners responded well to.

An addition that may have further enriched the lesson could have been bringing in my own personal photos of summer activities and asking learners to bring in theirs too. This could have provided a real-world basis for the initial brainstorming stage.

For me as a teacher, this lesson cemented the importance of learner-generated lexis, as the learners' engagement was so much greater than if I had given them a pre-decided list of summer activities or a pre-written survey. It was early on in my experimentation with how Dogme could work in my context and this lesson helped me gain confidence in my capacity as a teacher who could make Dogme a success with adolescent learners. I have gone on to make learner-generated lexis a cornerstone of my practice.

A NOTE FROM SCOTT:

*This is a '100% proof' Dogme lesson, it seems to me: it developed almost entirely out of the content that the learners themselves generated, with, of course, facilitative interventions on the part of the teacher.*

*The only pre-lesson planning – that I can detect – might have been creating the sentences for the 'charades' game (where learners act out sentences that their classmates have to guess). I'm a great fan of surveys as a way of generating interest but also a great deal of language.*

*The way you have structured this one seems to me the way to go: generating interest in the topic, after which students create their own questions, survey their classmates, and – very importantly – report the results in written form. This has the effect both of making the students a little more attentive at the interactive stage, but also of shifting the focus from fluency on to accuracy – never a bad idea!*

*And the idea of following this up with a quiz is inspired. Also, please note the level of the class: A2! This gives the lie to the idea that Dogme is only suitable for advanced learners who have a sufficient core of language to create their own content.*

# 13

# SEEING THE CLASS THROUGH A CHILD'S EYES

## JENNY GALLIGAN

## SPAIN | YOUNG LEARNERS | A1

There were six 4-year-olds in the group, who I met with twice a week for an hour. They were highly motivated and energetic, as four-year-olds tend to be. From the beginning of the academic year, they showed a strong capacity for picking up any language, especially phrases and expressions that they were using in L1.

The learners were in class as their parents wanted a complement to their mainstream education. A coursebook was used, although the main function was to provide a rough syllabus which I then expanded on (and sometimes abandoned!). As a monolingual group, they communicated with each other in their L1, but were happy to include any English I provided them with.

Sticking to the coursebook language rarely resulted in authentic communication with my students. I found myself teaching more and more what they were actually saying in their L1 as opposed to what the coursebook dictated. These expressions and phrases showed up in most classes, and so the learners showed real progress in learning them. I began to look out for these moments and to see how I could capitalise on them.

As we were doing a drawing dictation together, one of the learners took out a glue stick from her pencil case. She proudly displayed it to her class-mates, its star feature being that it no longer had glue inside and so was, in fact, a makeshift telescope. She proceeded to hold it up to her eye and pronounced, in L1, 'Yo veo L' (I see L). I quickly translated it for her, prompting her with 'I see L'. She slowly turned the 'telescope' on every student in the class, proclaiming, now in English, 'I see ...'.

I decided to go with the moment and let the students get fully distracted from what we were 'supposed' to be focused on. Another student asked to have a go, and she repeated the same procedure, without any instruction from me on what she should do and only some gentle prompting about how to say 'I see' in English.

The glue stick proceeded to pass from student to student, each of them holding it up to their eye and looking at their classmates. Some students were able to produce the phrase in English, others needed some prompt-ing. What was obvious was their sheer joy in this activity. It wasn't about English at all, but about exploration of the world and the objects around them.

Due to their interest, the next class I brought in some empty toilet rolls. Each student was given their own roll to decorate and draw on. We then repeated the activity from the previous class, but this time with all students participating at once! We focused on the other people in the classroom, but already some students were going further, incorporating classroom objects and the room around us. I collected the rolls for future use, rather than letting the students take them home.

One of the key elements of teaching very young learners (VYL) is repeti-tion, and so the toilet rolls became a staple in my classes with this group. By following their lead on what is interesting for them to 'see' and some teacher modeling, we began to play a guessing game with colours – 'I see something red/blue/green' – always with the toilet roll telescope. The other learners would use their telescopes to look around the class and find the object. It didn't matter that they didn't know the word in English –

they would happily shout it out in Spanish and I would provide the English for them. It was an authentic and joyful way for learners to explore the environment around them.

We went on some mini adventures with our telescopes (of course, I needed one too!), going into the corridor and even visiting another classroom.

Before this activity, I would have scoffed at the thought of Dogme for VYL. However, it opened my eyes to the possibilities that exist in the VYL classroom, if only we are willing to put ourselves in the shoes of the young learners and see what they would like to communicate. We may want to 'engineer' fun in the classroom, but often the most fun and joy comes from the learners themselves.

As mentioned above, the telescopes made frequent appearances in our classroom. Each time we took them out, I was reminded of the power of letting the learners take the lead and how free play at that age can nourish and enrich the possibilities of engagement with the English language.

This Dogme moment also encouraged me to look at how this element of 'freedom' could work with other levels and ages. I've begun to examine the interactions students have and how they play with each other, experimenting with how I can make the most of these moments in the classroom.

A NOTE FROM LUKE:

*Jenny says she used a coursebook mainly to provide a 'rough syllabus' to be enlarged upon or set aside. This flexibility means that when the light bulb moment occurs with the glue stick, it can be developed fully.*

*The creative use of an empty glue stick as a telescope made me think of the fundamental difference between language as a subject and, say, math. If you're teaching a math class and everyone starts talking about last night's football, you might be off topic. But in a language class, you're still right on topic! If the ultimate aim is communication, it doesn't matter what we're communicating about – providing that it's interesting.*

*The other day my wife (also an educator) showed me a clip of her four year-old nephew doing an activity for 'children's week' at school. And I asked – why isn't every week children's week? It's like having a wet week in a swimming pool.*

*This lesson is full of joy, as children are when we let them lead – as Jenny says, 'often the most fun and joy comes from the learners themselves.'*

# 14

# A MINIMAL MODEL FOR TRAINEE TEACHERS

### DYLAN GATES

## SPAIN | ADULTS | B2 – C1

The learners had signed up to receive classes taught by trainee teachers on an initial face-to-face teacher training course (Trinity CertTESOL) in Spain. The class consisted of eight mostly Spanish adult learners (B2).

I was working as a course trainer. It was the last teaching practice on the course and I was waiting for a struggling trainee teacher to arrive. Five minutes before the lesson was due to start, I received a text message informing me that she was dropping out of the course. Rather than let the learners down, I decided to teach the lesson. I now had only four minutes to come up with something!

I decided to hold a Dogme lesson for several reasons:

Firstly, during one of the input sessions, the trainees had asked me about Dogme so I thought it would be an ideal opportunity to demonstrate an unplugged approach as an alternative to following a course book or using published lesson plans.

Secondly, I felt confident in this situation. The trainee teachers had completed their guided observations of experienced teachers and their own teaching practice. There was no real pressure on me to demonstrate specific teaching techniques or skills; I could make it a far more learner-centred event.

Thirdly, I had always felt a sense of cognitive dissonance when giving demonstration lessons on initial teacher-training courses as I would often be required to deliver PPP (Presentation-Practice-Production) lessons that did not reflect my preferred teaching approach. This would provide me with the opportunity to teach in a more 'authentic' way.

Finally, in a previous lesson, I had witnessed a 'Dogme moment' when the learners started talking about their favourite childhood films. One learner mentioned 'Star Wars' and everybody's faces lit up. The trainee teacher, pressured by the requirements of completing her lesson plan' quickly curtailed the conversation but the learners continued to chat about the film.

I had a fairly clear aim for the lesson. I wanted the learners to talk about somebody who'd had a positive influence at some pivotal moment in their life: a mentor figure. I printed out a picture of Yoda and stuck it to the centre of the whiteboard. The learners walked in, noticed the picture, and commented on it. I elicited what they knew about Yoda and his relationship to Luke Skywalker. The words 'guide' and 'teacher' came up. I asked for similar words and boarded them as a spidergram.

We explored the 'teacher' synonyms and I put them in small groups to discuss the differences between them before asking them to check the meaning in their dictionaries. They were surprised by some of the nuances.

For the next stage, I told the learners that I was thinking about an influential figure in my own life and told them to ask me questions to find out more. We reformulated some questions: a useful few minutes dealing with emergent language.

Then, I asked the learners to think about a 'Yoda' figure in their own lives in preparation for a mingling activity in which they would speak with five other people. I invited the trainee teachers to join in. This was quiet time as I wanted to give the learners time to consider what they wanted to say and predict questions.

I decided to use a timer and change conversation partners every three minutes. The first round was a little stilted as the interaction followed a typical question-and-answer format. I reminded them to converse naturally.

The second round worked better but I noticed that the learners were making quite a few mistakes with verb patterns. I stopped the activity and quickly reviewed some common patterns related to the topic:

> He advised me to study X at university
> She encouraged me to keep practising
> He supported me when I was not able to...
> She prevented me from dropping out.

We were also able to briefly review the third and mixed conditionals.

> If she hadn't supported me, I wouldn't have gone to university
> I would have gotten fired if he hadn't helped me learn the process.
> If she hadn't encouraged me, I'm not sure I would be working as a nurse today.

I continued the activity until each learner had participated in five short conversations about mentors. I made a few notes about emergent language but for the most part I let the activity run without much interference.

We had a quick feedback session reviewing a few language points. After reviewing some emergent language points, I finished the class by asking the learners to choose five characteristics of effective mentors.

I was pleased with the way the lesson evolved. The lesson was materials-light (just the image of Yoda), conversation-driven (the learners spent most of the lesson having meaningful conversations) and we focused on some emergent language (question formation, verb patterns, and some lexical clarification).

Most importantly, the learners were engaged throughout and were given the opportunity to practise telling anecdotes (a valuable skill) and asking referential questions (a feature of meaning-driven conversations).

The learners responded positively and were particularly appreciative of the chance to have the time and space to have meaningful discussions and noticed that their language improved through task repetition.

The trainee teachers were also surprised by the quantity and quality of learner-generated language. One commented how Dogme lessons could save a fortune on photocopying costs! Another insightful comment came from one trainee who was surprised at how the learners had resolved any communication issues themselves by negotiating meaning.

I'd been teaching with an unplugged approach for several years at this stage but this experience changed my approach to several aspects of teacher training. Firstly, I ensure that my demonstration lessons include Dogme moments in which the learners' voices can be heard. During these Dogme moments, I ask the trainee teachers to join in giving themselves the chance to be responsive rather than preemptive.

Secondly, whenever possible, I help trainee teachers find room in their lesson plans for 'emergent language' slots so they can deal with any learner-generated language that comes up.

Finally, I encourage trainee teachers to limit the amount of materials they bring to the lesson. I remind them of one of the Dogme principles 'Students are engaged by content they have created rather than third-party content' and this often produces a 'lightbulb moment' when the trainee teachers realises that learners can generate much of the lesson content themselves.

I've given the same lesson on a number of occasions in different teaching contexts and it always works well. I've even used it as one of my demonstration lessons on Trinity CertTESOL courses so I'm doing my bit to introduce Dogme to trainee teachers.

A NOTE FROM LUKE:

> *It's interesting to reflect on Dylan's preparation for this lesson. On the face of it, it's hasty: five minutes at best. But it's actually a moment when attentiveness (to his trainees' interests), awareness (of the nature of the class), self-reflection (on demonstration lessons that didn't reflect his beliefs), and professional memory (Yoda, and that 'Dogme moment' that didn't happen), all come together. Purpose, context, opportunity – and a catalyst to set the ball rolling. Not all teaching interventions are deliberative and linear. Sometimes it all comes together. The same is true of learning.*

> *Having figured this out just before the lesson, the teacher needs to be alert during the lesson – advising on how to approach the conversation rounds, and feeding back on verb patterns.*

> *It's also fascinating to hear what the trainee teachers observing the lesson took out of it: the potential in minimal stimulus, the resourcefulness of the learners when given space to participate, and the benefits of task repetition. This lesson represents a model they can adopt and adapt in their own teaching.*

# 15

# THE BEST AND WORST WEEKEND
## PAOLO GHIDINI

## REPUBLIC OF GEORGIA | YOUNG LEARNERS | A1 – A2

My time in Georgia was an exciting and formative one. I joined as a freelance teacher with PPP imprinted in my daily practice, and I left with DELTA (Extended assignment on a DOGME course), tons of experience, a promotion, and a renewed passion for teaching and discovering approaches that challenge preconceived ideas.

The class was a group of 20 young learners, aged 11-13, at the British Council in Tbilisi, Republic of Georgia. They were placed in the same group based on their perceived level (CEFR A2) and were all fairly new to a communicative environment, having been exposed to plenty of traditional explicit instruction at school.

Have you ever noticed the change in mood in the classroom when you move from a communicative lead-in to "Now, open the book to page 16"? Well, with this group of learners, it wasn't subtle! The kids' facial expressions changed so dramatically that it was heartbreaking. So, I decided to give Dogme a go, with the hope that shifting away from the book would also help me with some classroom management issues (little did I know, I would end up becoming a fierce opponent of the whole concept of classroom management!)

As the kids entered the classroom, I asked, as usual, individually, how their weekend went. As more and more of them kept coming in, I said: 'You know what? I can't ask everyone! Why don't you tell each other?' So I put them in pairs and asked them to share with their partner what they had done over the previous couple of days. Soon, the pairs broke up as some learners were more interested in something others had done and joined others' conversations to listen or to ask questions (often in their L1, to this day a complete mystery to me). I resisted the instinct of 'forcing' them to speak English and to stick to their partner, and instead moved closer and just listened attentively while taking notes of what the kids were saying. Interestingly, in most cases, kids tried to revert to speaking English as soon as they realized I was listening.

After a good 15 minutes, while students were still talking, I went to the whiteboard and wrote a list of weekend activities based on the notes I took. The kids' production was a brilliant display of creativity and language inaccuracy at the same time:

I goed to the cinema
I was in mall with my brother
I was swimming, then i was eating McDonald's, then I was playing computer games, then...

And similar. I wrote a 'correct' version of these utterances on the board:

I went to the cinema
I went to the mall with my brother
I ate at McDonald's

I wrote about a dozen of them and also made sure to include my own weekend activities (going for a bike ride and studying), 'hidden' among the students' answers.

I then asked the students to stop talking and directed their attention to the board, saying that two of these activities were something I had done during my weekend. In pairs, they guessed what they were, a task in which they succeeded, very quickly (by that time they knew me pretty well).

I then started going through the other statements, one by one, asking if, in the previous conversation, they had heard of anyone who (for example), went to the cinema. This triggered an engaging whole class feedback, in which every learner was involved, either because they had heard of the activity done by another student, or because their curiosity was triggered and now they wanted to hear who went to the cinema, to which one and if it was 3D or not, to see what film, etc. All were expressed in very basic language surely, but all were incredibly communicative, incredibly spontaneous, and with very little need for support from the teacher.

I have to admit I was lost in the moment and completely forgot about a way to round it up, so when we ran out of statements to explore, I came up with a task on the spot for them to pick the best and the worst weekend (which, to my surprise, they enjoyed doing, and which generated some more production).

It seemed to me at the time that students had 'learnt' the correct form of many verbs in the past simple. I know better now, and they were probably just parroting what was on the board (learning takes much longer), but I am convinced that starting from the 'learner-generated text' created the conditions for learners to be ready to absorb language, or at the very least to be motivated to deal with it in the most accurate way possible. This lesson is also likely to have contributed positively to seeing second language learning as a way to communicate meaningful things rather than a subject to study in a book.

The perception that this lesson had a much bigger impact both motivationally and content-wise than any other lesson I had planned, made me think further and eventually brought me to the path of studying authenticity and focusing on how I can approach every activity or material with 'the real world' in mind. Moreover, the penny dropped, and the words of John Dewey: 'Education is not preparation for life, education is life itself' suddenly rang true, since those kids were not 'practicing communication' for subsequent use, they were actively communicating and sharing. Perhaps most importantly, at the end of that specific lesson, the students left class smiling, and giggling, with magically more energy than when they came in.

A NOTE FROM SCOTT:

> *This is a great insight, Paolo: 'Those kids were not 'practicing communication' for subsequent use, they were actively communicating and sharing.'*
>
> *Dogme shares with what are now called usage-based theories of language learning the belief that there is no real separation between learning and using.*
>
> *Using IS learning, and learning IS using – or, at least, it should be. The separation between the two has resulted in teaching approaches that have deferred real communication almost indefinitely – both in terms of the individual lesson and the whole of the learner/user's language education.*
>
> *What I like about this lesson is that it starts with real language use and doesn't really stop.*

# 16

# FACES BEHIND THE SCREENS
## MARIA GLAZUNOVA

## UKRAINE | TEENS | A1 – C1

This was an online class of four Ukrainian teenagers aged 15-17. Their English level ranged from B1 to B2. At the time, I was teaching Business English to German professionals at a German company. Interestingly, the Director of Studies of this company was a huge fan of Dogme. She enjoyed my book for teachers on Dogme, reducing over-prep and preventing burnout, and was excited to have me on their team. Besides German professionals, they had asked me to work with these teens.

At first, it was challenging. The students didn't speak hardly at all in the beginning, refusing to turn on their cameras, and were undergoing a tough period in their lives, just like me, due to the events in our country.

I had complete freedom over the curriculum. So, I combined the TBLT approach with Dogme and gradually transitioned entirely to Dogme. Step by step, I dived deeper into their interests and needs and found things to build on. And you know what? Magic happened.

Dogme is the most effective approach that I've ever applied to create an emotional connection and get the best results with my students. I love it! It opens up new perspectives.

Here's an analogy: I'm fascinated by Michelangelo's view that a sculpture is already complete in the marble. The sculptor's work is to find and release it by removing excess material. Similarly, our learners already have the lesson within them when they come to our class. They bring their experiences, feelings, dreams, and goals. Our job as teachers is to turn that into a learning opportunity and respond to their needs. We minimize reliance on external materials and instead focus on direct interaction with students to integrate language into their lives. They are the main protagonists of the story.

At the beginning of the class, for the first 10 minutes, the teens shared how they spent their weekend with family and friends. I always strive to connect my classes to the real lives of students. The topic of describing personality and physical appearance emerged, and we decided to explore this further. So, I asked them to share a photo of their best friend or relative in our shared Google Doc and gave them a few minutes to prepare a description. I also provided some guidelines:

- Who the person is
- What he/she looks like
- Describe his/her personality
- Explain "My friend is reliable because..."

When they were ready, we decided not to go into breakout rooms because everyone was interested in hearing the stories. One of the students began:

> This is my best friend. He is high and muscular...

I saw an opportunity for immediate correction:

> It's better to say 'tall'. By the way, in slang, 'he is high' means being on drugs.

> Haha, omg no no… He is TALL, not high. We go to the gym very often. He is kind because he is always ready to help and um.. loves giving…

> Generous.

> Thank you! He's generous. We get on very well. I know him all my life…

When the student finished the description, I commented:

> Wow, amazing. Thank you! It sounds like you admire him.

> Admire?

> When you really like and respect someone.

> Oh definitely. I admire my best friend.

> You mentioned some interesting phrases like 'we get on very well.' Guys, do you know this phrase? (They did not)

So I asked the student to explain the meaning. We also discussed the reason for using the Present Perfect in the sentence, 'I've known him all my life.'

Everyone took turns and talked about the special people in their photos. Sometimes, I made immediate corrections or I made them after they spoke to avoid interrupting the flow.

We were especially impressed by the youngest and most introverted student in the group. He never said much. But this time, he spoke passionately about his little brother and delivered a heart-warming description.

The students generated lots of new spontaneous language, and I also shared some relevant expressions: 'to take after', 'the life and soul of the party', 'to look up to someone', and so on. We wrote everything down in our Google Doc in two columns (phrases about physical appearance in one column and phrases about personality in another).

Next, I selected the ten most challenging new phrases/words, and we played a game. I asked one student to choose any phrase/word (but not to tell us!) and explain the meaning so we could guess the word. The first person to guess correctly earned a point. Then students took turns. This way, we could recycle new vocabulary.

At the end of the class, we still had some time, so I got an idea to extend the activity further. I suggested the following:

> Guys! You've never seen each other. You've only heard each other's voices. Let's describe how you think everybody looks based on their voice. Then, you'll turn on the cameras for the first time and see if you are close. It'll be so much fun!

They were thrilled by this idea and shared fascinating and completely different descriptions of each other. When they turned on the cameras, they were shocked.

> Omg, I thought you were much taller!

> You have curly hair!

> What's the color of your eyes? Blue?? I knew it!

It was a memorable and emotional experience for them. And I accomplished my mission, too – finally, they turned on their cameras! We even took a photo of that moment. In future classes, they would end up turning on their cameras more often.

To wrap up, I always asked two questions at the end of every class so we could reflect together:

1. What did you like during the class?
2. What would you like to change?

The students told me that it was easy to remember new vocabulary because the context helped a lot. And the last activity was fantastic because they felt so connected to each other.

What can I say? Dogme connects people and makes them feel heard, seen, and valued. What can be more important?

After that class, we became closer, and students began sharing more interests and preferred discussion topics, leading to increased motivation to speak and practice the language. This boosted my confidence to experiment with emergent language creatively.

A NOTE FROM SCOTT:

> *Applying Dogme principles online during the pandemic (and not just during the pandemic) turned out to be a challenge for even the most committed 'Dogmetists': the vital role that proximity and physicality play in forging and cementing relationships cannot be underestimated.*
>
> *The problem is made worse if learners resist turning on their webcams. Moreover, classrooms are (reasonably) insulated from the kinds of disruptions that occur in your home or workplace.*

*Maria's lesson triumphantly demonstrates how these constraints need not compromise the most basic Dogme principles, foremost of which is – in Maria's words: 'Our learners already have the lesson within them when they come to our class'.*

*'Releasing' that lesson, and 'uncovering' the language that best expresses it, is key. And if this can be done without risk to the learners' vulnerable emotional lives, but actually serves to make them 'feel seen, heard and valued', so much the better.*

# 17

# MOVING TO WHERE THE STUDENTS ARE

CAROL GOODEY

## UK I ADULTS I A2 – B2

This was a small group of adult ESOL learners who had come to live and work in Scotland. I had been working with some of them for a few months and others had recently joined. On this evening there were four learners – two women (one from Poland and one from Romania) and two men (both from Poland). They had been in Scotland for different lengths of time and varied in their knowledge of English. The Romanian woman had learned some English at school. The others had only started learning after arriving in Scotland.

It was a rural area, with two small towns and a number of smaller villages. I was the only ESOL worker there, working for the local authority and based in one of the towns. These sessions took place in the other town, nearer to where the learners lived and worked. Limited public transport meant it was difficult for them to get to me, so I went to them. I had arranged to use the local public library after closing time. I had a key, an alarm code, some ideas of what I would focus on that evening, and small pieces of paper that I used to record the language.

With learners at different levels in a group, with new people joining frequently, and with work shift patterns meaning that learners can't always come along, I have found that a Dogme approach works best. Working through a coursebook does not make sense in this context. Where possible, I like to work from the conversation that develops between the people in the room so that learners are more connected to the language that emerges, more focused on communicating and more ready to absorb new information.

As I arrived at the library door shortly before 6pm, two of the learners were waiting for me. Once inside, rather than sitting around our usual table, they suggested we sit in the armchairs in the other corner. We sat and started to talk about our day. As the other learners arrived, our conversation turned to jobs. This was the topic I had planned to focus on that evening. I had an activity that I could use if needed, but with the conversation already moving forward, it meant that it wasn't necessary.

I asked the learners about the jobs they had done in their life. We heard that one learner had just got an additional job. We found out that two had run their own businesses in their country and two were interested in doing some part-time study. Since the learners were at different levels, the language, and what I chose to focus on with each of them was different. For example, when one learner talked, I paid attention to his use of the past simple, recasting or eliciting self-correction. We had looked at that in previous sessions so the conversation provided a context to work on it further. With a more proficient learner, I introduced the present perfect continuous to help with what she was trying to say. Learners worked hard at expressing themselves, searching for the best way they could say something, and working with other learners to find the word or phrase they were looking for.

As words and phrases were needed, and as grammar points came up, I wrote them on small pieces of paper and put them on the low table we were sitting around. Towards the end of the session, we reviewed the language that had been recorded. I referred to things they had talked about and elicited the word or phrase that I had suggested to help them say it better.

As we looked back at the language used, patterns emerged. In addition to one learner telling us that she had been working since she was 18, we had heard that another had been living in his village for two years. One of us used to work as a shop assistant, while another used to live in a neighbouring town. Having the language on small pieces of paper meant that we could move it around and then build on it with further examples.

> I've been working since I was 18.
> I've been working at the hotel since November.
> I've been living in the village for 2 years.
> I used to live in the town.
> I used to be a shop assistant.
> I used to volunteer.

Much of the vocabulary related to employment or business. There were words we might anticipate in a conversation about jobs such as wages, contract, apprenticeship, accounting. We also needed words to describe a common aspect of the working environment that may not commonly be introduced to discuss the topic such as bully, intimidate and stressed.

I really enjoyed how this session flowed and how everyone was able to contribute and learn. As Mike Baynham and his colleagues suggested, "Talk is work in the ESOL classroom" with one of our main tasks being to "encourage classroom talk, transforming talk into learning and learning into talk"[1]. It doesn't always work this way. If the conversation doesn't develop spontaneously, I will have a quick activity or an object ready to prompt conversation. If that doesn't work, I'll have a more structured activity that we work through. This week, though, it worked!

---

1.   Baynham, M., Roberts, C., Cooke, M. and Simpson, J., Ananiadou, K., Callaghan, J., McGoldrick, J. and Wallace, C. (2007) Effective Teaching and Learning: ESOL. London: NRDC. Available at: https://dera.ioe.ac.uk/id/eprint/22304/1/doc_3341.pdf

Learners wanted to take home 'their' words that I'd recorded on the pieces of paper. Instead, I offered to type them up so that they could all have them, with links to further information. As a colleague commented, though, I could have taken a photo so that I still could create a shared record while not taking away 'ownership' of the language. Now when learners want to take their language, they can... after I've taken a photo.

A NOTE FROM LUKE:

> *ESOL students are often poorly paid or marginalised: classes are a vital bridge to using English in real-life situations. As such, Dogme – with its focus on locally situated discourse – was embraced by the ESOL teaching community quite early on.*
>
> *Carol recognises its fit to irregular attendance and different learner levels, too: sometimes Dogme is a pragmatic solution as well as a pedagogical choice. In an improvised setting, with a few bits of paper, the teacher adopts Candy van Olst's classic distillation of Dogme: 'Listen, Ask.'*
>
> *Carol's first problem is where to hold the class, and her solution – ' It was difficult for them to get to me, so I went to them' – is a nice analogy for the approach itself. Instead of trying to fit the learners to the plan, the teacher fits to the class. The result is a coherent but wide-ranging language set, yielding patterns as well as surprises, recorded on scraps of paper which – it turns out – can be photographed and shared.*
>
> *'Talk is work in the ESOL classroom', writes Carol, quoting from Effective Teaching and Learning – ESOL. And talk is the subject of any English language class. We don't just teach to get to the talk. We also talk to get to the teaching.*

# 18

# THAT'S MY STORY!

## CAROL GOODEY

## UK I TEENS I A1

This was a group of unaccompanied young people seeking asylum in Scotland – young people who have been separated from their parents or guardians and who are looked after by the local authority. The number in the group changed as people arrived or left but, on this day, there were five young people in the room from Eritrea, Somalia, Iran and Afghanistan – two girls and three boys – aged 15-17. This was one of my early sessions with them.

I was working in the local authority as an Adult Literacies and ESOL worker. Much of my work was in a rural area with adults but I had been asked to work with the young people by the social worker responsible for looking after them. Once a week, I travelled to their base in the city. We met in one of the meeting rooms, near to offices of youth workers and social workers and a drop-in area for local young people. The social worker had also arranged for a volunteer tutor to help with the group, something I'd not had before.

In the ESOL contexts I worked in, Dogme was the approach that made sense. People in the groups all came from different countries, spoke different languages, had different educational backgrounds, and were different ages. Some came with a strong knowledge of the grammar rules from years of language learning in school, others had learned what they knew informally, picking it up from the people around them. Shift patterns, other commitments, and new arrivals meant that planning to focus on specific needs in a particular session was, at the very least, difficult. Dogme had become the way I approached all my ESOL work.

I wanted to provide space for the young people to talk about themselves, without compelling them to open up about traumatic experiences. I also wanted to acknowledge the languages they brought with them.

I brought in a map of the world, some sheets of A4 paper, and a pile of small pieces of paper that I liked to use instead of a whiteboard. I shared my own experiences with language. I talked about how I was born in Scotland and learned English as my first language, how I'd grown up in Ireland where I'd learned Irish at school. I told them that I'd moved to France and learned French and later when I lived in Belgium, I learned Dutch. I accompanied this by drawing and by locating the different countries on the map. The other tutor talked about how she had learned French at school and how she had picked up some Spanish. The learners were very engaged, interested in us and our stories, and keen to see where the countries were on the map. Then it was their turn.

They started by saying where they were born and a bit about their first languages. At this stage, I helped with phrases such as, 'I was born in...', and words, the names of countries, and of the languages. As they communicated, often by pointing at the map, I provided language orally and kept a record of that language on the small pieces of paper.

As their story developed, they were soon telling the story of their journey to Scotland. As well as the languages they encountered, they communicated about the different countries they had travelled through, how long they had stayed in each place, and occasionally, how they had travelled. They showed interest in each other's experiences, asked questions, and provided support.

Using the small pieces of paper, we built up the story for each of them.

> I was born in....
> When I was 14, I went to...
> I was there for .... weeks/months/years.
> Then I went to....
> I came to Scotland in....

Capturing the stories in writing required further negotiation of meaning – How long were you in Italy? 3 weeks? Oh, 3 months! – using drawings and gestures to facilitate understanding.

We then used these simple, but powerful, stories to consolidate what we'd learned, with each learner working with their own stories. We didn't at this stage expand beyond what was needed unless learners asked about particular features or words; we could do that in a future session. The young people then practiced recounting their stories, prompted by the pieces of paper. We turned some of the pieces of paper over for the young people to work on remembering the language until each could tell their own story unaided.

At one point, one of the boys said, 'That's my story! Next week, you ask me, 'What's your story?'. Being able to tell his own story was important to him and he was keen to make sure he retained that ability. Because of where we were, there were other (non-ELT/ESOL) colleagues in the building. I asked a colleague – a youth worker – to pop in. Ask me 'What's your story?', they prompted her. She did and they had the opportunity to share their experiences with someone new. Later a manager also looked in and he too had the privilege of hearing about their journeys.

Being able to connect with people beyond the classroom is particularly valuable, especially when they can do so on their terms, telling their own stories. There is learning in this, not only for the language learner but also for those they interact with who are often not used to talking to speakers of other languages. The young people being able to initiate conversation, rather than waiting to be spoken to, makes connection and empathy easier. In future sessions, we continued to take opportunities that the environment offered us, connecting what was happening in the classroom to the people outside of it. After discussing a topic in class, for example, the learners formulated questions and surveyed people in the drop-in area, coming back to report what they'd found and talk about the new connections they'd made.

A NOTE FROM SCOTT:

> *The neurologist Oliver Sacks once wrote, "If we wish to know about a man [sic], we ask 'What is his story — his real, inmost story?' — for each of us is a biography, a story. Each of us is a singular narrative, which is constructed, continually, unconsciously, by, through, and in us — through our perceptions, our feelings, our thoughts, our actions; and, not least, our discourse, our spoken narrations. Biologically, physiologically, we are not so different from each other; historically, as narratives — we are each of us unique."[1]*

> *Using minimal means (a map, slips of paper) Carol's lesson sensitively explores this principle, endowing her immigrant learners with the capacity to voice their stories and thereby to ease their integration into a new life.*

> *In rejecting imposed and imported materials, Dogme offers a space for the learners' stories to emerge, take shape, and propagate.*

---

1.  Sacks, O. (1985). *The man who mistook his wife for a hat and other clinical tales.* Picador.

# 19

# SHARING THE WORLD OF DOGME
## VILTE GRIDASOVA-RUSEVIČIENĖ

## LITHUANIA I ADULTS I A1 – C1

Classes are usually held on Zoom or Teams, but there are in-classroom sessions as well. My typical class hosts 4-25 adults from a wide range of backgrounds and ages 25-75 plus. Several weeks into the course, we now cannot imagine anything but the Dogme conversation-based class. Yet, before joining the course, these same people sounded skeptical about the approach.

*"What do you mean by NO textbooks? Are you a teacher, seriously?"*

Despite coming from various backgrounds, my learners share one common need – practice in speaking fluently. To meet this need, Dogme becomes a game changer. Through learner-relevant topics – relationships, hobbies, work-life balance – my students naturally engage in a conversation. I can open the *ActivInspire*[1] interactive display and use images as a prompt for speaking. Or we can listen to and discuss a TED talk. Or create a text of our own. All of these will lead to plenty of

---

1. https://www.prometheanworld.com/gb/products/software/activinspire/

emerging language. After a while, the learners get used to a Dogme approach and appreciate its value.

Research shows that people love talking about themselves. That's why, for about 20 minutes in the first class, my students speak about themselves ... as learners (Which also serves as a needs analysis activity).

One by one, I reveal images featuring common learning environments and ways that people study. I ask, "What do you see? Where are they? What are they doing?"

As this is our first activity, we do it as a whole class to reduce stress. My beginners come up with words like "writing", "university", or phrases like "sunny weather", "in the café", and "late at night". To elicit learning-related vocabulary, I continue with: How do you learn best? The students shout out "read", "vocabulary", "questions and answers", "difficult" or make simple sentences ("I like read books"), all of which I write on the board. This language record is our first focus on the emerging language. Having praised some students for their output and mentioning even the silent ones ("Good, Snieguole, I saw you making notes – a great habit), we go over the notes. Here, I draw attention to the silent "w" in "answer". Another "popular" structure is – like + gerund. The language focus is light and encouraging and the students accept it naturally.

By now, the students will have become more confident so I can split them in groups to discuss the questions:

1. How do you learn best?
2. Who was/ is your favourite teacher and why?

Online or face-to-face (F2F), I rotate among the groups and remain as a listener for about 30 minutes, making notes of the emerging language. When we get back together, everyone's input deserves praise. I spend about 10 minutes on emerging language. My experience shows the learners accept this activity naturally and with enthusiasm – emphasizing the value of emerging language as it focuses on the learners' immediate needs.

By now, the students will be tired – so, it's my turn to speak. I usually start like this: "We've spoken about learning and now I'll tell you about our classroom. You can relax and listen. Is everyone comfortable? Do you have tea or coffee?"

I start with a slide featuring Scott Thornbury and his books. "This is my teacher, Scott. He is from New Zealand but lives in Barcelona. He is an author of books for teachers and travels around the world to teach other teachers..."

I say this to every new group and every time the students are impressed to learn I also have a teacher! Naturally, they are eager to ask questions. So, we engage in a genuine conversation about Scott and his books. After that, I continue, "Scott is the creator of the Dogme ELT approach that has three main principles and I'm going to explain what our Dogme classroom is like."

In response to the learners' questions, I outline the basic tenets of Dogme and encourage them to react with their own opinions and further questions. During this phase, I suggest that together we will create our own coursebook: "Our book will contain a) the notes from the board, b) the notes you make, and c) the learner's diary."

Introducing emerging language is simple! I open the earlier slides with the emerging language from our class and ask my students to assign each item to each area, e.g., I like making notes – grammar; silent "w" in "answer" /ˈɑːnsə/ – pronunciation, etc.

My experience tells me to allow at least 15 minutes for the learners to reflect, discuss or ask questions about Dogme and its benefits, which are:

1. interactive learning and active involvement;
2. meeting the ultimate needs of the learner; and
3. focusing on all four language areas.

We can spend time answering the learners' questions (in English or their native language), discuss the points in the visual above, or initiate further discussion in groups (with higher levels), e.g., What do you find most attractive in the Dogme ELT classroom? How will the Dogme ELT classroom be beneficial for you?

Dogme is more about genuine flow. At the end of every lesson, the learners see what they have learned. So, we open our Language Fridge – to fill it with language we're going to "consume" within several days! We fill the Vocabulary, Pronunciation, Grammar, and Discourse shelves with instances of the emerging language from the class. Located on *Padlet*[2], it enables students to access the Fridge from any device.

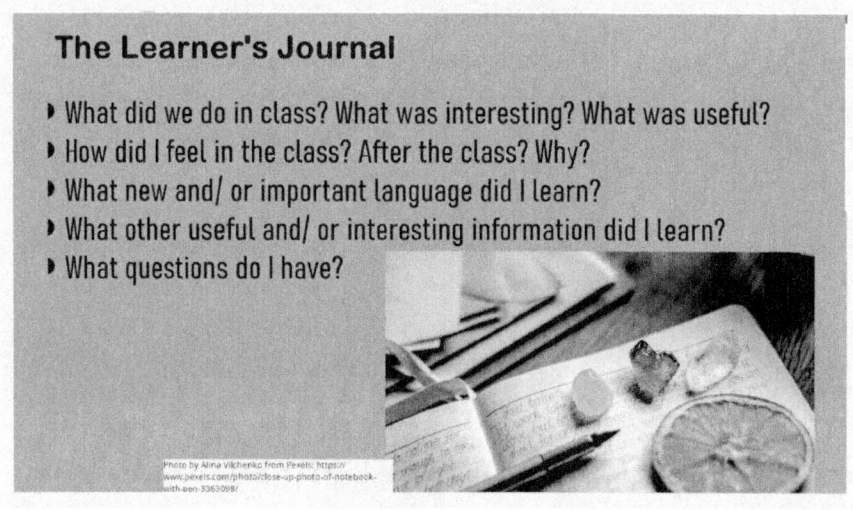

**The Learner's Journal**

▸ What did we do in class? What was interesting? What was useful?
▸ How did I feel in the class? After the class? Why?
▸ What new and/ or important language did I learn?
▸ What other useful and/ or interesting information did I learn?
▸ What questions do I have?

Photo by Alina Vilchenko from Pexels: https://www.pexels.com/photo/close-up-photo-of-notebook-with-pen-3363098/

In the beginning of our next lesson, either as a class or in smaller groups, we go through the journal notes and have another meaningful conversation. This results in another portion of the emerging language.

After focusing on form, we delve into our first topic. We laugh, speak up, take notes, and focus on form again. Dogme casts its spells with every

2.  https://padlet.com/

class – learning becomes light and natural, almost invisible, and yet so powerful.

A note from Scott:

> *A Dogme lesson about Dogme – how cool is that!*
>
> *Seriously though, it makes me wonder if we teachers really do enough to raise our learners' awareness about language learning, and in particular about the pedagogical choices we ourselves have made.*
>
> *I'm often asked if there is any resistance, on the part of learners, to working without either a coursebook or a predetermined syllabus of grammar structures, and, in all honesty, I have to say, 'Yes, probably'. It's not what most learners expect or are accustomed to. No point, then, in trying to impose it, against their will.*
>
> *Much better is to do what Vilte has done here, and demystify the approach by drawing on their common sense understandings of language learning, and – very importantly – revealing that many of the activities that they seem to enjoy (e.g. free-ranging discussions, asking the teacher questions – rather than being always asked questions by the teacher) are in fact perfect (and non-mystical) examples of Dogme practice.*

# 20

# A PERSONAL ANECDOTE

## NICK HAMILTON

UK I ADULT I A2 – C1

This Dogme moment emerged during a lesson with a one-to-one Italian learner at a pre-intermediate level, telling of a chance encounter with the Italian sculptor Antonio Berti.

This was one of my first attempts to go off-piste and respond spontaneously to learner content, after coming across Scott's article 'Dogme Vow of ELT Chastity' that introduced the application of Dogme principles to language teaching. Starting my teaching career in the 1980s and prompted by a whole-hearted embrace of task-based methodology 10 years later, I was ready for an approach that could balance preparation and spontaneity in a way that would allow learners to perceive a teacher genuinely interested in what they had to say – and not just how they were able to say it.

Dogme as an approach immediately made sense to me, having previously come across Michael Long's distinction between a Focus on Meaning and a Focus on Form, and realising the importance of using genuine language in the classroom in order to give real significance to subsequent language focus. It soon became the guiding principle of my teaching and teacher training.

What I value in the Dogme approach is the importance put on really listening and responding to what emerges in the classroom interaction – and seeing everything that happens in the lesson as part of the lesson. In doing so, I've learnt to trust that what the learners actually need to learn next will naturally emerge in the process.

I can no longer remember how this story emerged, but it happened spontaneously, and I could immediately see that it had enormous significance for the learner and also had a profound effect on his life. He was very keen to be able to tell it confidently in English.

This is why I kept a written record of it at the time. I have since heard other extraordinary stories from learners, and learnt the importance of giving space for these things to emerge and be explored and worked with.

This particular story occurred in a one-to-one lesson, but I've learnt that the focus on individual anecdotes works equally well in a group context where other learners can then practise relating an interesting story they have heard.

Having listened to the learner's telling of the story, I first related it back to him, reformulating the language and checking the details of what had been said, including requesting the actual words in Italian – see story text below.

I then boarded the following keywords on the board:

many   year   ago   I   travel   train   when   I   meet

famous   Italian   sculptor   who   tell   me   dream   he   have

Michelangelo   dream   Michelangelo   speak   him   and   say

one   who   not   know   not   do   it   fantastic   philosophy

(chi non sa non faccia!)

At this point, I was able to work more or less silently, allowing the learner to draw on his language resources, noting what he was and wasn't able to come up with, and writing up his suggestions but indicating where something wasn't appropriate. Which produced the following completed text:

many years ago I was travelling by train when I met a famous

Italian sculptor who told me about a dream he had of Michelangelo

in the dream Michelangelo spoke to him and said the one who does

not know does not do it is a fantastic philosophy!

I then demonstrated how when we tell an anecdote, we chunk our speech, pausing to take a breath and picking out prominent words. And again invited the learner to notice where the pauses and prominent words were, marking the text as below:

**many** years **ago** / I was **travelling** by **train** /

when I met a **famous** Italian **sculptor** / who

**told** me about a **dream** he had / of

**Michelangelo** // in the **dream** /

Michelangelo **spoke** to him and said / the

**one** who does not **know** / does not **do** // it is

a **fantastic philosophy** //

Finally, we worked on the fluent spoken production of the text, practising individual chunks and sequences ending in a falling intonation (indicated above by a double line). We finished with a progressive deletion activity, gradually removing the non-prominent words to enable the learner to commit it to memory.

What has stayed in my memory was the enthusiastic response of the learner to this whole process and the enormous satisfaction he got from it. It was immediately apparent that this was exactly what he needed in that moment to upgrade his language, providing the appropriate level of i + 1 input for him to move forward. This has prompted me to listen very carefully for these learning affordances that can be so easy to miss if hurrying to move on to the next thing planned. I have also come to reflect with learners on the usefulness of spontaneous responses to language needs as they emerge in the learning process. This was my first real moment of insight into this approach to teaching, and I've never looked back.

A NOTE FROM SCOTT:

> *This lesson perfectly embodies the progression from (as you note) a focus on meaning to a focus on form, and captures the meaning-driven nature of Dogme-style teaching.*
>
> *Moreover, it's not enough simply to have learners tell their own stories: it's the work the teacher does, first on checking their understanding of the story, then reformulating it (i.e. putting it into a more standard, or target-like, form), then having the learner reconstruct it from lexical prompts – doing the grammar work, in fact.*
>
> *There is so much discovery learning going on in this kind of activity – it's not just mindless memorization of the text. And, as you say, this could be done with a whole class: one student tells their story, and then the rest of the class reconstructs it.*

# 21

# STRATEGISING FOR IELTS
## ANNA HASPER

## NEW ZEALAND | ADULTS | B1 – B2

This was a class of 12 young adult learners, 7 males and 5 females from China, Korea and Japan who were all of B1- B2 level. Most had just finished school in their countries and had come to New Zealand with the aim of starting higher education there and were preparing to sit, or resit, their IELTS test.

None of my students had travelled much before and it was their first time living and learning in an English-speaking country. Some had strong reading skills and knew the grammar rules well, others had less language knowledge. What they all had in common was that speaking English was not something they were comfortable with yet.

This was one of my first teaching jobs, but I have never felt more enabled than working with Warwick[1], one of the owners of the language school. He welcomed me into his own classes, to observe not so much what he

---

1. I'd like to dedicate this lesson to Warwick Isaacs, a teacher, a mentor and a friend but above all an incredibly skilled educator and wonderful human being who believed in all his students. Sadly, Warwick left us too soon, but he lives on forever in my teaching practice and I will forever be grateful for the passion he ignited in me.

was doing but how he was teaching. He often walked into the classroom with a sheet of A4 paper filled with empty boxes or a short text full of gaps. He believed in a humanistic approach to teaching. He encouraged me to connect with learners according to their interests and needs. Observing his lessons truly developed my approach to teaching and dealing with students and sparked my interest in materials-light teaching.

We usually followed a textbook, but I was looking for something different for my one-hour IELTS Speaking class since learners were mostly half awake at 9:00 am! The focus was on IELTS Speaking Part 2, where learners are given a prompt card and one minute planning time before they are expected to talk for up to two minutes.

After a short connecting activity, we moved on to Speaking Part 2 when learners started to express their concerns about this task. I moved them into 3 groups, each group having one test expert who had sat the test previously. The expert explained how it had worked during the real test and I encouraged others to ask questions some of which I boarded up:

*What to do when you run out of ideas?*
*What can I do when I don't know what to say?*
*How can I talk for 2 minutes on a topic I don't like?*
*Can 2 minutes be too much time?*

After 15 minutes we reflected on the questions and reasoned that having vocabulary on a wide variety of topics would be more helpful them memorising possible topics as some students suggested. However, their main concern was how to keep going for 2 minutes.

Since students indicated that they were most worried about being able to talk for the expected two minutes on the IELTS speaking section, introducing some useful strategies to students seemed the way forward. So instead of moving on to my plan, I decided to go with the flow since students were offering this wonderful learning opportunity: they were giving, and I would be responding!

In teams students first brainstormed prompts. We boarded up 3 different prompts they recalled. Next, students moved groups and each team selected one prompt. Students took roles: the test taker, the examiner and the time-keeper/observer who would take notes. They performed the speaking task as usual, noting down what the test-takers had said and when they stopped. Students rotated so all had a chance to speak. I then asked students about their experience and indeed, no one had managed to keep going for 2 minutes. One observer mentioned that the longest turn observed was mostly due to repetition.

The next task was for students to work together and pool their ideas in relation to their topic. I created 2 columns on the board and elicited ideas for each column:

| What we TALKED about: | What we COULD HAVE TALKED about: |
|---|---|
| –The what, why, where, when, who | –How to do something |
| –Likes | –How it made you feel |
| –How long / beautiful / good etc. | –More details |

At this stage it seemed useful to prompt students so we could get some strategies in place to help students keep going. We all agreed one strategy would be "think of Wh-question words" to elaborate on once all bullets had been addressed. I then answered one of the prompts myself and asked them to listen for the tenses. We then agreed on a second strategy, "think past- present- future" and noted down different structures for this. Next, I asked them who they had talked about (themselves) and if other people would have similar or different views, which led us to identify and label a third strategy, "think from personal to general." We explored language to do this while trying to avoid overgeneralisation.

**From Personal to General**

Finally, I talked for two minutes on a third prompt whilst modelling the last strategy: Advantages-Disadvantages. We boarded some more useful phrases:

> *Adverbs: maybe, possibly, probably*
> *Adverbs of quantity: the majority of, a large percentage of...*
> *Modal verbs: It could be..., it may be...*
> *Verbs: seem (to), tends (to)*

**Advantages & Disadvantages**

> *One (huge) dis/advantage of (noun)... is*
> *One good thing about... (noun).*
> *The main dis/advantage of...*
> *The drawback of...*

Next it was the students' turn to start experimenting with the strategies and language themselves. They returned to the same prompts and had three minutes to think about how they could integrate their chosen strategies in their answers. Again, they took on roles, which was followed by discussing their timing and performance. I monitored purposefully, focusing on strategy use but above all pronunciation of the useful language related to the strategies. We ended with some drilling of intonation and praise for their willingness to keep going!

To wrap up, students shared how they felt about using the strategies and nearly all of them felt a bit more confident to talk for longer. I then provided one more task, "I'd like you to describe a challenge you have had in your life," for students to complete outside the classroom. Based on their enthusiasm I think they all had a topic in mind for this one!

Putting Dogme into practice exemplified that exploring the above strategies provided a genuine purpose for my students. Students being aware of "why" strategies are helpful enhanced their motivation to develop "how" to employ them.

A note from Luke:

> Talking for two minutes straight without visual prompts is rare in most real-life contexts (including work), so that part of the IELTS exam is a real challenge.
>
> In this lesson, Anna takes a refreshingly collaborative conversational approach to what is a rather performative conversation test.
>
> This collaborative approach is carefully staged. First students work in groups, with a 'test expert' placed in each one. Then, after a shared brainstorming and feedback phase, they break into teams: each student has a role, and they take turns trying the 2-minute test.
>
> Throughout these phases the teacher is acting as a guide, helping to shape student outputs via board work: I like the table with its binary rubric – what we talked about, and what we could have talked about. All of this leads to a final phase in which the teacher prompts and feeds in helpful exam strategies more explicitly. Earlier, Anna describes the students 'giving' and her 'responding' – by this stage, having placed them at the heart of the lesson, she is giving back.

# 22

# WINDOWS INTO INTERACTIVE TEACHING
## STEVEN HERDER

### JAPAN | TEENS | A1 – B1

As a young, inexperienced teacher in Japan, I got thrown into the deep end, being given full classes in a Catholic Girls' Junior and High School in the early 1990s. My partner Chris and I split classes of 40 students, and while she oozed with teacherness, seemingly born to teach and inspire young women, I was definitely feeling a lot of imposter syndrome for the first few years.

In my initial interview, I asked the vice-principal what he thought was a good teacher. He replied, "strict, but kind" and so that's what I promised to aim for. Armed with the best textbooks I could find, I had students do every single activity in every lesson of each of my six different textbooks. For too many years, I thought I was fulfilling the strict part of the promise.

Even though I soon realized that many activities either didn't work with my students or were not even remotely interesting for young Japanese students, I carried on. Then one day, some 15 years later, I decided to stop following and started to be a leader in my classroom.

It was a combination of observing my mistakes for over 10,000 contact hours, and the underlying tenets of Dogme that set me free. In 2007, I decided to stop using textbooks entirely. Dogme encouraged me to go materials light, put a focus on speaking output, and exploit emergent language whenever I could. What I discovered, changed my teaching forever.

Has this ever happened to you?

You discover some new thing, something you weren't really familiar with previously, and suddenly you notice it everywhere. This happened with the first car I bought: a 1964, baby blue VW beetle; 400 dollars and sporting a homemade wooden floor. It got me through my university summer job, and that's all that mattered. The funny thing was, though, that having bought a VW beetle, I suddenly noticed how many others were also out on the road. They were, in fact, everywhere. This very same phenomenon is happening in my high school EFL classroom in Japan, with what I have coined as, "S.L.O.W. moments".

**S.L.O.W. Down**

These "Spontaneous Learning Opportunity Windows (S.L.O.W.)" are moments that I have grown to love and cherish. I define them as those serendipitous moments when everyone is suddenly focused on exactly the same thing. It may be triggered by a student's comment, a joke, a mistaken answer, something from the textbook, or something the teacher has just said. At that moment, everyone's brain has stopped and a small window has opened. If the teacher is ready, it is very easy to slide something through that momentary window and into the student's head. It actually gets easier and easier the more you keep an eye or an ear open for these S.L.O.W. moments. After two years, I now get at least five or six chances per lesson. The bonus is that when they happen, the students think that I'm off-script and therefore something "fun" might happen – and it does! They all learn something – and that is about the most fun there is.

**Classroom Interaction**

This classroom interaction opportunity and strategy is a part of learning to improve your teaching techniques during a class. Richards and Lockhart[1] point out that "teaching is essentially a thinking process [which] involves making a great number of individual decisions." These decisions are planning decisions, interactive decisions or evaluative decisions. Certainly, decisions both before and after a lesson have a great advantage in terms of time. However busy one may be, there is still the luxury of time to think before having to take action. Since interactive decisions must be made immediately on the spot, it is in our interest to learn what we can here and spend time honing these interactive planning skills as quickly as we can in the "live" classroom. Among other researchers who have focused on classroom interaction, some of my favorite educators include: Dick Allwright, Kathleen Bailey, Ruth Wajnyrb, Amy Tsui, and David Nunan because they consistently deliver a clear and useful message.

So, how is a teacher to exploit a S.L.O.W. moment? I'll describe 5 types or scenarios that have all happened this year in one of my classes, and roughly how I've exploited them. First, though, there are three things necessary to become adept at exploiting a S.L.O.W. moment:  1) confidence, 2) syllabus awareness, and 3) riffing ability, like a jazz musician.

*Confidence* – If you don't believe in yourself when you go off-script, you risk the students also not believing in you in the S.L.O.W. moment. That's when things can go wrong: the most common problem is that the group loses its cohesiveness and chattering ensues. Then you've lost them – not forever – but certainly for this S.L.O.W. opportunity;

*Syllabus* – You need to know the syllabus so you can make sure that everyone succeeds in being able to do what you ask them to do, using

---

1.   Richards, J. & Lockhart, C. (1996). *Reflective teaching in second language classrooms.* Cambridge University Press.

meaningful language that isn't too far away from what you're doing or have done in the past.

*Riffing Ability* – riffing simply means improvising, but being able to stay on one track or one theme is important. If you ever watch comedians, they follow the rule of three – you can follow up a joke or a point in three ways or from three perspectives. After that people stop laughing, reacting, or listening, so knowing your limits is crucial.

Here are five examples of catalysts of S.L.O.W. moments that have all happened in my classroom:

### 1. Whining

Rumi complains in Japanese that she's hungry. Rumi is always hungry, every week, like clockwork. I call out, "Rumi is hungry again. Rumi, this morning I had a big breakfast. I had two pieces of toast – one with peanut butter and one with honey. I also had a cup of coffee and a glass of water. What did you have? Nothing? Really? Everyone – Why do you think Rumi didn't have any breakfast? (Elicit, elicit, feedback, etc) OK, let's give Rumi some good ideas to help her fix her life. Rumi, I think you should _____. Anyone else? What should Rumi do? Does anyone remember what I had for breakfast? Did anyone eat more than me today?"

### 2. Reporting

Chikako reports, "I went *to shopping and *studying English last night." I call out, "Chikako – Double chance! Can you or anyone find any small mistakes with [I went *to shopping and *studying English last night.]? Can anyone else give me a two-verb sentence about last night? Can anyone ask Chikako if she bought anything cool?"

### 3. Worrying

Miki asks, "What's on the test?" I call out, "Miki chan loves tests! Miki, what do you think is on the test? If you were Steven, what would you put on the test? Everyone, ask your partner, "What do you think TERRIBLE Steven will put on the test?" Ready... Go. (time passes...) OK, let's review what could be on the test" (Elicit, elicit, feedback, etc).

### 4. Killing time

Hiroko suggests, "Let's play a game today." I call out, "Hiroko is the queen of "killing time." What does that mean in Japanese? Yes, exactly, jikan wo tsubusu. In this class, who else is good at killing time? Oh, yeah. Which teachers are weak against students killing time? Everyone, ask your partner, "How do you sometimes kill time?" (Elicit, elicit, feedback, etc).

### 5. Writing

Yuri writes, "I take *on the train to school every day." I'm walking around the room, watching students during a writing assignment. When I see this mistake, I call out, "Wow, Yuri, you are a very macho girl. Everyone, do you know how macho Yuri is? Every morning, she takes on* the train (I gesture putting on a train like a backpack). There are two or three good ways to say this. Anyone? Yes, "take the train", "catch the train", and "get the train" – great answers. Everyone, be careful, though. Don't make Yuri angry.

This technique is actually full of hidden bonuses: it builds extra rapport with students, it teaches students to learn from other students, it promotes consciousness-raising of grammatical patterns, it feels like it isn't studying, and finally, it encourages active participation by both the instigators and students who respond to my questions.

The more you invest time into observing, recording, and reflecting on what is ACTUALLY happening in your classroom, the more you will learn to handle classroom interaction better, and the closer you will come to becoming a master of classroom interaction. Those 45 or 90 minutes with the students have a disproportionally high influence in determining what they do with English or how they think about English for the other 10,000 minutes of the week.

A note from Luke:

*Sometimes people say: "Oh, Dogme is only for great teachers."*
*Steven's account shows us that a new approach like Dogme can*
*help us become a better teacher.*

*Like him, I didn't take naturally to teaching. Like him, I 'armed'*
*myself with coursebooks. (This is such an interesting word to use,*
*because if we are 'arming' ourselves, what is the enemy? The*
*students? The syllabus? Language itself?) In my case, it was the*
*Lexical Approach that set me free to forge a new path that led in*
*time to Dogme. In his case, Dogme paved a way to a more sponta-*
*neous teaching practice focused on what he calls Spontaneous*
*Learning Opportunity Windows (S.L.O.W. moments).*

*In fact, these 'slow' moments – small, relatable moments when*
*everyone focuses on the same thing – demand quick thinking! The*
*rewards are significant, building rapport, learner autonomy and*
*collaboration, noticing, and participation. What did Simon and*
*Garfunkel sing in The 59th Street Bridge Song? 'Slow down, you*
*move too fast.' There's a lot to be said for living, and teaching, in*
*the moment.*

# 23

# SUSTAINABLE ELT
## PETER HOLLY

## HUNGARY | ADULTS | A2 – C2

For over 18 months I have been teaching 1:1 sessions, largely face-to-face, with around a dozen managers at a medium-sized food processing factory close to where I now live in southwest Hungary. These adult learners range from CEFR A2 level to lower C1 in spoken English, which is the skill we focus on in our sessions together.

I was asked to help with the learners' language development by the director of a foreign-owned company, as the language of communication at the higher levels is English. I have found that my time with these learners as an educator is often spent as anything ranging from teacher, to mentor, to advisor.

I first worked in Hungary in the late 1980's with the British Council, and there have been many changes since those days. I relocated as a free-lancer, finally, during the tail end of the Covid period in 2021. It took a while for me to sort out things to enable me to work as a teacher again, and since then Dogme has been my inspiration – with these learners and with other private students aged from 12 to 62 that I teach online to enhance their conversational skills in general English.

With such a diverse range of clients, language levels, and professional needs, it would have been impossible for me to identify any published coursebook which might have guided our time together. I also have to add that a significant part of my educational career has been spent teacher training and promoting for ELT publishers, and I have therefore become very wary of advocating a 'one size fits all' approach to any materials I use for language development – especially with individual learners. As such, it was almost inevitable that I would adopt a Dogme approach, even if I had no name for it initially.

With my corporate students I generally start off with a topic, such as a soft skill or specific business area relevant to their role in the organisation, and go with the flow as language is generated by us both as equal partners. We basically have a conversation focused on one of these themes, and English emerges from this fairly easily. Although my role is as a facilitator to their language development, I will occasionally intervene to 'teach' when a slip or error is repeated frequently – usually as a result of L1 interference.

However, what I am really passionate about these days is incorporating sustainability and green issues into ELT, and I have been able to do this in a Hungarian corporate setting as a result of an ongoing EU drive to focus on ESG ratings for companies (Environment, Social, and Governance). I have therefore turned to the United Nations Sustainable Development Goals (SDGs)[1] as a resource, and with 17 to choose from, these have all – at various times – worked as a springboard for discussion and conversation as ways to extend and develop my learners' English. Awareness-raising about these goals in global terms quite easily morphs into talking about the SDGs from a local perspective, and how these can relate to green initiatives being undertaken by the company itself at this time.

---

1.   United Nations. (2015). Transforming our world: The 2030 agenda for sustainable development. https://sdgs.un.org/2030agenda

As an introductory scenario I have used the SDG icons without their labels ( cut up ) to generate language about what the picture could represent – those of you familiar with these will know that the link between the image and the topic can be quite tenuous with some of them. In our experience this only helps to generate more language linked to sustainability as a general concept, especially speculative language. As a puzzle task, the labels are then given to the learner to match with a suitable icon until all 17 have been identified. This then leads to further discussion about the appropriacy of the image, and whether or not my language partner can come up with – and describe – a better icon to go with that particular goal.

To illustrate this, here are a few examples of spoken language generated by the learners:

- Solar panels are a great way for the company to save on electricity charges.
- I am really worried about climate change, even here I feel that winters are not so cold as before, and summers getting hotter.
- Transportation costs are less if we bring our livestock locally.

- I'm not sure if ESG regulations is a good thing for the company.
- I don't think this picture is matched with the words.
- How I can describe this ?
- The company don't spend many money on that.
- What I like best is quality education for my children.
- In my opinion the environment is a big problem.
- Some thing about electric cars is good, others not as good.

I relish the freedom I have been given to develop individualised learning paths in my current role, and the potential for utilising real world issues to facilitate English language development. I love these discussions best of all, as I believe – through language development – that we are putting something back in to the world which we have 'borrowed from our children'. It is particularly rewarding when these managers become so motivated that they take these topics home to discuss with their own children.

I have been able to adapt the SDG theme and some of these language development activities to general English lessons I have had online, as well as two intensive week-long summer courses for underprivileged teenagers, and also a week-long training course for Erasmus-funded teachers from Central Europe – which were especially rewarding. There seems no end to the possibility of using discussion of the goals to generate English at any language level, and with learners of all ages.

A NOTE FROM LUKE:

> This account articulates a very nuanced sense of the 'teacher' role: Peter describes this as encompassing teaching, facilitating, mentoring and even a kind of therapy.
>
> A fundamental link between these last three roles is the act of listening: being present, but not necessarily directing. Peter's

*description of his student as a 'language partner' is a nice way to reframe the traditionally hierarchical 'teacher>learner' dynamic.*

*Interestingly, the act of teaching in an explicit, explanatory sense is seen as one behaviour within the wider scope of being a teacher: 'I will occasionally intervene to 'teach' when a slip or error is repeated frequently.'*

*In other words, stepping back from a delivery method teaching role doesn't mean we stop being a teacher. It means becoming a different kind of teacher, rethinking when and how we articulate our expertise.*

# 24

# MAGICKING GRAMMAR OUT OF STUDENT TALK

## JANCILEIDI HÜBNER

### BRAZIL | TEENS | B2 - C1

This was a class of 11 high school students in Brazil. They were around 15 years old and their English classes were included in the curriculum. Most of the students were somewhere between B2 and C1. Unfortunately, I didn't feel that they were very motivated for the classes. Sometimes they came to my classroom with other topics in mind and keeping their attention was a difficult task.

This was a private school in the South of Brazil where I have been working for around 18 years. In this context, the students are offered extended hours of English instruction and use materials from a globally-renowned publisher. The large groups of students are divided into smaller ones and shared among teachers for the English classes. This way, each student can get the chance to develop the skills and abilities necessary to advance their language knowledge and use. For this reason, most learners succeed and their English level is much higher when they leave the school compared to other contexts in the same region.

I chose the Dogme approach in this teaching moment as it seemed the perfect opportunity to make my grammar class more meaningful. Making use of emergent language rather than my pre-planned examples would help create a more conversational tone and prevent me from having to force students to change their focus from a real situation they were experiencing to a boring out-of-context sentence on the board.

I was in my classroom, waiting for my group to come with all my weapons: the teacher's book, my notes of pre-made examples to use, my markers, and a video about nothing less than the mixed conditionals! It would be a battle, for sure! A grammar class about such a complex structure based on an international book with examples and exercises that sometimes are far from my learners' culture and life.

So, they came. Lively, talkative, and (or but) upset. They had had a very hard Physics test that day and were complaining about it in Portuguese. As soon as they stepped inside the classroom, I told them, "If you keep complaining, this has to be done in English!".

How could I redirect their attention from the commotion and engage them in my grammar class? With this question in mind, I had an insight and decided to use what they were talking about to teach what I was supposed to. I started a conversation by asking, "What happened that made you so upset?" and joined them by sitting around the big oval table we use in our classes. The moment felt like a conversation among friends instead of a class on conditionals.

Throughout the conversation, they told me what had happened. In a nutshell, they shared the fact that most of them were feeling they had failed the Physics test and were very worried about that. So, I started asking follow-up questions (with the future grammar explanation in mind, but without showing that.) Having talked for some minutes, I had the two things I needed: their attention and real examples to use. They told me things like, "I didn't study enough," "I didn't think the test would be this hard," "My family will be really mad at me," "I was never good at Physics after all," and other similar things.

I stood up, approached the board, invited them to analyze the situation, and listed some facts they had shared with me below two headings:

| PAST | PRESENT |
|---|---|
| I didn't study enough. | I am not good at Physics. |
| I thought the test would be easier. | I am worried about the difficult test. |
| I didn't do all the test activities. | I feel my family will be mad at me. |

I then said, "This is the reality we have right now. But we are not happy with it. Let's imagine how everything could be different." I followed up with, "You didn't study enough. What if you had?" and wrote on the board, "If I had studied enough, ...". So, I invited the class to complete my sentence with a possible imaginary result based on the second column on the board. One girl said, "I wouldn't be worried now!" and I immediately completed the sentence by writing it on the board.

I went on by inviting them to imagine they were excellent in physics. I asked, "Can you express that by starting the sentence with 'if'?" We had some experimental sentences with mistaken structures until one student said, "If I were good at Physics...". I copied the example on the board and asked, "What's a possible result of that from our list?" Some students then tried to say, "I would do all the test activities," to which I promptly responded, "But the test is over. It has already finished. Your example is referring to the present moment. How can we imagine this result in the past?". After some inaccurate clauses, I heard, "I would have done all the test activities".

I smiled happily with the two perfect examples on the board. We then analyzed the sentences together focusing on the mixing of present and past imaginary conditions and results and the verb form we should use to express those kinds of ideas in other sentences. Eventually, the group took notes of the examples and verb forms we highlighted on the board and used their notes to guide them in the exercises provided by the student's book.

It was a strategic freeing of class "space" so that we could generate learning from conversation. I don't think I would be able to teach completely unplugged as I am a bit enthusiastic about the benefits of the intentional use of technology in class. However, whenever I see that dialogue can bring us collaborative learning, I don't hesitate to let go of the pre-planned framework.

Unplugging from the plan and integrating their real-life concerns into my teaching of grammar helped me avoid uncomfortably cutting into their conversation in order to move into the class itself. The conversation became the class and maintaining this flow increased my students' receptiveness to my explanations.

A NOTE FROM SCOTT:

> Jancileidi writes: "I had an insight and decided to use what they were talking about to teach what I was supposed to." This is a profoundly Dogme insight.

> What's more, to develop a grammar point out of the students' immediate concerns is one thing – but to develop the grammar point that was the original aim of the lesson out of the student's talk is true artistry – testimony of which was the class's engagement and receptiveness.

> Of course, it's not always possible to craft a lesson so elegantly in this way, but training oneself to listen out for student utterances that can become the focus of a mini grammar lesson is a step in that direction.

# 25

# CIRCLE TIME
## RUTH IIDA

## JAPAN I YOUNG LEARNERS I A1 – B2

I'd like to write about a class of EFL learners who are currently nine and ten years old. There are eight students, seven of whom have been studying together in the same class since age five. These seven children entered the school with no prior English experience and came from monolingual families. The eighth child entered the class later, at age nine. This child has one non-Japanese parent and entered with a basic receptive knowledge of English gained from YouTube, English TV programs, and movies. The learners, three boys, and five girls, attend different elementary schools and look forward to seeing each other every Tuesday in English class.

Lessons take place in a private language school in Japan, featuring typical once-a-week 60-75 minute English lessons. The location is a two-story house, rather than an office space, and children move from room to room during the course of one lesson. Learners play and watch videos in the waiting room, sit on the carpet in the "speaking room", and work at a long table in the "writing room". Flowers and small vegetables grow in the attached garden area, which is used for events as well as for bird watching. The atmosphere is informal; although some children hesitate to drop the use of "Sensei", others feel quite comfortable calling teachers by their first names. I, myself, am "Ruthie" to my students.

Last year, I chose a Dogme approach for this class of eight because these children were particularly outgoing and spontaneous. This is not always the case in Japan, so I was determined to take full advantage of my learners' willingness to speak up. Also, the period of online lessons during the Coronavirus had come to an end and masks were beginning to come off. Children were happy to be together and ready to be active participants, rather than passive watchers.

A year ago, my learners, sitting together on the soft blue carpet of the "speaking room", could easily tell me when they were good, great, happy, excellent, wonderful, not so good, tired, sleepy, hungry, hot, cold, or sometimes sad. But the whole "How are you today?" dialogue had lost its spark. It was a dead-end activity. Hoping to breathe some new life into a tired routine, my assistant and I began introducing more colorful adjectives, spiced with intensifiers. For example, when a student politely asked, "How are you today, Ruthie?" I might answer, "I'm AMAZING!" or "I'm SUPER WONDERFUL!" In no time, students' answers become more playful and creative as well. One child was inevitably, "SUPER-EXCELLENT!" while others became more quantitative in expressing mood. "I'm FIVE TIRED!" or "I'm TEN HAPPYS!" Qualitative learners tacked on vocabulary that suited their positive mood, such as "I'm CHOCOLATE FIRE WONDERFUL!" On good days, the more outrageous the answer, the more determined other children were to outdo their peers. Descriptors flew back and forth as children laughed and I took mental notes.

Over the course of that year, my eight students embraced big numbers, employing them with often reckless abandon. They demanded to push past the hundreds. "What comes next?" they asked me in Japanese. So I taught the concept of "thousands" which they immediately adapted to circle time. The answer to "How are you today?" became, "I'm ten thousand AMAZINGS!" or "I'm forty four thousand EXCELLENTS!" If a student offered a modest "ten happys", others pretended shock, urging the speaker to choose "Higher!!" Soon thousands were not enough. I gave them "millions", protesting that I was not numerically fluent in anything larger, but even this was not enough to satisfy. I capitulated, giving them "zillions", and waited for the response. To my relief, they seemed to intuit that words beginning with Z are likely to be a product of the teacher's imagination. Zillions were popular for the next few weeks, along with "willions" and "quillions", which have an equally satisfying sound. When I noticed students glancing up at the alphabet chart on the wall contemplating what initial letter to tack on to "illion", I saw every teacher's dream: on-the-spot student-initiated phonics practice.

These students have just entered the fourth grade of elementary school. We do not reflect together on how circle time conversational patterns have changed, but as they develop intellectually and emotionally, we will. I predict that they will be half-amused and half-embarrassed to recall their enthusiasm during circle time. Adults might doubt the practicality of teaching imaginary numbers, as did a teacher friend who witnessed the circle time spontaneous language exchange. "They can't talk like that in the real world!" she said. And this is, to a large extent, true. Yet I can see that this stage of magical realism is already at its peak, and will soon be replaced by more prosaic descriptions including longer chunks of language.

I believe that part of the reason these eight students continue to be highly motivated learners is because I have allowed them to help shape the direction of their curriculum. Their language experiments have not been ridiculed or ignored; on the contrary, I have done my best to catch their ideas and work them into subsequent lessons. Circle time is fun and exciting, and they tell me so directly. As a teacher, I have been stretched, both by the unpredictability of student language and by the timing of its usage. While listening intently, I'm also thinking, "Is this an interruption or a valuable contribution? Is this irrelevant or is it a potentially exciting detour?" This Dogme-style approach has allowed me to become part of the language journeys of my students, enjoying the scenery as I go. How's the weather along the way? Sometimes sunny, and sometimes cloudy with occasional showers. I own a sturdy umbrella, so it's all good.

Third graders on the speaking room carpet

A NOTE FROM SCOTT:

> *Ruth's account challenges at least two perceptions of Dogme: that it is not appropriate for Japanese learners and that it doesn't work with young learners.*

*What helps to counter resistance to a fluency-first approach, on the one hand, and child-centred learning, on the other, includes such factors as the physical environment (that blue carpet!) and the teacher's attitude and example.*

*But what also comes across strongly in this account is the 'permission' that learners have been given to use language playfully, even irreverently. Vygotsky wrote that "play creates a zone of proximal development of the child. In play a child always behaves beyond his [sic] average age, above his daily behavior; in play it is as though he were a head taller than himself..."*[1]

*The creative and collaborative use of language in these greeting exchanges allows the children to 'outperform their competence', and it is basic to a Dogme approach that learners' expressivity should not be constrained within the narrow bounds of the traditional syllabus.*

---

1.   Vygotsky, L. (1978) *Mind in society: The development of higher psychological processes.* Cambridge, Mass: Harvard University Press.

# 26

# TALKING THROUGH TRICKY TIMES

## HENRY JONES

## COLOMBIA | ADULT | B2

This was an online one-to-one class with a Colombian lawyer, Paula, who is in her early 30s. We worked together for about a year. She was a solid B2-level student, able to communicate fluently while discussing a range of topics – and believe me, we talked about everything from business, fitness, and music through to love, religion, and politics. Paula is highly driven, always with several projects on the go, and always looking to improve her professional profile. So, naturally, improving her English is an important part of this.

We would meet once or twice a week over Zoom and converse freely while I took notes on what she was saying, either for later corrective feedback or to keep note of useful emergent language in context. In the case of highly-talkative learners like Paula, I tend to lean more towards focusing on using the affordances of the conversation and on emergent lexis rather than pausing the lesson too often to offer corrections or mini grammar and pronunciation tutorials.

Dogme is my default mode of teaching for one-to-one classes! Years of lesson planning, following coursebooks, and course design have given me the tools to teach reactively rather than pro-actively. I find lessons more engaging and valuable when I'm in the moment, responding to what's in front of me, and 'teaching at the point of need', rather than following a lesson plan on autopilot. This is especially true with chatty people like Paula who have a lot to talk about and thus produce a lot of language to work with, 'grade up', and discuss.

I started the class by asking her how she'd been, and she proceeded to tell me that both her sister and her dad had been in hospital! After expressing my sympathy, I asked her if it was something she'd feel comfortable talking about, she said yes, and then immediately proceeded to go into more detail.

Thankfully, Paula started by reassuring me that her sister and dad were both OK, then went on to explain what had happened to each of them. While she talked, I prompted her with questions to find out more details.

At times, I gave her immediate feedback, while at other times, when she was in full flow, I took note of errors in our shared document for later discussion. She would often recognise gaps in her own lexis, ask me for a word, or how to translate something from Spanish, and I would record this too. Sometimes I would let her know that while I understood what she was saying, I'd suggest lexis that I would use to express the same idea, saying "... but this is how I'd say it ... " before modelling and recording it.

I shared my screen at intervals to show her the notes I was taking so that we could discuss useful language that she could use to help her express herself. I would sometimes prompt her to repeat or retell parts of her story; often she would do this unprompted, especially when she found the vocabulary particularly useful for filling a gap.

Vocabulary

| Word / Phrase: | Part of Speech: | Copied and Personalised? |
|---|---|---|
| • At the moment, he's **stable**. / He's in a **stable** condition.<br>• He's not **in pain**.<br>• He's **getting better**.<br>• **All in all**, he's much better now.<br>• I have a weekly **check up** with my doctor.<br>• **Over** the last 2 days, my mum**'s been able to** stay with him.<br>• She's **been able to lift his spirits**. | Adjective ▾<br>Adjective ▾<br>Collocation ▾<br>Adverb ▾<br>Noun ▾<br>Verb ▾<br>Other/Phr... ▾ | ☐ |

The conversation transitioned from her talking about her dad 'getting better' after being hospitalised with high blood pressure into talking about how her sister had avoided being 'mugged' in a 'sketchy neighbourhood', but had 'lost her balance and fallen off her scooter'. She wasn't wearing a 'helmet', but 'wasn't hurt that badly, only ending up with some 'cuts and bruises'.

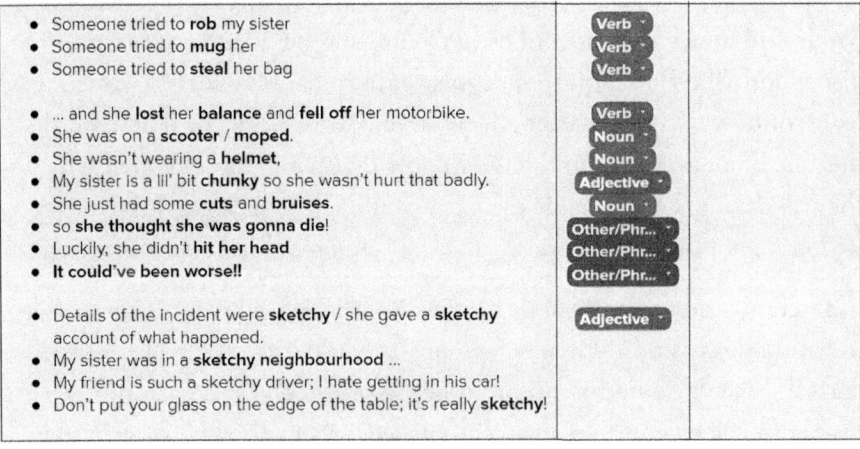

| | | |
|---|---|---|
| • Someone tried to **rob** my sister<br>• Someone tried to **mug** her<br>• Someone tried to **steal** her bag | Verb ▾<br>Verb ▾<br>Verb ▾ | |
| • ... and she **lost** her **balance** and **fell off** her motorbike.<br>• She was on a **scooter** / **moped**.<br>• She wasn't wearing a **helmet**,<br>• My sister is a lil' bit **chunky** so she wasn't hurt that badly.<br>• She just had some **cuts** and **bruises**.<br>• so **she thought she was gonna die!**<br>• Luckily, she didn't **hit her head**<br>• **It could've been worse!!** | Verb ▾<br>Noun ▾<br>Noun ▾<br>Adjective ▾<br>Noun ▾<br>Other/Phr... ▾<br>Other/Phr... ▾<br>Other/Phr... ▾ | |
| • Details of the incident were **sketchy** / she gave a **sketchy** account of what happened.<br>• My sister was in a **sketchy neighbourhood** ...<br>• My friend is such a sketchy driver; I hate getting in his car!<br>• Don't put your glass on the edge of the table; it's really **sketchy**! | Adjective ▾ | |

At the end of the session, we looked at some grammar, vocabulary, and pronunciation errors that she had made and I elicited the corrections from her. I then prompted her to transfer all of the notes I'd taken into her own notebook, recontextualising the lexis and writing more example sentences with the same language.

**Learning Opportunities**

| He has high presion | He has high blood pressure |
|---|---|
| My dad is in the hospital since the 28th | My dad has been in the hospital since the 28th<br>My dad's been in the hospital since the 28th |
| At these last 2 days | Over these last 2 days ... |
| It's probably that he can go home on Friday. | We can probably go home on Friday.<br>We might be able to go home on Friday. |
| She was OK, thanks god. | She was OK, thank god. |

Reflecting on this now, I feel blessed that a student would share these stories about a worrying moment in her personal life. Despite the seriousness of what she was talking about, the conversation was engaging without being heavy, and she was noticeably energized by talking about something so meaningful.

Aside from the interaction having a potentially therapeutic effect (arguably the most important outcome), I also hope that the emotional connection to the topic also made the emergent language more memorable. These types of conversations are certainly memorable to me as a teacher.

A NOTE FROM LUKE:

*Henry makes a useful connection between the way we are taught to teach, and the way we choose to teach. These paths are not mutually exclusive – there is plenty of good practice we can take from orthodox models like coursebooks, and repurpose in a Dogme setting.*

*One key difference is that Dogme is responsive, not prescriptive. To respond fully we need to be fully present, which means being alive to the language, and sensitive to the context it emerges from. There's a nice balance here between interest in language, and concern for the student and the health issues in her family. Crucially, the teacher sense checks that the student is comfortable pursuing this subject.*

*There are clear stages in this lesson: the teacher listens, prompts, notes, gives feedback on emergent language, and helps adjust or upgrade it in the moment. The notes are referenced against language forms that are familiar to the teacher and student, and the student is encouraged to recycle the emergent language into new sentences. All of this is not just replicable but transferable to other students, including – I would note – quieter 1-1 students, and busy classroom settings.*

# 27

# A HARRY POTTER MOMENT
## DANI KABBANI

UK I ADULTS I B2

The class took place in a language institute in London during a three-hour General English session that I was covering last minute. There were nine adult B2 learners from diverse linguistic backgrounds including Korean, Japanese, French and Arabic. I hadn't met the students previously and while the suggested topic was the passive voice, I was given free rein in how to approach the lesson.

Being on standby and covering at the last minute can be stressful and I've often been in a panic about what to do. However, thanks to the time I've spent working with a team of passionate teachers in a collaborative and creative atmosphere, I've gained the confidence to go with the flow and be more responsive to emergent learning opportunities. For me, stepping back and trusting in that process has always proved to be a successful approach.

For this lesson, my immediate goal was to get to know the students and hopefully engage them through some meaningful discussion. Although I hadn't planned to go all out with an unplanned Dogme lesson, I aimed to be open and responsive to whatever arose and if all else failed, I had a pile of coursebooks at hand!

Over the years, I've increasingly valued spontaneous interactions which are core to the Dogme approach. Where once I would have viewed them as deviations from the plan and the learning outcomes, I now eagerly anticipate these off-piste moments and see them as golden opportunities that are central to learning. In my experience, it's so often those unexpected instances of heightened student interest or even controversy in the classroom that provide the perfect opportunity to seize on a topic and maximise engagement. That was certainly the case in this class.

I began the lesson by asking some questions to find out how they were settling into their day and learning more about their backgrounds. Through this discussion, I discovered that most were relatively new to living in London. Given their varied experiences of the city so far, I steered the conversation toward asking what each enjoyed about London to get a sense of their interests and perspectives.

This conversation helped us relax into a dialogue and our discussion was flowing pretty smoothly when one student mentioned her recent trip to Soho. She then animatedly told us about spotting a famous actress there. Intrigued by this, I asked her to tell us more about the celebrity sighting.

After doing her best to describe the actress another student suggested it was Helena Bonham Carter. Other students didn't know the name, so I showed them a picture on my phone. There was immediate recognition from the class and one of them said, "Ah, from Harry Potter!". I then made what I thought was a pretty innocuous comment about never having seen the Harry Potter films. Gasps of disbelief and shock reverberated around the room. The outrage and blasphemy! An Englishman who's never watched Harry Potter! I was tempted to go one further and tell them that I never ate fish and chips either, but I thought better of it given the magnitude of this bombshell so early in the morning. Though they were clearly aghast and horrified, there was a palpable energy in the room, and it would have been remiss not to seize on that and make my 'faux-pas' a fortuitous one.

Riding the wave of this new energy led to a lively discussion about film preferences, generating lots of language for preferences and describing films from having a soft spot for tear-jerkers to enjoying unnerving films that fill you with dread.

As the discussion unfolded, one student mentioned having recently seen the film 'Napoleon'. This shifted our focus to analysing the trailer, discussing reactions to it, and, thanks to insights from a history buff in the class, reflecting on the merits of historical accuracy in films. We also practiced decoding strategies to help us understand Joaquin Phoenix's almost incomprehensible mumbling Napoleon.

As our discussions had touched on several films, I thought it would be good for the students to share their top recommendations. Firstly, I told them about one of my favourite films, recording our conversation on my iPad. I then sent the audio file to the students so they could listen to it through their headphones and make notes on useful language for describing films. After this, they took time to prepare and before telling each other about their favourite films. To wrap up, we regrouped and discussed their choices and voted on which sounded the most appealing, allowing for further input on film preferences and genres.

To my surprise, at the end of the class, a student approached me to ask if I had planned to discuss films or if it was because of the Harry Potter moment. I said that they seemed interested in the topic, so I went along with that. To my great satisfaction, he said how much he had enjoyed the lesson and found it useful, particularly because it had engaging topics they wanted to talk about. I can't think of a much better stamp of approval for Dogme than that! The class really underscored for me the power of being attentive to those peaks in student engagement and having the flexibility to run with them. What was personally of most interest however was the spontaneous use of modest technology such as the trailers on YouTube and the audio recording I sent the students, which I felt had really enhanced the lesson.

This has got me thinking about how we might harness technology to enrich Dogme moments by supplementing the type of interactions that bring about so much emergent language with what we might term 'emergent materials'. The extraordinary pace at which generative AI is developing offers rich ground for experimentation and creating materials in response to the real-time needs and output of learners. I'm excited to experiment with this idea and test out some of these tools in class.

A note from Scott:

> *There are a number of interesting points that this vivid description suggests to me: first of all, the fact that, as a substitute teacher, you had little or no time to plan a lesson, and hence had to work from whatever the learners provided.*
>
> *This kind of experience was very formative for me, too, and it was through doing a lot of stand-bys that I learned (a) to trust the learners and (b) that you can do a lot with very little.*
>
> *I also like the way you integrated the available technology, but without letting the technology disrupt the flow of what was essentially a conversation-driven lesson. The notion of 'emergent materials' is perfectly compatible with Dogme principles.*
>
> *Finally, the unsolicited feedback you got from one of the students suggests that the students themselves recognize the validity of an approach that allows them at least some control of the content and direction of the lesson.*

# 28

# A TEACHER TRAINING LENS ON DOGME

### ELENA KAPSHUTAR

## RUSSIA | ADULTS | C1 – C2

This was an online Zoom class of four language teachers, Russian women from their early twenties to forties. Their level of English was at least C1 CEFR at the time, and several of them had been my trainees on the CELTA courses I had tutored.

In 2020 I became a certified Cambridge CELTA trainer, and a year later I launched my first online teacher training course in which I wanted to address topics and issues that go beyond the traditional staple diet of CELTA training. The participants were very inspired and motivated, and, as they had already had three teacher training sessions before this course, they knew one another and worked comfortably together.

At the needs analysis stage, the teachers expressed particular interest towards Dogme ELT. As I had tried it in my Cambridge Delta Module 2 Experimental Practice a few years earlier[1], I was familiar with the main tenets of the approach, and, I must say, instantly became its fan.

---

1.  https://www.academia.edu/100551162/Using_Dogme_ELT_for_improving_interme diate_level_students_fluency?source=swp_share

One of the main issues that the teachers on the course were concerned about was whether Dogme ELT is a suitable approach in their class-rooms. With the help of this demo lesson, I decided to demonstrate how this could be integrated into a class.

I began with a famous *pecha kucha* activity: I used several items that were lying around my table at the time of the lesson (curtains' holder, ink cartridges for pens, unusually shaped pencil sharpener) and elicited ideas from the teachers. While they were quite experienced teachers them-selves, they used various modal, semi-modal verbs and modal phrases to make guesses about the items, which defined the language focus for the lesson early on.

In the second round, the teachers were talking about the items that they had at their disposal. Some exciting and unusual things such as a laptop cooler, cigar guillotine, miniature table lamp, and an octopus head massager were demonstrated, and participants tried to guess what they were and what they could be used for.

Teachers were asked to retrieve, record and research the items that they used and heard from one another during the previous phase. They came up with a table on a shared Google Doc:

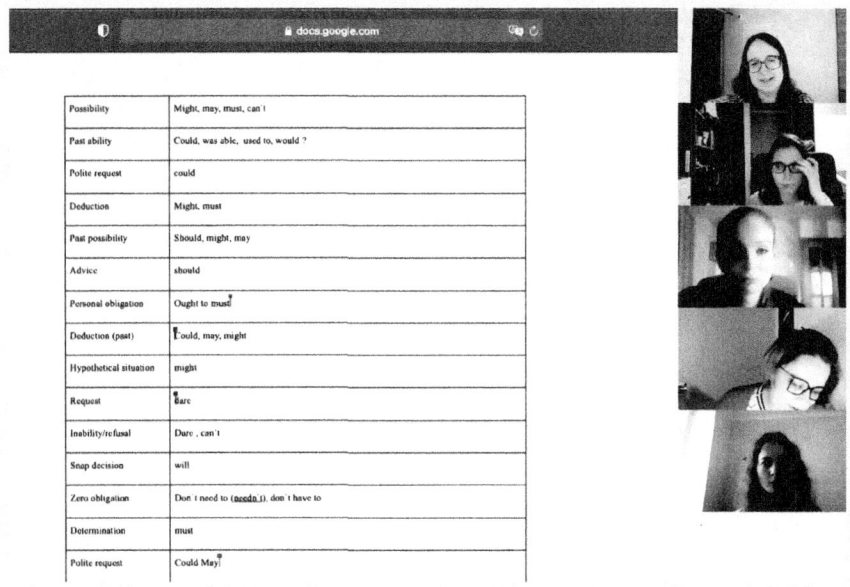

| | |
|---|---|
| Possibility | Might, may, must, can't |
| Past ability | Could, was able, used to, would ? |
| Polite request | could |
| Deduction | Might, must |
| Past possibility | Should, might, may |
| Advice | should |
| Personal obligation | Ought to must |
| Deduction (past) | Could, may, might |
| Hypothetical situation | might |
| Request | Bare |
| Inability/refusal | Dare , can't |
| Snap decision | will |
| Zero obligation | Don t need to (needn t), don t have to |
| Determination | must |
| Polite request | Could May |

Having checked the ideas together, the participants moved on to a discussion of things they would like to change in their life, or what they think they should be doing. I arranged them in pairs and, after about five minutes, swapped them to form new pairs. While they were discussing various aspects of their lives, I was taking notes on the language produced by turning them into gap-fill sentences, and then, in the main session with the whole group, we filled them out and compared our ideas.

For the final part, quite spontaneously the teachers began discussing the DOs and DON'Ts of lesson planning and teaching. This is what they produced:

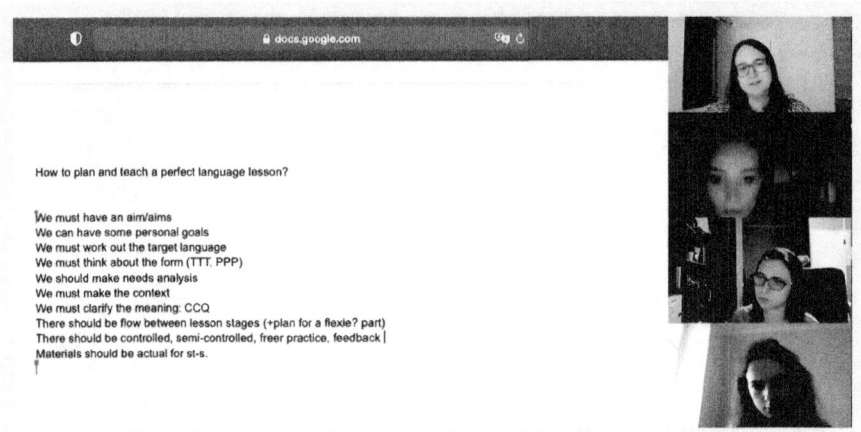

How to plan and teach a perfect language lesson?

We must have an aim/aims
We can have some personal goals
We must work out the target language
We must think about the form (TTT, PPP)
We should make needs analysis
We must make the context
We must clarify the meaning: CCQ
There should be flow between lesson stages (+plan for a flexie? part)
There should be controlled, semi-controlled, freer practice, feedback
Materials should be actual for st-s.

As often happens with Dogme, the lesson took an unexpected turn. However, as I was working with experienced language teachers who were highly motivated and engaged, we naturally came to the discussion of things that were most relevant for them and for the course overall, coupling it with a thorough yet learner-centered language focus.

After the demo lesson, we had a short 20-minute discussion about the main principles of Dogme ELT and reflected on the lesson, which was certainly beneficial for them and their future teaching.

As a follow-up for this lesson, the teachers were asked to plan 2-3 lessons using the Dogme ELT techniques for the students they were teaching at that moment. If they had a chance, they were encouraged to teach at least one of them and then reflect upon the strengths and weaknesses in planning and teaching that they encountered. For the final part, they were asked to prepare an action plan that would help them develop further in understanding and applying the Dogme ELT in teaching.

I believe that this experience was a successful lesson that demonstrated various possibilities for teaching language. Apart from providing opportunities for spontaneous and natural communication, the class techniques showed how teachers can not only help their students develop fluency in a standard 60-minute class, but also focus on accuracy and language points that pose difficulty even for highly-proficient experienced learners of English.

A NOTE FROM LUKE:

> *On one level this account shows how much can be generated by minimal, non-verbal stimulus – all the language here is generated by the participants from personal items.*
>
> *On another level, there's an interesting dialogue between spontaneity and control. The learners here are also teachers, familiar with published materials built around a grammar syllabus, and quickly identify modality – rather than any language used to describe these curious physical items – as the focus of the lesson.*
>
> *We can see the same tension in their list of do's and don'ts. While this includes relevant materials and 'flex', it also includes target language and classic PPP sequencing.*
>
> *This is natural: we see new ideas through the window of the old. That's why Elena's extended follow-up task for her trainees – to teach two or three dogme-style lessons with their own students, and to come up with an action plan for further development – is so important and interesting. I'd love to know what happened next!*

# 29

# TEACHER TRAINEES EMPOWERED BY DOGME

### KHANH-DUC KUTTIG

## GERMANY | ADULTS | B2 – C1

This is a language development course for pre-service teachers. There are three parallel groups in the course and each group has about 20 students per session. The average level of the class is mid- to high B2. Very few of them have had any extensive classroom experience.

'Classroom Language Skills' is a compulsory course for students in the teacher education program at our university. This is a course where students learn to teach English through English, focusing on the language needed for classroom interaction. Since language is best learned when practiced in the context of its use, the pedagogical and content knowledge that students bring with them from their other modules becomes part of what we do in class. Assessment is by active participation and a reflective journal. All sessions are student-led.

Dogme seemed the perfect approach for this course as it would ensure learner-generated content, focusing on the future language needs of my students who would be teaching EFL in homogenous groups in German secondary schools.

Every session begins with a student taking attendance, and sometimes, the student has the additional task of rearranging the physical classroom, doing a warmer activity with the class, or checking some written homework that had been previously assigned. This would take no longer than ten minutes. In this short segment of between two and fifteen minutes, so much language is produced and this then becomes the basis of our language development.

From here, we moved to verbal and non-verbal language. There will always be an initial discussion on the particular classroom routine or event – for instance, the use of gesture and eye contact, questioning strategies, managing behaviour, rearranging the classroom, or giving instructions. Each session has four groups of students with four to five students per group, all seated at group tables.

Each group is given a discussion card that gets students talking about the particular classroom routine for the session. The card describes a scenario and asks for language or has a question that gets students thinking about the classroom routine. Groups always first choose a discussion leader before beginning their discussion. After two minutes, the cards move in a clockwise direction to the next table, and a new discussion leader is chosen. This repeats until all groups have completed four discussions. This part of the lesson takes about 20 minutes. During this stage, I walk around the classroom, monitor for language, and make notes on what we might work on in the next stage. After the series of discussions, we are usually at the halfway mark of our 90-minute lesson.

After a short break, the next stage focuses on language and this includes language structures and where necessary, classroom-specific vocabulary. With one classroom routine as our main focus per session, I elicit from students the language they feel would be useful in their future classrooms. For instance, in the session on rearranging the classroom, students provided examples that were put on the board:

- <u>Move</u> the desks, to form some rows....
- <u>I need</u> 3 brave students to....
- <u>Could you</u> find a seat/place where
- You have 2 minutes to form___
  you can -----
- I need a teacher's assisstant ....
- Put the chairs back to the
  <u>original place.</u>
- I need 3 strong kids to <u>help me</u>
- Each table needs 4 chair
- Please <u>take your chair</u> and----
- Everybody <u>grab</u> a chair and.---

As a class, we then looked at these structures, grouping them into different patterns:

1. Imperatives
2. We/I need/want + noun phrase
3. We/I need/want + (you) to-infinitive
4. Modals for requesting: Could/Would/ Can

The structures then served as prompts and students would add their own examples.

Students also discussed how to personalize the instructions – by adding names, or addressing groups of students (You boys at the back, move the chairs ...), making it more polite with 'Please', showing displeasure or frustration, and adjusting their instructions according to the language abilities of different learners. Our board looked like this:

| I / We | need / want | noun phrase<br>tables in a circle<br>+ tables joined up<br>a free space /<br>space in the middle<br>3 in front | please<br>now<br>after the break<br>: |

The final stage is in two parts. First, each student is given a card and writes a prompt that would elicit language from their peer. For instance, 'The previous class left the room in a mess. Ask your students to put the tables and chairs back in order. Your students are in Year 5.' With 20 students, we get about 20 prompts. In the second part, students pull a name out of a bag and address the prompt to the student they've pulled. The student who has been addressed responds with what they would say in that particular scenario. The language structures that had been elicited in the previous segment remain on the board for reference. For the previous example, a response might be: 'Let's move the tables and chairs back. I want everyone to help, please.'

We finish the lesson with students writing the language stems and any other new expressions into their notebooks. I encourage students to consider which expressions they would actually use, write possible alternatives, and to avoid those expressions that they find problematic.

Rearranging the classroom   25.04.24

1. use imperatives:
  • come to the front
  • [name] [group] [gesture] line up against the wall [please]
  • now get into pairs [please]
  • get into pairs now

2. use questions:

| • would | | return to your desk | |
| could | you | help Jim with his desk | now, please |
| can | | | |

  • I need | groups of three
    I want | pairs, circles for discussion

For their reflection, they write a paragraph answering the following questions:

1. What was the most important learning you have gained today?
2. What questions do you still have about language use in this particular classroom event or routine?
3. What could you do yourself to answer these questions?

Students have responded positively to the Dogme approach, despite initial reservations about the absence of a pre-determined weekly syllabus. Their reflections and the mid-course evaluations showed that students felt that they were finally learning language that was relevant to their future needs. They felt empowered when they provided examples

of classroom language, and more so, enjoyed sharing their knowledge of
the local classroom and school culture with me.

Entry 25.04.2024

I like the material used which are this journal
and the cards given to us with the different
situations described to us. It helped us
think about age-related language. The
materials also pushed us to have meaningful
discussions with the other students.

40 Minutes Reflection.                               26.4.24
I really liked the idea of using this exercisebook
to write down important phrases / words and
useful grammar because it helps us with keeping
information together. I also like that we get
exercises every week that help us get confident
and experience.
I am inspired by the conversation game we did
because in my opinion it is a great way to get
pupils to use english and the vocabulary they
learn in a conversational way.
I really agreed with the use of clear instructions,
less words and better articulation.
I did not disagree with anything that happened
in todays session

While I provided the formal language input to my students, they
supplied the contextual and cultural knowledge to me. Our lessons
evolved from being top-down and instructional to sharing sessions where
we learnt from each other. As a group, we were able to determine what
may or may not be appropriate in our EFL classrooms, and we learnt
about challenges teachers faced at different levels in German schools.
Every semester, I bring the knowledge I gained from previous students
into the next course, showing a greater sensitivity to the context of my
students' future careers.

A NOTE FROM SCOTT:

> *While this account describes a course rather than a single lesson, it
> scores lots of Dogme points. For a start, it helps answer the ques-
> tion: Can you design a whole course along Dogme lines? Khanh-
> Duc demonstrates that, indeed, you can, if you commit yourself to
> these three principles:*

1. *Jettison the coursebook and work with what the learners bring to class ('Since language is best learned when practiced in the context of its use, the pedagogical and content knowledge that students bring with them from their other modules becomes part of what we do in class');*

2. *Adopt a clear lesson structure that offers the learners a secure and predictable frame within which to experiment with language;*

3. *Incorporate a clearly demarcated focus-on-form stage, where the learner-generated language is 'tidied up' and then recycled through activities with a high volume of output.*

*Moreover, there's a wonderfully symbiotic relationship established: 'While I provided the formal language input to my students, they supplied the contextual and cultural knowledge to me' – redolent of Freire's dictum that 'the teacher is no longer merely the-one-who-teaches, but one who is [herself] taught in dialogue with the students, who in turn while being taught also teach' (Pedagogy of the Oppressed, 1970/1993, p. 71).*

# 30

# COLLABORATIVE PUZZLE SOLVING
## ANASTASIIA LOLLO

## SERBIA | ADULT | B1

This was a one-on-one class with a B1 student. The class had a certain ESP flavour to it as my student was a software developer and most of his English use took place in online meetings with the members of his international team. Although he had been studying English on and off through his school and university years, he was still seemingly unable to understand authentic speech.

The student took this course in response to being transferred to a new work project where most of his teammates turned out to be native speakers of English. It was a course in listening skills heavily based on the authentic communications he had at work. Classes were held online in the format of video conference with the use of an interactive board, which to a certain degree mirrored the conditions of the student's daily English use.

The part of the class described below is best characterized as a "Dogme moment," as it was a listening practice that turned into a wider learning opportunity. All in all, it took around 25 minutes of our time. My original intention was merely to liven up our listening classes and to have the student adopt more authentic ways of expressing himself.

We were listening to a recording of a meeting the student and his colleagues had the day before when the following portion made my student visibly puzzled.

> **Speaker 1:** [00:00:00.45] Hi there. Well, things sound a lot easier since we've actually hired some people on a remote basis so er... I gather we'll be sort of creating more meeting rooms and then staying in the office. Are there going to be sort of facilities there? Are there going to be TVs with the ability to do teleconferencing? Because I think that's going to be quite important for these teams.

The student had difficulty understanding "sort of" because he interpreted the utterance literally as a type or category of things. By way of analogy, I pointed his attention to the word "well" asking whether it denoted something done properly. Eventually, we arrived at the conclusion that these words didn't serve to convey specific meanings but rather to perform a certain function: give the speaker time to gather their thoughts without interrupting the flow of communication.

The student immediately fell in love with them, as oftentimes, when speaking spontaneously, he got frustrated with his inability to formulate precisely what he intended to say. We also had a chance to compare using these words with simply saying "er".

First, we tried to come up with alternative filler words together that could be used in the passage (e.g. like, kind of, right, I mean, you know). We then brainstormed situations where he could have spoken or would like to speak this way. For him, those were meetings in which deadlines and progress on certain tasks were discussed, as well as situations when he had to explain how certain technologies worked.

To give him a more focused practice, I then asked him to explain to me the technologies that had been mentioned in our previous conversations.

As it was an ESP course and I didn't know a lot about his area of expertise, our situation naturally lent itself to this type of activity. The only condition was not to extend explanations over three sentences. The activity turned into a sort of ping pong where I would ask him to explain something from Javascript development and then he would ask me to explain something from language teaching.

What is API?

What is a gerund?

What is Node.js?

What is the accent?

What is the event loop?

This part of the class closed with a brief discussion on the level of precision expected of him in various work situations, and whether overuse of fillers could make him appear too hesitant.

One of the things my student did between our classes was to keep a language log, where he would jot down peculiar aspects of his colleagues' speech. Building on this established practice, I asked him to track them using fillers. Over the following weeks, his observations proved quite beneficial for his cultural awareness, as he noticed that filler words were in fact used for a range of reasons (e.g. being vague, being polite, etc.).

The fragment of the class described here took place in the first weeks of our course. The course was paid for by my student's employers and it was their idea to design it strictly for listening skills practice. Later on, our classes evolved into a full-fledged ESP course aimed at enhancing the student's general ability to perform his professional tasks in English. Such moments probably had their fair share of influence on our decision to change the focus of our studies.

I am not convinced that the described intervention was solely conversation-driven. It can be clearly seen that a couple of lexical items were the springboard and what we wanted to do was to explore how these items could be used.

I really appreciate that this course was an ESP course and the materials we used were mostly provided by my student. Those were written and oral real-life conversations people had when they were focused on using language to get things done. The language they spoke contrasted starkly with the examples my student had encountered in textbooks.

After this intervention, I didn't observe any immediate changes in the student's language production. The effect it had would better be described as a change in expectations. As a person with many years of studying English, my student had held rather rigid views on fluency. For him, fluency meant rapid-fire production of complete, grammatically correct sentences, ideally following the subject-verb-object pattern. Noticing what authentic utterances looked like helped him realize that fluency in a foreign language had a lot in common with fluency in his mother tongue.

A NOTE FROM SCOTT:

> *One-to-one teaching is an ideal context for engineering Dogme 'moments' and for using these to explore aspects of language use that are not necessarily targeted in conventional materials.*
>
> *In this case, the student himself identified a 'puzzle' in the authentic data that he himself had sourced from his work context. By providing the lesson content AND choosing the language focus, the student is exercising maximum agency; the teacher's role is very much 'the guide on the side', prompting, directing atten-*

*tion, giving feedback, and expediting a heightened awareness on the part of the student as to the nature of fluency.*

*While the one-to-one situation lends itself to this approach, it's not impossible to imagine how this kind of awareness-raising activity could be transferred to a classroom context, with students in small groups studying short extracts of authentic data, and attempting to solve language 'puzzles' collaboratively.*

# 31

# FINDING A NEW RHYTHM
## CLARIANA LUCAS

### ITALY | TEENS | B2 – C1

This is a class of six teenagers aged 14-18 attending the first year of a two-year B2 exam preparation course. Though hardworking and dedicated to eventually getting their First Certificate, they were initially more comfortable directing their communication exclusively my way – the teacher zone.

Italy, at least in the south where I have been living for over five years now, is very keen on exams and certificates, so it is no surprise that most of my time teaching is spent on exam classes. While this passive, teacher-centered learning style might have sufficed for these students in lower-level courses, it becomes a hindrance to their progress in higher levels. Beyond that point, student ownership of their learning journey becomes not just a choice, but an absolute necessity. This group needed to increase their vocabulary, sharpen their accuracy, and, most importantly, find their voice within the classroom.

I had already dipped my toes into Dogme through the Teaching Unplugged book with one-on-one sessions and general English classes, so I felt emboldened to bring Dogme to this exam preparation class.

Initially, it was all about diligently testing the waters – trying different activities, taking notes on what worked (and what ideas were abandoned halfway through and why), and honing my ability to seamlessly and systematically recycle the language that emerged.

To my pleasant surprise, things flowed better and more easily than I had anticipated. A lesson that incorporates what students bring to class, all their experiences and interests, becomes a shared journey, a vivid memory that not only resides in everyone's minds but also comes alive in unexpected moments. The whiteboard became our collective workspace. We would jot down interesting bits of language, and tweak as necessary, then students would copy them, snap photos, or when the interactive board was used, we'd save everything as PDFs. We fell into a rhythm of collaborative exploration of their language.

It soon dawned on me, that Dogme was the ideal pathway to guide these students towards owning their English skills, both for the demanding tasks students faced in the First Certificate exam and beyond.

The lesson started with one student dragging himself in, visibly exhausted from a particularly intense sports practice session. The conversation quickly drifted towards sports. Instead of steering the conversation in a different direction, I let it unfold. Five out of the six were actively committed to training in various sports, some even participating in competitions, so this was obviously something they could just keep talking about without losing interest. I wrote the following questions on the board:

*Why sports?*
*What are the highs and lows?*

As conversations kept on going, brimming with real-life experience, a gold mine of interesting vocabulary and collocations was unveiled. I chose to focus on language that:

- I suspected to be unknown to the rest of the group.
- Could improve their fluency when talking about sports, giving reasons, and expressing opinions.

This time though, instead of directly recording this language on the board or presenting in some other way, an idea sparked: I took some paper slips, wrote the language gems down on small bits of paper, and attached them onto each student's back. There was a consistent effort with this group to get them to interact – and rely on each other more. So, the goal was to foster peer teaching, as they had to explain the word on their partner's back for others to guess. Besides that, the idea was inspired by a word-guessing game show they had told me they all watched, so it was no surprise when they enthusiastically embraced the challenge. The activity became a meaning-focused puzzle. They collaborated to decipher each word/collocation through definitions and examples.

I retreated and silently observed them (I could have easily snuck out for coffee). I witnessed remarkable teamwork as these teenagers would contextualize, clarify, and rephrase to elicit meaning. Then came the moment the "weakest" student, with "weightlifting" on her back, struggled. I held my breath, anticipating the moment I might need to step in. "Give them time," I whispered to myself.

"It's two words."

"The second one is like 'carry'," another student offered, mimicking lifting a heavy object.

"Get?"

"No"

Silence.

"No, if you don't wanna use the stairs, you take the....?"

"Elevator?"

"Yes, the other word."

"Lift?"

"Yes, but like swimming, climbing." Elongating the /ŋ/ sound

"Lifting."

Their teamwork, their non-stop conversation, the palpable joy in the air – it was incredible. We still had "weight" to uncover, which was brilliantly done by using homophones (".... a minute" while gesturing with their hands). Witnessing this interaction was truly inspiring. They were unknowingly using many of the communication skills (paraphrasing, circumlocution, active listening, turn-taking,) which are essential for success in exams like the First Certificate in English. Afterward, when I pointed out their strategies, they were quite surprised to learn how much they were already applying these skills.

To this point, word games and sports had dominated the lesson, so a natural progression was that each pair created their own "taboo" cards with relevant vocabulary. We had already played the game, but that time with cards I had created myself. As this is a two-year course, this initiative aimed to establish a student-generated resource they could continually develop and use. After an initial round of playing "taboo" with the cards they had made, they were encouraged to discuss and edit them, creating a refined vocabulary bank we kept 'making deposits' to until the end of the year.

The Weightlifting lesson remains a vivid reminder that the people before you are the richest resource a teacher can have. Witnessing these teenagers actively employ exam-taking strategies like paraphrasing and peer teaching demonstrated how Dogme fosters real communication, naturally leading to the development of skills essential for both exams and real-world scenarios. This solidified my confidence in implementing Dogme with exam-focused classes. It has shown me that authentic engagement and exam goals can coexist, allowing students to develop valuable communication skills without relying solely on textbooks.

A note from Luke:

*This lesson leaps off the page, full of joy, love of learning, and smart connections made between organic communication and the demands of the curriculum.*

*There's also plenty of technique on display. We see many core Dogme teaching behaviours in play: noticing the opportunity, allowing it to unfold, shaping the interaction, choosing which language to focus on, and waiting for students to find their voice.*

*But it isn't just about technique. This practice also benefits from true empathy with the learners: the teacher is on their side, can see that they need to own their own learning journey, and happily records falling into 'a rhythm of collaborative exploration of their language'*

*This embodies the paradigm shift which truly learner-centred education demands. The account begins with a mention of Clariana's compatriot Paulo Freire, and concludes by subverting his 'banking' model of delivery-led education: here, instead of the teacher making 'deposits' which the learners 'receive', the learners make deposits in a shared vocabulary bank which they can all use.*

# 32

# COOKING UP AN IMPROMPTU LESSON

## ANNA LYONS

## UK I ADULTS I C1

T he class was C1 level with 12 students, most of whom had gotten to know each other throughout the first three weeks of the month-long course. There was a mix of L1s – mainly Arabic, Korean and Spanish – and the average student was in their early twenties looking to study at an English-speaking university.

Initially classes were based loosely on the topics and/or grammar points from the assigned coursebook, though as the month went on I moved further away from the book. Analysing authentic texts and completing tasks proved more challenging and satisfying for the class. For example, we had a very interesting discussion about the themes of Pink Floyd's Another Brick In the Wall Part 2.

The rolling onboarding of students at International House London keeps the classes dynamic. The fluctuation of the class make-up calls for flexible planning. While I often give the students a survey at the beginning of the month, asking about their perceived needs and weaknesses, by the end of the four weeks it is rare to have all of the same students. This encourages me to be responsive to the students throughout the course and change weekly plans as needs or interests arise.

While I have often used a Dogme approach to begin a class – sometimes in response to a student question or conversation or sometimes as a deliberately chosen prompt to account for late-arrivers – I don't usually plan or account for improvisation during the class proper.

That is not to say I will never "go off-piste" if something comes up naturally in response to material I've brought to class – as together the class can get a nice lexical set and opportunity to share their personal experiences – just that I'd never look at something I'd planned and consider if or how these moments would arise.

In this lesson, we were following a few pages from the coursebook: vocabulary and reading exercises about anti-aging treatments. The warmer before the reading was the question "would you like to live forever?" and I'd grouped students to discuss it together.

As I was monitoring the groups, I overheard one group discussing how much they hated induction hobs. None of them could remember how they'd landed on the topic, so it remains a mystery.

We did class feedback about the assigned question and then I asked the induction hob group to explain their discussion to the class by displaying an induction hob on the board to help the others understand.

From there students from other groups chimed in with dis/agreements and their cooking equipment preferences with most sitting up and becoming more engaged. To stretch the moment, I asked about V60 coffee, which had been mentioned in passing a few lessons earlier, then using a rice cooker versus a normal pan.

Once that discussion petered out and I couldn't think of a natural continuation, I decided the moment had passed and returned to the book activities. The Dogme moment had lasted perhaps fifteen minutes but in that time the atmosphere had completely changed.

Though a brief moment in the class, this represented a huge moment for me and how I saw my role as a teacher.

At first, my feelings about the moment had been disappointment. I thought that perhaps I should have been able to take it further in some way, such as providing students with a full lexical set around the topic of cooking preferences or a follow-up task with opportunities to use any useful chunks that had come up in the discussion. However, in a discussion with other teachers I came to realise that that wasn't necessary. A Dogme moment can be just that – a moment.

Indeed, on reflection, a discussion about the practicalities of cooking for young adults – some of whom were living away from home for the first time – is much more relatable than such an existential one like "Would you like to live forever?". The fact that it only took a few moments was not important. It was good they had time to talk about it.

This has shifted my perception of what a successful class looks like and of my role as a teacher. I considered if small moments that satisfied an immediate need could be just as valuable as big 'aha!' moments and further, if I could allow my students more control in these small moments.

The main questions I've come away with are:

- How much do I need to direct the class and how much could I let students take charge?
- Is there a way to encourage Dogme moments or is it only possible to respond when they come up?

Recently I have made a conscious effort to step back from time to time and subsequently I have been surprised by some shyer students taking control of the pause to continue or re-direct the conversation.

Additionally, I have occasionally let group discussions go for longer than usual, paying attention to where students go and asking them about any diversions in-class feedback as well as mining some lexical nuggets for the whole class in the process. I haven't radically changed my approach, but I'm happier to let the students have their moments.

A NOTE FROM LUKE:

> *I love how random this lesson is – from living forever, to pour-over coffee!*
>
> *I also like the way Anna describes her thought processes during the class in such detail – this is exactly what it means to 'reflect in action', or think on your feet. By putting ourselves in a position of uncertainty more often during lessons, we get better at finding our own answers.*
>
> *The spontaneous decision to stretch the moment by referring back to a previous conversation is smart – as is the later realisation that the energy was gone, and it was time to go back to the book.*
>
> *Fifteen minutes of engaging conversation is a good stretch of time, a real win. Also, I agree with the students – induction hobs suck. They are much less responsive than gas hobs, and shut down when things don't go to plan (a few drops of water, in my experience). Is that an analogy for rigid, coursebook-led teaching?*

# 33

# PLUGGED IN: MUSIC IS MAGIC
## LIZ MCFARLAND

## SPAIN | ADULTS | A2 – B1

A few years ago, Dogme started out as just a fun idea I thought I'd experiment with, but it has ended up being an indispensable tool and springboard for producing emergent language, developing my students' motivation, and ultimately making their learning experience more personalised, enjoyable, and memorable. The fact that these activities are directly based on what the learners themselves bring to class and find interesting means that they are by nature spontaneous; we never know what might come up, which keeps things interesting.

This was with a group of six 30-50-year-old adult speakers of Spanish and Catalan dotted around Spain and learning general English on Zoom. They were working for an international building solutions company. At the A2 level, having to communicate in English professionally means often feeling overwhelmed with the level of language input.

I have focused on learning strategies for autonomous learning in my online classroom. Small groups carry out tasks in class based on noticing and recycling language items through activities they might carry out at home. They are learning how to learn, while actively using and practicing the language that emerges as the lesson develops. We do one-hour classes twice a week. For this particular class, students had been told to add a couple of English songs they liked to our group chat.

Three out of the six students played their songs and we started off by discussing them. This produced about ten minutes of lively conversation in a mix of English and Spanish. At the same time, I was secretly on the hunt for an appropriate language item to focus on.

I eased them into just using English through comical reproachful facial expressions and asking open questions like 'Where/when did you first hear the song?' 'Why do you like the song?' etc. They produced some nice language, although with some typical errors at this level:

I send a video with subtitles for to understand
Is the sing old?
Do you understand the letters?
Have you listened it?
I listen in spotify.

Together we decided on one of the students' songs to review together in class. This couldn't have worked out better. Just as I realized that the chorus of the song they had chosen contained 'I'm gonna,' one of the students said 'I listen it at home this night' instead of "I'm gonna listen to it..."

So at that point, I jumped on my student's error and put it up on the board. We had already done some peer correction where between the three of them, they had corrected mistakes they weren't aware they had made. The students fixed 'tonight' but I skimmed over the fact that the structure was incorrect.

I was sharing my screen with the lyrics displayed while the song was playing. We stopped and played the track back a few times.  They were all suddenly leaning forwards, talking over each other excitedly, bombarding me with questions (in English!) about the meaning of 'I'm gonna' and also commenting on the missing auxiliary 'have' with 'got', which I told them is typically omitted in songs and speech because of the rhythm English has.

After a quick explanation of 'going to' being 'gonna' all I had to do was remind them about the whiteboard being interactive and all three immediately started typing madly without me even asking!

```
I'm gonna to go to shopping
I'm gonna go to the office
I'm gonna to call to my boss
```

And the list went on...

Then we focused on form. They first had to correct the sentences they had written themselves on the whiteboard by noticing the difference between the language structure in the chosen chorus and their own sentences; for example, the extra 'to' was noticed spectacularly quickly. They also noticed that two of their sentences were actually correct!

We then thought of other songs they liked containing "gonna" and discussed why English speakers use so many contractions in speech, which led to some direct practice of 'I'm gonna' reduced to '/ɒmənə/ (UK) and /ɑmənə/ (US pronunciation)' combined with time adverbials for events planned for the coming evening.

We were way over the 45-minute mark at this point when, the student who had made the 'trigger mistake' still not corrected, had a eureka moment and literally shouted out "I'm gonna listen to it tonight!" They were euphoric in their understanding and spent the last 10 minutes trying to build questions (seen as an example in another song) to ask each other about their upcoming weekends, both orally and written on the board. I just sat back and marvelled.

We spent the last few minutes discussing what they thought about the activity and class as a whole. They vowed that in the next class they would tell the other three about just how much conversation and learning the chorus of one song had elicited. They realised that the more interesting the activity was to them, the more they learned.

These three students are experts in using 'gonna' now. Furthermore, they have taken it as a springboard for exploring contractions in English and regularly request we work on songs as well as film scenes in order to further expose themselves to authentic speech.

A note from Scott:

*This lesson really captures the excitement and engagement that can be triggered by material that the learners themselves have chosen and brought to class – even if the language that is evoked is (initially, at least) a mixture of the L1 and the target.*

*The teacher's role is critical here: firstly, allowing the ideas to bubble out, then 'harnessing the communication' in order to exploit the language learning affordances that have emerged. 'I eased them into just using English...' nicely expresses that transitional point in the lesson where the focus moves almost imperceptibly (and, to my mind, quite magically) from content to code.*

*And the lesson wonderfully demonstrates how engagement can be maintained, even when the focus is on language, evidenced by the fact that the students themselves were asking all the questions, which, to me, is an unambiguous indicator of optimal attention, a necessary condition for learning.*

*And not only were the learners attentive to the language that was generated, but they also demonstrated metacognitive awareness –*

*that is to say, awareness about their own learning processes –*
*when they acknowledged how productive the lesson had been.*

*In short, 'they realised that the more interesting the activity was to*
*them, the more they learned.'*

# 34

## MY LOVELY NEIGHBOURS
### STELLA MUNTIAN

## UKRAINE | ADULTS | B1

This was a one-hour afternoon class of 12 international students of different ages, backgrounds, and life experiences, but of similar intermediate level. Classes focus on enriching vocabulary and developing communication skills. I really enjoyed teaching the class, as the students were open-minded and observant, discussing any suggested topic with keen enthusiasm. To better describe them, I would say that they like going deep into topics, but also going beyond them.

I was not supposed to stick to a particular course book, so I was free to design bespoke lessons for this group and choose my own topics based on their needs and interests. The topic for debate on this day was 'Neighbours'. From my perspective, it could spark curiosity and kick-start a lively discussion with 'sunny spells' of humour and jokes since people normally can remember some funny situations related to their neighbours. I thought this would provide me with lots of opportunities to work with emergent language. I didn't plan to use Dogme, but it gelled at an appropriate moment later in the lesson.

The lesson started with a short video of two guys dealing with noisy upstairs neighbours. I boarded two questions for the students to discuss to get the ball rolling.

1 *What kind of noise can you hear in the video?*
2 *What do you think the neighbours are doing?*

Through this task, a lot of interesting emergent language came up, for example,

- *stomping feet*
- *moving the furniture*
- *scattering the toys*
- *dropping the dishes.*
- *hoovering*
- *slamming the door*
- *hammering things*

After the video, I shared some useful phrases for talking to noisy neighbours and suggested the students make up dialogues imagining they are speaking with 'naughty' neighbours. It was where my prediction for the fun came true. I then encouraged the students to share any stories about their neighbours to wrap up the lesson.

In the feedback, this is where the lesson took an unexpected and memorable turn. One of the students shared a story about a difficult time in her life that ended with her dog passing away. She told the class that a few weeks later, her next-door neighbours' dog started coming up to her door and asking to come in, so she started to think that her dog might have been reincarnated into that one. She told her neighbour, and they ended up becoming very special to each other. What followed that touching yet inspiring story? A Dogme moment! We were all touched by this heartwarming story and lots of us felt quite emotional, and our discussion flowed into a discussion about the necessity of sharing feelings with someone and the importance of asking yourself: 'How do I feel today?' The students started recollecting when they felt dreadful, how it was, and what helped them to fix their state of mind. As students shared their feelings and personal stories, I was able to help them with emergent language that was rich and personal to them:

- *I felt really empty.*
- *I was really on edge.*
- *I was feeling really down in the dumps, when....*
- *I felt really low/blue.*
- *I still hold a grudge.*
- *I still feel a little bitter.*
- *It was the last straw.*
- *I was so fed up with it, I...., but she's still my friend.*

I knew it would be a well-rounded lesson, but I never expected it to be so emotionally packed. I also never expected how it helped the students in other ways. For some students, there was a chance to reflect on their emotions which some students said they had never done before. The students also became closer to each other as well as to me, which is always beneficial. They felt safe and enthusiastic while doing pair and group work, and it goes without saying that they enriched their vocabulary with words and phrases they wanted to use. I could see them writing everything down in their notebooks. For me, as the teacher, the most valuable part was the atmosphere of sincerity that developed an emotional connection inside the group and that stayed throughout the course. It enabled the students to speak out when they wanted to and continued to enhance both their language and personal confidence.

The lesson and its special atmosphere helped me choose the next topic: 'What is more important: our feelings and emotions or our achievements and results? When I told them this, I could see that they were looking forward to it.

We enjoyed being lovely neighbours!

A NOTE FROM SCOTT:

*This is a great example of a 'Dogme moment', that is, a spontaneous and sometimes prolonged episode of learner-generated talk, often triggered by an unexpected event (a bee in the room!), or an individual learner's anecdote, or (and let's not discount this) a text or activity in the coursebook.*

*But, for these moments to occur with relative frequency, certain classroom conditions have to be met, the most important of which is, in Stella's own words, 'the atmosphere of sincerity that develop[s] an emotional connection inside the group and that stay[s] throughout the course.'*

*And, of course, the teacher is key in terms of creating and fostering such an atmosphere: it doesn't happen overnight but must be nourished by the teacher's own preparedness to allow each learner a voice.*

# 35

# AN "ON-THE-SPOT" LESSON

## HANG NGUYEN

### VIETNAM I TEENS I B1

It was a class of 45 grade 10 students. In Viet Nam, a high school class usually has such a big number of students. The 45 students of this grade 10 class had different levels of English language proficiency. All they knew of English was mostly grammatical knowledge.

One day, a colleague of mine was suddenly sick and asked me to take over her class for 45 minutes. I didn't bring the textbook of English 10 with me, so she said I could do whatever I wanted with them, even if it was far beyond what was written in the textbook. What she told me made me think of Dogme ELT.

Having no textbook with me at that time, I decided to let the students experience a textbook-free lesson and check if such a method would yield positive results as had been described in various articles I had read in the past.

As usual, we did the greetings, and I asked students to choose one special thing they had in their school bags and tell the class who gave it to them, when they got it, and where they got it. To make sure students understand it, I myself gave an example about the watch I was wearing. After some moments of thinking, the first student raised her hand and talked about her pen case. Then another student shared with me his special thing, and I wrote the sentences on the board.

As the lesson went on, I drew the students' attention to the point of "Simple past" and reminded them of regular and irregular verbs. During that "long conversation", I noticed that the students could improve their language fluency and accuracy when talking about events happening in the past. For example, the first student who told me "I getted my pen case on my birthday. My close friend gave it to me." now knew how to make her sentence correct by changing "getted" to "got". I wrote some more verbs on the board and asked the students to give the appropriate past forms of them and luckily, they did it the right way.

To help students practice further, I asked them to work in pairs. At this point, they closed their eyes and picked up anything they could in the schoolbag, then talked about it, using the simple past to answer the three questions that had been raised at the very beginning.

Who gave it to you?
When did you get it?
Where did you get it?

When it was time for pairs to stand up and talk, it was obvious that each of them – regardless of their proficiency levels – tried to come up with some ideas about the thing they picked up from their school bags.

It completely took me by surprise that the students were really willing to talk during the short lesson though it had been assumed that Vietnamese students, particularly those living in the countryside, were not confident to speak English. The reason for their willingness to talk lay in the fact that what they talked about was something familiar to them and they shared with the class the real truth about it, instead of making up a story to meet the request of the teacher. When they see that English is not only a subject but also a language – a means of communication to convey their meaningful messages, students feel more motivated in their learning process.

This first-time-ever use of Dogme ELT – though not perfect – is a really memorable lesson in my teaching career up to now. It helps foster the assumption that without textbooks, students can also have meaningful lessons and Dogme ELT really creates teaching and learning contexts, which leads to more students' success in language learning.

Up to now, I have used Dogme ELT at least once every semester, or when time allows, I integrate it into speaking classes so my students can experience such a new and interesting learning approach.

A NOTE FROM SCOTT:

> *The power of physical objects can't be underestimated – whether they're the things that the learners have on them or carry with them, or the special thing they bring from home for the purpose of a 'show and tell' activity – which works equally well online, I should add.*

> *To which we could add all the exploitable material they each carry on their phones – not just the photos but the text messages and music that they have saved.*

> *Testimony to the interest that is generated by these things, and the language that is produced as a consequence, is the fact that Hang Nguyen was able to engage a class of 45 students of diverse levels for a full 45 minutes.*

# 36

# DISCUSSING GENDER, DOGME STYLE

## SANDRA GUADALUPE OJEDA

### ARGENTINA | ADULTS | A2 – B2

The activity I want to share was carried out by a group of 34 students, ranging from 18 to 30 years old. These students were doing a subject called Art and Culture. In this subject, they are supposed to improve their linguistic skills while learning about the English-speaking culture. This was a crowded class and most students had demonstrated certain difficulties in using English when they had to produce it orally.

The institution where I work is located in the eastern central part of Argentina. Spanish is our mother tongue and we do not have frequent opportunities to use English outside the classroom to communicate in real situations. These students enrolled in the Teaching and Translator Training Programmes but many of them have not acquired the threshold level yet.

In order to help this group of students acquire the language and give them opportunities to develop their communicative competence, I decided to work with group discussion activities and debates following the Dogme approach. Students have other subjects like "Language and

Grammar" in which they study rules about the language but they do not have many chances to interact freely and discover by themselves how much they can produce.

The activity was planned after watching a TikTok video about gender differences. In this video, a girl showed the results of two different web searches. She entered the words "men" and "women" in a search engine to see which words appeared associated with them. The search produced quite surprising results since the words clearly depicted gendered differences. For example, while the word "men" showed positive words like "courageous, brave, bold," the words associated with "women" were gender biased, for example, "curvaceous, matriarchal, dainty."

I thought it would be interesting to see the selection of words my students would choose to be associated with the words "men" and "women" and analyse if there were any similarities or differences compared to the words provided by the search engine. I asked them to work in groups of not more than 5 students and they were supposed to be grouped by gender, giving them the freedom to choose any group according to their gender identity. They had to write down any word they would associate with "men" or "women," and women had to write words about "men" and men about "women."

In each group, they had to debate their choices to see if the other members of the group agreed on the word selection. Students got so engaged in trying to justify their choices and back up their ideas that they started producing language I had not heard before in class. Thanks to this activity I could have a better understanding of the range of vocabulary and structures they could actually produce.

After finishing this stage of the task, they shared their word selections with the rest of the class, providing reflections to justify their choices. I wrote the words each group chose on the board, and as a final stage, I showed them the TikTok video so that they could compare their choices and the results of the web search. They could also reflect upon gender discrimination in discourse.

Students reported that they really enjoyed the activity since they did not have many chances to use the language in uncontrolled activities like this one. It was interesting to see how they managed to find words they did not know autonomously and how motivated they were to get their ideas across. This involvement in the task pushed them to make extra efforts in order to communicate. Having been able to witness this was fantastic.

The results of this experience encouraged me to reflect upon several issues. The first and most important is the fact that students need to have a purpose for communication, and they perform tasks a lot better when they are involved in and motivated by the task itself. Another point worth mentioning is the importance of reflecting upon social issues in order to foster reflection and tolerance. After all, we teachers are supposed to be agents of change. These kinds of activities give students the opportunity to negotiate meaning, debate, and reflect and learn not only the foreign language but also the power to embrace differences and reject discrimination.

A NOTE FROM LUKE:

> *This lesson shows how much can happen when a speaking task is clear and motivating, and the language parameters are broad.*
>
> *Unconstrained by the need to deploy a small number of specific language items, Sandra's students venture to the limits of their capacity, finding new words on their own initiative and producing language she hasn't heard in class before.*
>
> *This helps her assess their ability. Instead of needs analysis being processed outside regular class in a tick box setting, it is done qualitatively during the class: the processes of teaching and learning are aligned.*

*This lesson also shows how Dogme is not just about waiting for a spark from the students. Here the teacher has an idea and figures out how to shape it into a materials-light activity. While in a task-based setting, we might expect the learners to watch the TikTok video before they start. Sandra leaves the students free to create their own outputs and only shows them the video at the end. Instead of trying to emulate the model the students are free to create, and then compare.*

# 37

# IF YOU WERE A DOGME, WOULD YOU REGRET BARKING?

### CHRIS OŻÓG

## COSTA RICA | ADULTS | B1 – B2

This was originally a class of 12 adults just starting B2, which was then split into two groups of six and then became more or less a group of three for me as two never showed up, and there's usually one of the remaining four off. This lesson had the three who usually attend and who are fast becoming one of my favourite ever classes.

My three years with International House in Costa Rica, a private language school, will probably always be the happiest professional years of my life. I learned so much, developed my career so much, presented at my first conferences, became a CELTA tutor, IHCYLT tutor, IH LAC tutor and an IELTS examiner, met so many good teachers and stole all their ideas.

**Why did you choose to use Dogme?**

It might be better to ask—why did Dogme choose me! The particular 'ecology' I was working in—both in terms of the school and this specific class—really lent itself to experimenting with less course book-driven lessons and encouraging learner-generated content. Plus my own development as a teacher and teacher trainer had given me the confidence to work with the kind of spontaneity that a Dogme approach promotes: I don't think I would have taken such risks as a first-year teacher!

Out of a start-of-class chat the subject of 'dogs' came up. It has become a class joke the amount of moaning I do about the amount of barking the dogs in my barrio of San José, Sabanilla, do. Taking the dogs as our basis, I asked individuals to come up with five solutions to my dog/noise problem. Then, as a three, they had to discuss the merits of each problem, justifying their opinions, and selecting a group top five. This was a lively 20-minute discussion in which there was loads of language flying around. The group then reported their top five solutions to me, which I wrote on the board and discussed with them as they were read out.

At this point, we got to the focus on form. We were 70 minutes into the lesson and it had been pure conversation with lexis fed in where appropriate (sometimes the learners are surprised by how long and how much they speak in the class). In the end, I noticed that they could improve their range and accuracy of sentences such as *"if he do that, then he would to be happy"* and so went for 2nd conditionals as a point of emergent language to focus on. Using the solutions the group had agreed on, we rewrote them as 2nd conditional sentences, highlighting the use of past simple and continuous tenses as well as the modals *would, could, might + infinitive*. We discussed the contractions and drilled them, as well as going over ways to start conditionals that aren't *if*, such as *providing that/as long as...* We also looked at changing the order of the clauses and removing the comma.

Having taken a quick break, it was time for some practice. I asked the group to take their original five solutions and re-write them using the language we had just discussed, with me buzzing around and helping out where they needed it.

Next, they had to analyse these re-written sentences and decide if they were correct, as well as deciding on a favourite of each person. This led to a highly amusing feedback session that largely took care of itself as they debated the merits of each sentence. Who would have thought that 2nd conditionals could make students laugh so much?

They then wrote these favourite sentences on the board and we discussed each one in turn, highlighting excellent use of language such as collocations, as well as correct grammar. We also went through what parts of the sentences could be changed while keeping the same meaning i.e. replacing *if* with *suppose* in questions and writing up these options too. Some collocations that came up included *sleep deeply, beat sth/sb to death*, and *stop + Ving*. The group then copied down these sentences with the highlighted language.

The final practice involved me asking the group to close their eyes. I then rubbed off some select language. First of all, all the past tenses and modals. The group then opened their eyes and re-created the sentences together.

We then repeated this, until almost all the language had been removed. In feedback to each reconstruction, we highlighted the alternatives for if and the meanings of using different modals.

By this stage, we had regrettably run out of time. This was a real shame as I wanted to complete the task cycle with another related task which, in the end, had to wait until the next class (not that there's any harm in that). To finish in the last 8 minutes, I asked the group to select the lexis they wanted to keep for the vocab envelope and write these words down on the cards. Everyone went home happy, except that I gave them two exercises from the course book for homework (they have bought it after all and at $40, that's no snip in Costa Rica).[1]

---

1. *This chapter is an adapted version of a blog post originally published on* The Portable TEFList *on October 7, 2011, under the title* "If You Were a Dogme, Would You Regret Barking?" *by Chris Ożóg. It is included here with permission from the author.* https://thep ortableteflist.wordpress.com/2011/10/07/if-you-were-a-dogme-would-you-regret-barking/

A NOTE FROM SCOTT:

*I have to say, it was one of the most enjoyable classes I can recall and one in which there was so much language floating around, it was tricky to know what to focus on. You simply do not see the humour and creativity in people when you force them to work with language form a course book. I believe that doing things this way makes the language more memorable and the study of it more enjoyable.*

*This lesson is now part of the class 'folklore' and the themes recur in almost every class. While I have no actual proof, it certainly 'confirm[s] [my] own intuitions that Dogme, if not more effective, is more engaging, more memorable, more motivating – more fun!'*

# 38

# BUILDING BLOCKS WITH BEGINNERS
## SINALIE RITHMA PERERA

## SRI LANKA I ADULTS I PRE-A1 – A1

This is a class of 11 students who are engaged in a vocational program with an integrated module to learn basic English skills. They are from underprivileged backgrounds in Sri Lanka and have not had a strong foundation in the English language. Therefore, these learners are Pre-A1 or Low A1 levels on the CEFR scale.

Most students have either dropped out of school after the first 11 years (after only completing the O/L exam) or they have completed school but due to various circumstances, have found it difficult to pursue further education. We have set up programs to equip them with vocational training as well as adequate English skills so that they may secure a good job. We run full-time on weekdays and conduct largely digital sessions, but we have whiteboards and other materials if required.

There were two reasons to employ a Dogme approach. First, given the beginner level of learners I hoped the Dogme approach would help them organically emerge out of their shells and explore the language together. Secondly, even though I have always been interested in Dogme, I haven't tried it out before so I thought, it's now or never! A risk with the hope of a reward.

Students had just started off the course after a small holiday period. As an icebreaker of sorts, I asked the students to think about the following question:

*What did you do last week?*

I gave students a minute to think and discuss with a partner. However, a couple of minutes into the discussion, I realised they were struggling to answer the rather broad question and did not have the language to do so. In order to narrow it down for them, I added three more questions to the board.

*What did you eat?*
*Where did you go?*
*What activities did you do?*

Having been given a narrower scope, the students carried out the discussion with some encouragement to use full sentences. After the discussion, I asked the students to write their answers in their books as well. Finally, as a whole class, we went through a few answers for the three questions.

During the discussion, I had noted that students did not have the required language to describe events of the past. A lot of their answers to the questions were rather similar and as follows:

What did you eat?

I eat rice and curry/I eating rice and curry.

Where did you go?

I go to school/I going to school.

What activities did you do?

I play cricket.

All their sentences had used present tenses which led me to believe the students would benefit from exploring the simple past tense.

Using the sentence "I play cricket" as an example, I drew a timeline and asked a couple of students to mark when they thought the incident had occurred. Both students made a mark on the past section. Then, I questioned whether the verb "play" belonged to the past. With visual help from the timeline, most students quickly realised that it did not. As the light bulb went off in their heads, a few students provided the past tense of the verb. I then elicited that "-ed" needed to be added to the verb to turn it to past tense.

We explored the past tense form of a few more verbs such as jump, joke, help, etc. I didn't want to confuse the students so at this I stage we didn't dissect regular or irregular verbs. We used the example sentence and broke it down to the form of subject + verb-ed.

However, I soon realised confusion was overtaking them as they tried to fit their other sentences to the form. To avoid a total mind meltdown, we looked at "I eat rice and curry" as another example. Students knew the past tense of "eat" was "ate". We discussed how there were different patterns to turn verbs into past tense and segued into regular and irregular verbs. To avoid being bogged down with too much grammar, they played a competitive game to identify regular/irregular verbs and turn them into past tense.

Finally, I asked the students to look at the sentences they had written earlier and correct them if needed. I also asked them to add two new answers to each question. While some students needed help with some irregular verbs and longer sentences they had attempted, most were successful in correcting and creating new sentences using the past simple tense. Afterwards, we explored negative and question forms as well.

We finished off with another discussion on "What did you do last year?" Even though a few students needed encouragement and some eliciting, most were able to successfully produce language to talk about past events.

Given the students' limited exposure to English, I believe they made great strides during this session producing new language. However, I believe I made a mistake delving into the negative and question forms as students started losing interest due to too much input. It would've served better to have saved this for a later date.

Having never been given the opportunity to discover the language properly, students are very enthusiastic participants of all English sessions. As a first-time experience for both me and the students, we agreed that it was a productive session. Our main takeaway with Dogme is that it's prudent to take it slow and steady with beginner-level learners as they have very limited language. They need to be given a lot of space and encouragement to explore and keep building on it.

I've made it a point to ask students "What did you do yesterday?" whenever I pass by their class. Even though some of them now tend to make a run for it when they see me coming, almost all have happily and actively answered with simple, accurate sentences. I've also encouraged students to ask the question to each other. I'm hoping to build on what they now already know with another Dogme adventure!

A NOTE FROM LUKE:

*This account starts with a great example of 'reflection in action' (also known as thinking on your feet). Sinalie quickly realises that her first question was too broad, so she decides to break it down into three more manageable options.*

*The answers the students give are relevant to themselves as individuals, but also – because they are from a similar linguistic, social and contextual background – to one another. The material the teacher now starts to work with belongs to them, which makes the language work more meaningful.*

*After starting with reflection in action (during the event), the account concludes with what Schön calls reflection on action (after the event). Sinalie realises that introducing negative and question forms was a step too far.*

*The breakthrough moment of this lesson was not to teach the full grammatical scope of the past simple, but to link the students' latent knowledge of past forms in English to their existing conceptual understanding (the human understanding, which we all share, whatever our first language) of past and present.*

# 39
# NEXT-LEVEL MOTIVATION FOR TEENAGERS
## VIDA RAHPEIMA

## IRAN I TEENS I B1

Welcome to Room 205 at my high school, where the air is filled with the anticipation of learning. The walls are adorned with colorful posters, showcasing grammar rules and literary quotes, while student artwork adds a personal touch to the space. Rows of desks are arranged facing the front, where a whiteboard stands ready to capture ideas and spark discussions.

In this vibrant classroom, two teenage boys, Ahmed and Murat, stand out for their mischievous antics and disinterest in traditional teaching methods. Despite their potential, they struggle to stay engaged during lessons, often succumbing to the allure of daydreams whenever textbooks are opened. As their teacher, I am determined to find a way to reignite their curiosity and passion for learning.

The decision to adopt the Dogme ELT approach for this class stemmed from my desire to connect with Ahmed and Murat on a deeper level and make learning more meaningful for them. Traditional methods were failing to capture their interest, and I believed that by embracing a more organic and student-centered approach, I could create an environment where they felt empowered to engage with the material in a way that resonated with them.

The activity began with a simple question: "What interests you?" As the students shared their passions and hobbies, I listened intently, making mental notes of potential avenues for exploration. With textbooks set aside, I encouraged open dialogue and collaboration, inviting the students to take ownership of their learning journey.

As the class progressed, we delved into topics that piqued the students' curiosity, using real-life examples and experiences as the foundation for our discussions. From analyzing song lyrics to debating current events, each lesson was a dynamic exchange of ideas and perspectives.

During one session, the topic of their favorite video games emerged organically. Ahmed and Murat, who were avid gamers, eagerly shared their insights and opinions, using gaming terminology to express themselves in English. Phrases like "level up," "power-up," and "boss battle" became part of our vocabulary, as we explored the concept of overcoming challenges and achieving success both in-game and in real life.

In another class, we discussed their experiences with social media and the impact it had on their lives. Ahmed and Murat shared anecdotes about their interactions online, using hashtags and emojis to convey their emotions and experiences. As we explored the nuances of digital communication, they experimented with new words and structures, incorporating slang and informal language to reflect the casual nature of online interactions.

Role-plays and group activities allowed the learners to apply their language skills in context, and this led to their sense of confidence and accomplishment. Through simulated scenarios like ordering food at a restaurant or negotiating with a friend, they practiced conversational English in a low-pressure environment, experimenting with different expressions and intonations to convey meaning effectively.

Grammar structures naturally emerged as we engaged in these activities. For example, during role-plays, Ahmed and Murat used modal verbs such as "can," "should," and "would" to make requests and suggestions. In discussions about social media, they practiced using present perfect tense to describe their online experiences, such as "I have posted many photos on Instagram." Through guided practice and feedback, they honed their grammar skills while also building fluency and confidence in speaking.

As the weeks went by, I witnessed a remarkable transformation in the young boys. Their confidence grew, their vocabulary expanded, and their willingness to participate in class skyrocketed. By embracing topics that resonated with their interests and experiences, they became active participants in their own learning journey, demonstrating a newfound enthusiasm for English language acquisition.

At the end of the activity, I asked the students to reflect on their experience with the Dogme ELT approach. To my delight, Ahmed and Murat expressed enthusiasm for the class, noting how much more engaged they felt compared to traditional lessons. They appreciated the opportunity to explore topics that were relevant to their lives and found the interactive nature of the activities both stimulating and enjoyable.

As a teacher, I also reflected on the activity, recognizing the value of student-centered learning and the importance of adapting my teaching approach to meet the needs of individual students. The feedback from the two boys reaffirmed my belief in the power of Dogme ELT to foster meaningful learning experiences and ignite a passion for language acquisition.

The experience of using the Dogme ELT approach had a profound impact on both my teaching practice and the students' learning. Moving forward, I continued to incorporate elements of student-centered learning into my lessons, striving to create a dynamic and inclusive classroom environment where all students felt valued and supported in their educational journey.

This story serves as a poignant reminder of the transformative power of innovative teaching approaches such as Dogme ELT. By prioritizing student engagement and embracing a more organic and collaborative learning environment, I was able to create a space where the boys felt empowered to take ownership of their learning and explore topics that resonated with their interests and experiences.

The decision to adopt the Dogme ELT approach was driven by a desire to connect with Ahmed and Murat on a deeper level and make learning more relevant and meaningful for them. By stepping away from traditional teaching methods and embracing a more dynamic and student-centered approach, I was able to create an environment where these two learners thrived, ultimately igniting a passion for learning that extended far beyond the confines of the classroom.

As a teacher, the experience reinforced the importance of flexibility and adaptability in the classroom. By listening to the needs and interests of my students and tailoring my approach accordingly, I was able to create a learning environment that was both engaging and effective. Moving forward, I will continue to draw upon the principles of Dogme ELT to inform my teaching practice and ensure that all students have the opportunity to reach their full potential.

A NOTE FROM LUKE:

> *This is such an interesting sequence of lessons, and Vida's reflections on it are so acute, that it really comes with its own commentary – I almost don't need to add anything! 'By stepping away from traditional teaching methods and embracing a more dynamic and student-centred approach,' she writes, 'I was able to create an environment where these two learners thrived, ultimately igniting a passion for learning that extended far beyond the confines of the classroom.'*

*I love the way Vida embraces her teenage students' real-life communication behaviours and modes. So often teachers make students play their game, the unmotivating 'game' of the curriculum in which texts and communication activities bear little resemblance to the way we interact in everyday life.*

*But here she listens to and includes the language the students use in their own actual gaming lives, including slang, informal language, hashtags, and emojis. These are the multimodal communication paths of today, which makes this sequence of lessons – spanning weeks and months – truly conversation-driven for our times.*

# 40

# TALKING WITHOUT LIMITS
## MAHDI RAMEZANI

## CANADA | ADULTS | B1 – B2

The class, consisting of 6 international students aged 19 to 23, took place five days a week at a university in Halifax, Canada. My friends (learners) were individuals from Japan, Ivory Coast, Iraq, and Korea, with English proficiency levels ranging from B1+ to B2, four of whom are now studying at the University. Despite being an English for Academic Purposes (EAP) course, as a pure proponent of TBLT, my sessions were structured around TBLT. As usual, at the beginning of the course I explained my approach and explained the objectives. This time Dogme was going to build the pillars of my TBLT. They seemed to like it very much, as was evident in the feedback notes I collected from my students at the end of the semester. This is the practice that I have been doing for a long time.

Dogme was part of my action research; years ago around 2018, in my several email correspondences with Scott Thornbury, I shared my thoughts that Dogme is the offspring of TBLT considering the theory of learning and teaching. Clearly, a TBLT session is full of Dogme moments. I also prefer to use Dogme moments rather than Language Focus/ Focus on Form (FOF).

As mentioned before, TBLT was going to be shown to be teeming with a huge number of Dogme moments. Once early in the morning, I tasked my students to think of academic challenges they encountered while studying at university or secondary school (which would be relevant to my two Ivorian friends as they were recent high school graduates).

The first phase involved brainstorming. I invited them to jot down challenges they had encountered and encouraged them to prepare themselves for how they would explain them.

In the second stage, I wanted them to think about how things could have been different if they had known how to deal with issues. Finally, after grouping them in two groups of 3, I asked them to explain the situation to their partners.

While observing their discussions, I took notes on emergent language that could be perfect points to be dissected and resolved as Dogme moments.

It is important to use a specific task as a technique to attract your learners to a certain language item; However, this approach may not work for every situation and learner.

When finishing their discussions, I asked everyone to write a couple of sentences regarding what could have been done to eliminate their academic challenges. The examples below were collected from my learners:

1. I could take notes in class to be more free at the time of the final test.
2. It might be good to revise my lessons with my classmates.
3. If I had a voice recording device, I wouldn't have a hard time studying my lessons for the final exam.
4. If I had a wiser course consultant at school, I would choose another field. And I shouldn't study more to change my field now.

In fact, I intended for them to use language and then reflect on what they wanted to mention, communicate, or express. Every sentence was transferred to the board, and we analysed every single problematic or in-question item. I also used Concept Check Questions (CCQ) to expand their knowledge (i.e., is this about past, present, or future?/ Does this sentence express probability or ability?/Which word is better to be used in an academic context? Formal or informal?/How many syllables does it have? Long or short adjective?). This encouraged them to be engaged with the feedback process. Meanwhile, I provided simultaneous and spontaneous explanations for any unforeseen questions:

- How 'test' and 'examination' are different in an Academic context?
- I heard something about mixed conditionals — can you give an example?
- When I am writing a paper, what other words can I use instead of change? — I don't want to be repetitive.

However, for some responses I hesitated to dig down and engage them, being mindful of overwhelming them with too much perplex language.

*The basic idea is that the teacher provides 'better ways of saying' whatever the learners are trying to express through a meaning-focused task (e.g. describing their home town). The teacher will use his/her discretion in terms of what he/she chooses to focus on – probably ignoring constructions that would be way beyond the learners' current or potential competence. Similarly, the teacher will make choices as to the degree of explicitness he/she will adopt when re-formulating the learner's utterance – e.g. a simple re-wording, with no explanation; a re-wording with short explanation; a re-wording with detailed explanation, forming a kind of mini-lesson.*

Email communication with Scott Thornbury (May 8, 2019)

Regarding the statement mentioned by Scott, it can be interpreted that during Dogme moments, the teacher can decide how deeply to pursue an issue since it might cause greater confusion due to learners' proficiency level.

After a 25-minute break, we came back, and I wanted them to extend their thoughts and think more about various related examples of this kind, including their lives and studies. Through this, they were able to negotiate what had been learnt, picked up, and discussed.

I used a real-world task as a frame and then my learners filled this frame full of Dogme moments. During Dogme, we talked about the language since their proficiency and age allowed me to turn the implicit processing into an explicit one. However, with lower-level students, I believe we (teachers and learners) would still be able to talk about the language.

Regarding this Dogme rich session, I believe what I did was open my arms to the spontaneous needs of my learners. TBLT provided an opportunity to allow my learners to shape the direction of my instruction. Dogme is truly a learner-centered approach, which is orchestrated by the teacher as an artist.

Comment from a student from Iraq:

> When Mahdi (the teacher) told us about Dogme, the name was a bit strange. But today I think I had a very great experience in this class. I was free to talk, and Mahdi didn't limit us. I became brave and I was not afraid of talking. In other classes, I had to focus on only one grammar point and some words to practice a conversation. My brain was so limited to one topic or idea.

A NOTE FROM LUKE:

*Task-based language teaching (TBLT), with its emphasis on meaning over form, is a cousin of Dogme. But it isn't the same thing. One could say that Dogme is less focused on an outcome (completing the task), because it sees interaction as the task. Interaction is not a means to an end, but an end in itself.*

*In Dogme, interaction is the work of the classroom: if we are really interacting, using all the language at our disposal rather than trying to mobilise only those parts of the language dictated by the syllabus, we are – as therapists say – doing the work.*

*This is why my favourite part of Mahdi's account, which represents a kind of dialogue between TBLT and Dogme, is the closing comment from an Iraqi student: 'I was free to talk, and Mahdi didn't limit us.' This freedom is not just a 'nice to have'. It relates directly to the very thing our students study English for and the very thing we as teachers should be promoting. The scenario the student describes in other classes – focusing on 'only one grammar point and some words to practice a conversation' – is not enough.*

# 41

# LIFE LESSONS FOR 1–1
## DEBORA ROCHA

### BRAZIL | ADULT | A2 – B1

My student is a doctoral candidate, a public servant, and a law professor at a university in Rio de Janeiro. We have been working together for approximately a year. While her goal is to eventually take a proficiency exam, it's not our main focus at the moment. I've been using the Dogme approach in all of her classes from the very beginning. We primarily discuss her work, the political situation in Brazil, and occasionally veer off into other topics that pique her interest.

I teach English online as a freelancer to adults. This particular class was a one-hour private lesson. There's no specific goal with this student, so the class structure is completely up to us. She doesn't have a need to use English in her daily life; our classes are probably the only time she speaks English. We both speak Portuguese as our native language.

I chose Dogme for this class because my student seemed tired, likely from preparing for her upcoming lecture on fundamental rights in culture and education. I thought a less structured, more conversation-driven class would be a refreshing change, especially since she recently celebrated her birthday. Instead of focusing on grammar, I decided to delve into her life lessons from the past 28 years, inspired by an online forum I had read[1].

The class began with our usual greetings. She mentioned her busy week and preparations for her lecture. I asked her about her birthday, she told me it was great and joked about feeling old. Since it was her birthday week, I proposed exploring the lessons she's learned in life so far, specifically 28 lessons for her 28 years. She laughed at the challenge but agreed to give it a shot. We brainstormed topics together and I shared a link to the Quora forum for reference and language input.

About 15 minutes later, she had written nine sentences but was struggling to continue. I suggested a couple of topics to help her, and she completed the last two sentences. We then went through each sentence together. I orally reviewed each sentence, facilitating self-correction through guiding questions and eliciting alternative phrasings. For example, when she stumbled over the phrase "as fast as," we discussed alternatives, I introduced distinctions between "fast" and "quick," clarified grammatical structures, and refined her sentence construction collaboratively. Additionally, we explored her preference for home-cooked meals over dining out. She told me that she only goes out for dinner on special occasions. We talked about specific restaurants in Rio that we like and dislike.

For sentences 9 and 10, which we thought about together in class, I introduced the structure "more likely to". She didn't know how to say it in English so she told me in Portuguese, then repeated the sentence in English and continued telling me about it. We came to the end of the class and the remaining sentences became homework. Our next class is in two days and I plan to go over all of her sentences and in the end, have her write a small text summarizing her main learnings, adding a few examples to illustrate.

In the final 10 minutes, we reflected on the complexity of the task and

---

1.   https://www.quora.com/What-are-the-things-that-I-should-learn-before-turning-30

her feelings about it. She found it challenging to dissect her life lessons but noticed her own mistakes, particularly with past tense usage. We ended on a lighter note, with her planning to share the exercise with her sister. In this class, I feel as though I was wearing "two hats", transitioning between having an authentic conversation and providing pedagogical guidance, which I believe facilitates immediate feedback at the point of need and promotes self-correction.

This instructional experience has significantly informed my teaching methodology. Integrating creative exercises with text production and language exploration fosters a seamless classroom dynamic akin to conversational exchanges between friends, enriched by scaffolded linguistic support tailored to the task at hand. By centering lessons around the learner's life experiences, the curriculum inherently priori- tizes student engagement and relevance. Furthermore, having the student do written tasks affords both time for thoughtful composition and oppor- tunities to observe cognitive processes, thereby enabling targeted linguistic interventions during subsequent oral exchanges. This holistic approach, blending content with language acquisition, cultivates mean- ingful communication reflective of real-world interactions, thereby fostering collaborative learning within a supportive environment.

This experience has influenced my teaching approach in several ways. Mixing creative exercises with language exploration made the class engaging and relevant. By focusing on my student's life experiences, the class felt personalized, student-centered, and had plenty of scaffolding, which seems to be well received because of the nature of the task. Writing down her thoughts allowed for reflection and focus on form and accuracy, while our discussions helped refine her fluency skills. It's a collaborative learning experience that mirrors real-world conversations. My student benefits from a supportive environment where she can express herself freely and receive immediate feedback, which I hope instills confidence in her communicative abilities. I also hope that this format fosters her autonomy and cultivates her intrinsic motivation for learning. Access to external language resources, such as online forums, further increases her linguistic repertoire, offering a model for language use.

## STUDENT WORK – CLASS NOTES
28 lessons I've learned in 28 years

Debora's examples:

1. I've learned that I can be afraid of something and still do it.
2. The best day to go out to eat is Tuesday because that's when restaurants usually buy fresh produce.

Isabela's sentences:

1. Reading time is relative. (fast/slow) "When I was a teenager I thought I needed to read as fast as I could."
2. Dinner at home is better than dinner at a restaurant.
3. Doing nothing is essential.
4. Skin care is not as bad as I used to think.
5. Not planning everything is ok.
6. At work, it's better to encourage the people than serve compliments.
7. We had to make choices and it always have good consequences and bad consequences.
8. Sometimes, it's necessary to do things faster than doing things with perfection.
9. When we cook our food, we are more likely to try all the vegetables and everything.
10. The friendship doesn't need frequent contact.
11. When we are professors, we don't have all the knowledge of the world and it's normal.

A note from Luke:

*This is a nice example of a teacher responding to a student's needs (Debora knows her student has just turned 28) and setting a task that shapes the lesson (the '28 lessons for 28 years' challenge).*

*Dogme can thrive on thoughtful preparation and task design. The key is not to overload the learners with content or task instructions and to leave room for them to create texts, written or spoken, that express their language capacity and potential. This in turn creates the space for meaningful instruction.*

*This is beautifully articulated in the reflection section, where Debora really nails the nature of student-teacher interaction in the Dogme classroom: I agree with her that the teacher needs to wear two hats, cycling between authentic conversation and pedagogical input.*

*Also, things don't have to be perfect to work. The student couldn't think of 28 life lessons. But she had enough for one motivating English lesson – and I love that she wanted to ask her sister the same question!*

# 42

# HARNESSING THE COMMUNICATION
## CHRIS ROLAND

## SPAIN | YOUNG LEARNERS | A1 – A2

The lesson described here was first included as part of a Modern English Teacher article I wrote entitled *Question time! Can't we just talk to them?*[1]

We were halfway through the academic year of 21/22 and I had been working a group of seven and eight-year-olds quite hard, in an effort to cover the structural part of our syllabus ready for their mid-course exam which was a standardised test set across our language academy.

To this end we had been doing a lot of worksheets. They involved ordering words to make sentences (positive and negative ones, and questions), categorising vocabulary items, completing dialogues, describing pictures, and correcting spelling. The worksheets were very well designed but through my bullish overuse of them, I was starting to lose touch with the group and perhaps even dampen their enthusiasm for English classes a little bit.

---

1. Roland, C. (2022). Question time! Can't we just talk to them? *Modern English Teacher,* 31(1), 6–9.

**Beginning**

"Esas son botas de campo?" (Are those field boots?) asked Alejandro, as we settled into our seats at the start of a class. I was about to deflect the question but a little voice in my head said: "Come on Christopher, at least give the lad an answer."

"Alejandro," I said, "wait..." I wrote at the top of the board:

*Are those boots for the countryside?*

It certainly was not my best ever recast from a learner's L1 utterance and in retrospect, I could have put "Are those walking boots?", but that is what I came up with in the three steps it took me to get to the whiteboard. In a young learners' class, we try to keep things moving along as indecision on the part of the teacher does not generally benefit classroom management.

"Can you repeat that after me?"

He did.

"Can everyone repeat it?"

They did.

Now Alejandro, can you say it on your own? He managed to, and then I answered:

"Yes, they are. Problem?"

"No problem," he replied, smiling, because –Problem? *No problem* was one of our established adjacency pairs, often employed to defuse drama.

"Qué te ha pasa'o en en dedo profe?" asked another student, Sofía.

"Mmmm. Okay Sofía, hang on a sec..."

Under Alejandro's sentence, I wrote:

## What happened to your finger, teacher?

I was wearing a plaster (*band-aid* to some readers) on my index finger. Anyone teaching younger learners will attest to how observant they can be when it comes to changes in their teacher's appearance.

We followed the exact same steps. Sofía repeated the sentence. Everyone repeated. Then she tried saying it on her own and finally, I answered, explaining that I had a new knife in the kitchen and it was very sharp. I translated sharp and mimed it with an "Ow!".

"Lo vas a usar otra vez?" (Are you going to use it again?) asked another child.

The sub-vocalised narrative inside my head returned. *"So, is this what we're doing today – taking questions?"*

"It seems to be," I answered.

*"And for how long do you think you can keep this up?"*

"Let's see."

Perhaps it was the aforementioned sense that something had been missing from recent classes that prompted me to switch into Dogmetician mode. Maybe it was watching Scott's online plenary, *When the Learners Ask the Questions?*,[2] for APPI – the Portuguese teachers' association – the year before, which had rekindled some of my deeper methodological convictions. What I do remember clearly, though, is leading this third learner through the previous steps, responding with a measured, "Yes, but carefully," and consciously deciding to let things unfold and see where they would lead. Apparently, the children had decided that we were doing the same, and soon, hands began rising into the air en masse. I took questions for 45 minutes. They included:

---

2.  Thornbury, S. (2021, June 17). *When the learners ask the questions* [Online plenary]. APPI.

Can we watch the panda cheese commercial?

Which classroom do you prefer, this one or the other one we use?

How do you write so quickly in English?

Can you write my name in Arabic?

Throughout the development of this extended questions phase, I followed the same steps as for the first two questions. This was certainly conversation/text-driven (both, in fact), materials light, and resulted in two boards' worth of emergent language. I would also like to highlight two additional features here, which helped me map Dogme style teaching over to a young learner context.

Firstly, there was acceptance of L1. If we want to go off-road and allow learners to participate in a deeper communicative exchange than normal, they may need to go above their linguistic threshold. Here we can use L1 in a principled way as an entry point to interactions.

Secondly, one of the main challenges of having an extended conversation with a group of primary-aged learners is that they are not always interested in, and willing to listen to, questions that their classmates have fielded – or the answers to those questions. This is why I have heard the assertion, from time to time, that "...you can't do Dogme with kids' classes". My answer to that is: Yes, you can, but you need an additional layer of structure.

Here, the shift from individual repetition to class drilling helped share each question and make it common property – and hence of more interest to all. The shift back to the individual restored the communicative element, and the withholding of the answer until all those linguistic hoops had been jumped through, helped maintain engagement.

That particular lesson provided a real sense of reconnection. From that point on, I have regularly included a shortened slot like this, often for 10 minutes or so, or until the board fills up, every few classes, or whenever there seems to be something of a barrage of learner questions at the start of a lesson.

I have found this in no way incompatible with having a coursebook to get through. In fact, it has a calming and reassuring effect on the learners, as their curiosities are, at least once in a while, satisfied, and they feel they are being heard. It increases teacher-learner connection and, if the boarded language is recorded (I tend to take a photo of the board), allows the recycling of commonly occurring language as a valuable addition to any set syllabus.

A NOTE FROM SCOTT:

> *Reading Chris's account, I'm reminded of the visionary New Zealand educationalist, Sylvia Ashton-Warner, and her book, Teacher,[3] in which she charts the development of her teaching approach, grounded 100 percent in the lives of her primary age learners: 'I talk to them all day. I answer thousands and thousands of questions. Mainly they teach themselves. More and more I think that my converse with them is the main consideration' (p. 132).*

> *Elsewhere, she writes, 'I harness the communication, because I can't control it, and base my method on it' (p. 104).*

> *Chris's alternating between individual repetition and class drilling of the learners' questions, and ultimately of boarding them, are all a form of 'harnessing.' Of course, Ashton-Warner's children were developing literacy in their first language.*

> *Teaching a second language to young learners requires a degree of mediation between the two languages, so, as Chris points out, 'we can use L1 in a principled way as an entry point to interactions.'*

---

3.   Ashton-Warner, S. (1963/1985) *Teacher*. Virgo.

# 43

# CRITICAL THINKING FOR TRAINEE MECHANICS

## VALERIA RUSSO

## ITALY | TEENS | A1 – B1

This was a class of 14 Italian students aged between 15 and 16 in a vocational secondary school within the Italian public school system, specializing in mechanics. Most students were at A level, with just a few at B1 lower level. They were all male and had recently started working in local mechanic workshops or in family-owned production activities.

Our classroom was pretty standard but comfortable, equipped with both a whiteboard and an interactive board connected to the Internet. English lessons had to cover a scheduled syllabus of key mechanics vocabulary and useful functional expressions. The students were not particularly ambitious and did not display a motivation for English, as it was not seen as a tool to enhance their future jobs as labourers in factories and work-shops. Therefore, they tended to focus on essential and highly technical input, especially relying on the ESP textbook which was at B1-B2 level and consequently frustrating for them to navigate.

I used Dogme a lot for this class because I wanted them to get used to more natural and spontaneous English language usage. In particular, I created various Dogme moments to try to make them more independent from the textbook and more relaxed using English. Starting from cross-cutting topics, I encouraged them to reflect and share personal experiences and opinions.

The activity began with small talk about their weekend, during which they worked part-time in factories and workshops. We discussed their risks and responsibilities. Then, I shifted the focus to the responsibilities the factory owners may have, encouraging them to imagine themselves in this role. So, I wrote on the whiteboard:

*YOU ARE THE FACTORY OWNER*
*What would you do?*

I kept the atmosphere on a critical level, brainstorming ideas with questions such as:

*What are your priorities?*
*Would you bring cakes and pizzas?*
*What about the electricity bills?*

I instructed them to share their opinions and write a keyword on the board from their contribution. Some of them were great: one student suggested "I would have solar panels" writing GREEN ENERGY on the board. Another said "I would do maintenance because it's the key of saving energy", writing MAINTENANCE. A shy one said, " want to give workers more coffee break", writing COFFEE BREAK. Other good ideas emerged from their real-life experiences, even if they had to step into the role of someone they saw as different from themselves. I stood in the out-of-shape student circle eliciting practical ideas, scaffolding their language, and subtly adjusting the form by recasting what they said. For instance, I paraphrased contributions by saying 'Oh, nice, so you would opt for solar panels!' or 'You would give more coffee breaks, wouldn't you!'. The result was a colourful spidergram on the board with every-body's ideas, some of which were brand new to some students.

Through this lesson, I realized I had to create more opportunities for crit-ical thinking where students could utilize a broader range of English, even if they felt reluctant to do so. I think they came to realize that they were naturally and skillfully using the modal "would" and the phrasal verb "opt for" towards the end of the activity, and they were proud of that.

This activity is one of the most memorable Dogme excursions I've had with the mechanics students. It convinced me to start from real-life prob-lems and to assign simulated responsibilities within a specific "what if" scenario that had few but coherent guidelines.

A note from Luke:

> *This is a very interesting step outside the classic 'Business English' context of suits in skyscrapers, and into a working-class environ-ment where English feels irrelevant – a reminder that not all work takes place in offices and that not all work demands English.*

> *Given limited motivational space to work in, Valeria finds a way into the students' world by focusing on their experience of the workplace. She uses a nice projective technique to get them started: when she says that good ideas emerged from this, 'even if they had to step into the role of someone they saw as different from themselves,' I would suggest the ideas emerged because they had to step into this role. And I like the use of 'few but coherent guide-lines' for this activity – just enough control, not too much.*

> *The teacher's role in a dogme lesson or classroom is neatly summarised: standing in the 'out of shape student circle', Valeria*

*elicits ideas, scaffolds language, and adjusts form by recasting what has been said.*

*Maybe some of these trainee mechanics will go on to run their own workshops and small businesses, joining a supply economy where they will need English – even if they can't see a use for it now.*

# 44

# ADAPTING OLD ACTIVITIES TO NEW CONTEXTS

## KEVIN RYAN

### JAPAN | ADULTS | B1

W eek three of my first-year university classes in Tokyo is the sweet spot for an activity taken from *Teaching Unplugged*: "*Best in 24*" (p.27).[1] Over the last decade or so I have been using this Dogme activity because it fits both pragmatically and linguistically. *Best in 24* builds trust because students get to know each other on a personal level. Food is a concrete topic, making it easier for my A2 and B1 students. I used this activity in six of my nine classes last month.

You couldn't find a set of more typical first-year General English classes than the nine I have at a large university in Tokyo. These are required non-major classes, 90 minutes for 30 weeks over 2 semesters. I am free to focus on communicative language and learning skills to develop a student toolkit so that they may continue learning languages on their own.

All students have had twice-weekly English classes for the six years of junior and senior high school. These classes tend to focus on university

---

1. Meddings, L., & Thornbury, S. (2009). *Teaching unplugged: Dogme in English language teaching*. Delta Publishing.

entrance exam preparation, so students come with a wealth of grammar and vocabulary that they have not had the chance to use in real communication. This is where Dogme comes to the rescue. Through communication practice, they have the opportunity to turn their usage into use. Week after week, they learn to invest more of themselves as these emergent activities include parts of their lives. In this case, the topic is food.

*Best of 24* asks students to think of all the food they have eaten in the last 24 hours. This is surprisingly hard for some students, who need scaffolding to be able to translate some of the foods. Natto and Tonkatsu don't necessarily need to be translated to "fermented soybeans" or "breaded pork cutlet," for example. Harder to handle are the students who forget what they have eaten, or only eat two or three things a day. Ask them to imagine a weekend feed instead.

Once the students have a list of food, ask them to pick one; the best one. Ask them to prepare to explain why it is the best, giving them a minute to prepare. At this point, some help with comparative language may be helpful, as is a set of adjectives for the senses. Using *Memory Stars* (ibid p. 44) the previous week can also be helpful.

Often this starts out as mini-presentations with no interaction. Once the students become comfortable presenting, we mix up the groups and try it again, this time with questions. As we move the focus from speaking to questions, I usually see a spark in the groups. The idea that this funny language can be used to convey meaning and interact with others creates a literal buzz in the classroom. I usually keep mixing the groups until that happens.

I go around the room and collect especially good answers and questions either to go over later or to put up on the screen (whiteboard) for others to see. My Wednesday 2nd period, just before lunch, morphed into a discussion of which cafeteria served the best meal on campus.

The flexibility of this activity allows for many different directions. A2s may want to cover comparative language. Ask them to make a list of foods they like better than others and share that. Higher groups usually want to focus on talking about food in general. I often ask them to extend the period from 24 hours to a week or longer. Expansion to a new topic has often yielded more practice (sports venues in the last year, convenience stores, public transport). If they are in a sharing mood, narrowing the topic to "mom's best food" has also worked.

I use these kinds of activities to gently nudge the class culture from native to target language. It takes weeks, sometimes semesters, to make a noticeable change. Students get used to our weekly "practice" sessions, which include the following chapters from Teaching Unplugged (ibid) : *Same Time Different Day, All About Us, Slices of Life, Good News Bad News, Predicting the Text Type, What Did I Say?* and *Schwa Wars.*

For A2 students, I've found more guidance helps at first. Getting them to recognize interaction patterns helps. *The Unplanned Lesson*[2] helps with these. Hall Houston's *101 EFL Activities for Teaching University Students*[3] is another useful resource to extend the ideas of Dogme.

I discovered Dogme a decade ago, and it changed the way I teach. I hope it does for you too.

A NOTE FROM SCOTT:

> *It's always gratifying to hear how our ideas (such as this one from* Teaching Unplugged) *are adopted, adapted, extended, and even, at times, abandoned.*
>
> *One thing I have learned, after years of editing other people's*

---

2.   Roth, I., & Wicking, P. (2023). *The unplanned lesson: How to stop searching for activities and start engaging students.* University of Michigan Press ELT.
3.   Houston, H. (2023). *101 EFL activities for teaching university students.* iTDi Publishing.

*activities, or writing my own, is that activities, too, are emergent phenomena: they take on a life of their own as they adjust to a different educational ecosystem.*

*Kevin's description of how he has adapted 'Best in 24' is a good example. It serves to remind us that there is no 'one way' of doing anything, least of all of teaching a second language.*

*It's also a useful reminder that the lessons you have read about in this book cannot necessarily be uprooted and transplanted to your own context without some extra watering, trimming, and nourishing.*

# 45

# FROM A FROWN TO A SMILE: CONVERSATION AS CONNECTION

## NADINE SAASSOUH

## LEBANON | TEENS | A1 – A2

This was a class of 15 high school students in Grade 11 with English proficiency levels ranging from fair (A2) to below fair (A1) on the CEFR scale. All were eager to achieve fluency in speaking English. Despite their enthusiasm, many of them struggled to effectively communicate and express their ideas. Traditional classroom settings had left them feeling demotivated and unsure of their abilities. However, they were determined to overcome these challenges and unlock their full potential.

As an EFL teacher for secondary classes since 2003, I've noticed a common struggle among students in expressing their ideas effectively. Additionally, the abundance of heavy materials and resources hinders real communication. Many students become demotivated when tasked with activities that don't align with their interests, particularly when these activities are imposed by teachers. In 11th grade, students are expected to follow textbooks approved by the Lebanese Center of Research and Development (CRDP), covering specific topics required for their upcoming 12th-grade exams.

According to Thornbury (2000), "teaching – like talk – should center on the local and relevant concerns of the people in the room, not on the remote world of coursebook characters, nor the contrived world of grammatical structures" (p. 2). It can be difficult for EFL learners to express their ideas, and a heavy reliance on materials and resources can make real communication impossible. Learners may feel demotivated when having to engage in artificial speaking activities. Research has established that the key to improving students' communication skills is to provide the students with tasks that are meaningful, relevant, and engaging (Cooper, 2012). Considering this, the absence of speaking opportunities that simulate real-life and spontaneous interactions in L2 classes has led me to consider Dogme as a potential solution.

In my context, traditional teaching approaches are prevalent, and both EFL teachers and learners are often unfamiliar with the Dogme ELT approach. As previously mentioned, both my students and I are shackled by a syllabus, so we cannot practice the target language freely. Recognizing this gap, I have proposed implementing Dogme ELT to enhance 11th graders' speaking skills and reshape their attitudes towards speaking tasks.

This particular lesson was the first period on March 26, and the weather was unusually warm. As we all entered the classroom, one person was notably absent—Samir. He had to explain to the supervisor why he wasn't wearing his school uniform. A few minutes later, Samir finally joined us, sporting a Juventus T-shirt and a frown on his face. While everyone else settled in and grabbed their textbooks, I took the opportunity to jot down some questions on the board:

1. Can you guess the story behind this special T-shirt?

2. What do you think makes it so meaningful to him?

3. Do you believe it was a gift, or did he acquire it in a unique way?

*4. What memories or experiences do you think wearing this T-shirt evokes for Samir?*

*5. What interesting encounters or reactions do you expect others to have when they see Samir wearing this special T-shirt?*

I instructed everyone, including Samir, to write answers to the questions listed above. I offered assistance with words and structures as needed. Samir was then invited to come to the board. I posed the first question, and students shared their predictions while Samir revealed the correct answer. We continued this engaging and lighthearted learning activity for the remaining questions. To wrap it up, I asked each student about a special T-shirt they own and to share interesting stories about it.

The students reflected positively on this enriching and engaging learning setting, finding the topic particularly interesting and relevant. They appreciated the opportunity to delve into the story behind Samir's special T-shirt and were intrigued by the insights shared by their classmates. Moreover, many students noted that the activity helped lift Samir's spirits, as he transitioned from wearing a frown to sporting a smile throughout the discussion. By exploring the significance of his T-shirt in a supportive and interactive environment, Samir felt validated and valued, contributing to his overall sense of belonging in the classroom. The activity not only deepened the students' understanding of Samir's personal story but also strengthened the bonds of empathy and friendship within the class. Overall, students felt that the activity not only enhanced their learning experience but also fostered a sense of connection and positivity among classmates.

A note from Luke:

*This account says so much about the interpersonal impact of lightening the syllabus load and focusing on the people in the room. It also helps build Samir's intrapersonal intelligence – as he is gently encouraged to come out of his shell and join in.*

*Nadine's introduction is richly reflective, rooted in her local experience in Lebanon, and carefully referenced against Dogme ELT and classroom research.*

*But the account really comes to life when we hear that: 'The weather was unusually warm .. one person was notably absent – Samir.' It sounds like the beginning of a story, and it is the beginning of a story: wonderful things happen as the activity engages the students, meaningful language use ensues, and Samir is recuperated into the group.*

*Lesson design is often channeled into micro-planning around tasks and phases of tasks, and we risk missing the broader goal. Here, the teacher is clear about the need to break free of the syllabus and has researched ways of doing so. This broader sense of aims and goals is what helps shape the activity that emerges from Samir's football shirt and anxious frown, ending in a smile.*

46

# ONE OF MY FAVORITE SOUVENIRS
## BARBARA SAKAMOTO

## JAPAN | ADULTS | A2 – B1

This was a class of 12-15 Japanese women ranging in age from their late 50s to early 70s. The women all belonged to the same group (New Women's Association, a women's rights organization founded in 1919). They came to the class with amazing life experiences, a lot of fossilized English, and a hesitation to trust their own ability to learn. Their English level ranged from high A1 to low B1 on the CEFR.

While ostensibly a Travel English course, members rarely needed to use English because they traveled with group tours. The community center where our bi-weekly classes were held provided a room with tables and a whiteboard, but no WI-FI, so our lessons were decidedly low tech. Students and I had complete autonomy over curriculum and content. They preferred having a textbook because they could "see" what had been covered, but didn't mind if we went off on tangents to follow interesting topics as they arose.

I was hoping that the topic of souvenirs would be engaging for my globe-trotting seniors because they didn't have many "real life" reasons to use

English. When the topic came up in pre-class conversation, it was the perfect opportunity.

Before the start of class, Mrs. O shared a box of cookies she'd brought back from a tour to Germany and classmates asked about her trip in Japanese. I wrote some of the questions on the board, in English.

> *Where did you go?*
> *What did you do in ~?*
> *What did you eat/drink?*
> *How was it?*
> *How was the hotel?*
> *How were the public toilets?*
> *What did you buy?*

This was a frequent topic in class, but students had never really developed the habit of using English to talk about their travels. I nudged students to use the English questions to have a similar discussion about Mrs. O's trip. Since they had just finished talking about it in Japanese, this was a chance to discover some useful travel English, encourage everyone to participate, and to work on expanding responses. I added language to the board as needed or requested.

After about 15 minutes, we stopped, and we went over the language that had emerged in the discussion. I circled the word "souvenirs" and moved to the main focus of the lesson.

Souvenirs are important to my students. They spend a lot of time thinking about what to buy for themselves and for others when they travel. We started by talking about Mrs. O's souvenirs and then began to talk about our own.

I erased the board and wrote "Souvenirs" at the top. I showed students my brightly colored glasses case." This is one of my favorite souvenirs. I bought this in Poland a long time ago. I found it in a small shop that sold handicrafts. It was very colorful and cheerful, and every time I take out my glasses, I remember my trip. It's also very practical. I often lose my glasses. This case is very difficult to forget!"

I asked, "Why is this case one of my favorite souvenirs?" I wrote some of the ideas on the board:

> *happy memory*
> *beautiful*
> *useful*

I asked students to think about some of their souvenirs over the years and add some other reasons.

They came up with ideas such as the following:

> bargain (something they couldn't get in Japan easily)
> thoughtfulness (a gift that showed someone was thinking of them)
> small (doesn't take up space in a suitcase)

Next, it was the students' turn to talk about their favorite souvenirs. I gave them five minutes to think, make notes in English or Japanese, ask for language, and imagine what they would say.

To develop fluency, students talked about their souvenirs three times in pairs, first for three minutes, then for two minutes, and finally for one minute. Each time they spoke with a different person, and in between conversations we added useful language to the board.

To wrap up, students shared what they remembered about each other's souvenirs, using language from their discussions.

The time constraint of the 3-2-1 activity helped students focus on what they were trying to say and less on whether or not they were making mistakes. Students had a wide range of English ability, and it was always challenging to create speaking opportunities that provided enough support for the less fluent or confident students to succeed as well as enough space for the more fluent students to challenge themselves. This lesson approach worked pretty well for both goals. If I were to do this lesson again, I'd try to plan it so that students could begin with physical objects to share. They often seemed to find it easier to show something while speaking than describing something AND talking about it.

After the activity, students said they'd like to see the souvenirs their class-mates had talked about, and we agreed to have a sharing time at the start of each class. This allowed us to continue using and building language to talk about things that actually motivated them about traveling.

A NOTE FROM SCOTT:

*I love that this lesson led to a sharing time at the start of each class. The personal, tactile example of the glasses case (not to mention the cookies!) is a great way to open the subject and make it accessible to everyone.*

*The note that 'every time I take out my glasses, I remember my trip' also suggests the ideal outcome: language memorisation being triggered by relevance, and students remembering a lesson because it was personal.*

*I also like the fact that you allowed them the opportunity to brainstorm ideas in their first language (Japanese) in advance of rendering these ideas into the target language (English).*

# 47

# THERE IS NO SUCH THING AS A
# BAD QUESTION

## MARIA SAMPIO

## SPAIN I ADULTS I B2 – C2

This was a 60-minute in-company business English class (retail
segment) with six adult students of B2 level on the CEFR.
Currently teaching in Alicante, Spain, my students are native speakers of
Spanish (Castellano) aged from 20 to 28. From the beginning, they
wanted to practice using English in authentic situations they are likely to
encounter in the workplace to enhance their ability to communicate
fluently and confidently with clients, colleagues, and stakeholders.

My role as the business English trainer extends to imparting both business skills and the English language for effective intercultural communication. At the time this lesson took place, my students were attending
annual individual meetings with their managers and preparing inten-
sively for the summer season, and they could sometimes be disturbed
during the lessons by emails and phone calls. Recognising this busy
period for the students, integrating mobile-friendly activities could potentially enhance engagement and effectiveness.

Dogme came absolutely naturally into my teaching! In business English
training, learners are often self-directed and motivated business people

who have specific goals related to their professional roles. This approach allows me to tailor lessons that address those needs directly, right here and now. Whether it's negotiating contracts, writing emails, or whatever my students come up with in the unpredictable rapidly-changing business environment, Dogme allows me to focus on the language skills most relevant to the students.

Right before the start of the lesson, one of the student's phones beeped, announcing the arrival of a new email. He sighed loudly and remarked, "It's not a business conversation; it's literally becoming a chat. What does he want from me?" The other students joined in, asking for more details. The student explained that his colleague from another store department had requested additional numbers missing in presentations, stating, "He wants to ask where can he find these figures in the presentation. Could you please tell me what the cost of this service is?" as my student quoted the email. The rest of the students shared with me that they could totally relate to the described problem and summed up the conversation with a rhetorical question, 'When we will stop having problems with the CRM system?!" And that was the way direct and indirect questions came as a point of emergent language to focus on.

I intentionally wrote down the questions the students came up with on the board in two separate columns: direct and indirect questions. We discussed the form, and I highlighted that they already had knowledge about the concepts but struggled to formulate explanations. Eventually, they identified the grammar structures of both types of questions and provided correct versions of the original sentences. Then, I asked the students to identify other introductory expressions of indirect questions, and they mentioned phrases like "I would like to know," "Could you tell me," "Do you know" and "I wonder," which we listed on the board.

Next, I suggested that we analyse authentic job-related emails on their phones to see which type of questions, direct or indirect, was more commonly used and in which part of the emails they appeared. We wrote down examples of both types of questions from their own and their colleagues' emails on the board, corrected where necessary, and transformed direct questions into indirect ones and vice versa.

Regarding the meaning and function, I prompted the students to reflect on the differences in register, tone, and the types of texts where direct and indirect questions were used. They concluded that they rarely heard managers or themselves using indirect questions in daily conversations but mostly encountered them in formal and semi-formal emails of inquiry to sound more polite and more tentative.

After a short break, during which a store customer accidentally entered our meeting room (as sometimes happens), we engaged in the final activity. The students practiced interviewing each other in pairs, preparing for individual meetings and role-playing conversations with their managers, using both indirect and direct question forms.

As the lesson drew to a close, the students expressed their satisfaction with its productivity and relevance. One student mentioned on leaving the meeting room that he had realised anything could serve as material for language learning—not just course books or abstract texts, but also content retrieved from their own phones, and that "impressed him a lot".

Considering that indirect and direct questions are typically learned at lower levels, students' errors in asking questions at B2 level may be attributed to fossilisation. If I were to teach this lesson again, I would incorporate a writing practice activity where students write responses to the emails discussed, allowing them to practice using the question forms in written business communication.

What truly touched me was the genuine emotion and feedback from my students. This lesson struck a chord with them because it revealed that our time together wasn't just about distant future outcomes; it was about making an immediate impact, right from the moment they stepped out of the classroom.

In the subsequent lesson, the students expressed a desire for all future lessons to mirror the last one. They felt a tangible sense of progress in their language skills, noting that throughout the week, they became more mindful of their question-asking habits and found themselves during lunch breaks discussing with colleagues who didn't attend English classes how they could improve the efficiency of written communication through strategic questioning in emails.

A NOTE FROM SCOTT:

> *This lesson is a great example of how technology (in this case the students' phones) can be integrated into what is essentially a Dogme lesson.*

> *Why is it a Dogme lesson? Because the content of the lesson was generated from the learners' own texts (specifically the emails on their phones) and because, in Maria's words, it 'wasn't just about distant future outcomes; it was about making an immediate impact".*

> *This is what some scholars, such as Leo van Lier, call 'contingency' – the sense of connectedness, where the texts that stimulated the lesson were connected to the learners' lives, where the learners were connected to one another by a shared professional context, and where the language that emerged was strongly connected to the texts that generated it and to the learners' immediate needs and interests.*

> *The teacher's expertise in highlighting and exploiting this network of connections is what no doubt motivated the learners to request lessons of a similar type.*

# 48

# I WONDER WHY...

## SAEID SARABI ASL

### CANADA | ADULTS | B2 – C1

This was a multicultural class of 16 adult students (aged 20-25) from Japan, South Korea, Taiwan, France, Belgium, Spain, Mexico, and Columbia attending a cultural immersion program at a private language school in Toronto, Canada. In this language school, each CEFR level is broken down into three sub-levels, and these students had just started the first stage of the B2 level. The class consisted of two blocks of 80 minutes with a 20-minute break time in between.

Like many other language schools in Toronto, my workplace is known for providing cultural immersion programs for international students from many countries around the world. The students in this class were all college students who wanted to use their gap year to come to Canada to improve their English quickly. Thanks to their varied backgrounds and motivation, they always had ideas for speaking activities, discussions, and writing tasks.

I have been a huge fan of Dogme ELT and encouraged my teacher trainees and colleagues to lower their dependencies on materials. I tend to go unplugged in many classes to avoid overplanning and the difficulties of navigating my lessons through textbooks. However, teachers are obligated to use at least 40% of the materials since students have purchased the books.

After a greeting and warm-up discussion, I started the class by reviewing the grammar points from the day before, which were about indirect questions in English. I had my students do focus-on-form grammar exercises in their textbook. While students were busy answering them, I looked at the next exercise in the book, which had the aim of helping students generate similar questions. I felt that the exercise did not make logical sense for the next part of my lesson and didn't provide a real-life purpose for learning question forms. I wanted my students to feel that the grammar points they learned in class were commonly used by English speakers. As I was thinking about a better plan for the next part of the lesson, one of the questions in the exercise caught my attention. In that particular question, students were supposed to spot errors in this indirect question: "I wonder where did the vandal target last night." Upon a quick reflection, I realized that questions starting with "I wonder why....." are very common indirect questions in English.

After we checked the answers to the exercise, I asked them to close their books and come up with three big questions for which they were curious to find an answer. The questions had to start with the question word "why". Once they wrote their questions, I put them in groups of four and told them to convert their regular questions to indirect form, starting with "I wonder why....." and have a 5-minute discussion around each question. I reminded them they didn't need to give factual answers and could just share their hypotheses.

As the discussions started, I was fascinated by the questions in each group. Here are some samples:

I wonder why women are more emotional than men.
I wonder why there is still a significant gender gap, even in developed countries.

I wonder why some countries have official religions.

Apart from world knowledge, students needed help with vocabulary to share their ideas. So, I stood in the middle of the class, and when someone raised their hand, I joined the group, fed in the necessary vocabulary, and wrote it on the board. To my surprise, at the end of the discussions, there were around 60 new words and collocations, such as evolutionary reasons, middle-age crisis, gender discrimination, etc. Most of the words were above their level (C1 or C2), but students managed to understand them and use them naturally in their discussions.

When the discussions finished, I quickly reviewed the words on the board and asked them to write a paragraph based on the answers they received for one of their questions. To do so, they needed to use the new vocabulary items, which meant they also used the words in a written form. Next, I asked them to exchange their writing with a partner and do some peer corrections before collecting them. As the time was up, I read their paragraphs later and returned their papers to them the following day. Here is a sample after correction with the new words highlighted:

> "I always wondered why Japanese people are shy. My Japanese classmates shared with me that they have a 'collective society'. They think that group work is more important than 'individuals'. Their society has an 'altruistic nature', and they help each other a lot. But this good thing has an 'unpleasant consequence'. It makes people less 'self-confident', so maybe that is why they are 'reluctant' to speak in front of the class."

Students found the lesson enjoyable and memorable. They found some tentative answers to the questions they always had in mind (especially about other countries), had a chance to share their knowledge when answering other people's questions, and learned many collocations.

A NOTE FROM SCOTT:

*This is a great example of how an almost random example in a coursebook can inspire a highly interactive and productive speaking activity, incorporating a grammar focus, a vocabulary review, and following up with writing and reading activities – that is to say, a lesson that integrates all four skills and includes a focus on both grammar and lexis.*

*Not only that, the texts that were generated from the activity (as the example shows) are intrinsically interesting and more likely to engage the learners than the somewhat bland texts typical of most coursebooks.*

# 49

# TEACHING WITH THE STUDENTS
## ALLY VICTORIA SHEPHERD

## UK I ADULTS I B1 – C2

This was an Intermediate adult ESOL class at a refugee community centre in the North of England. Students ranged from age 21 to 67 and were from various countries. There were around 10-15 students in the class, depending on the week, with up to half from Ukraine and others from Algeria, Eritrea, Iran, Spain, Sudan, and Vietnam. As a result, we were a 'super-diverse' class in terms of languages, nationality, religion, educational background, and migration journeys. We met once a week for 1.5 hours.

Being in community-based education, we did not have a set curriculum or textbook. As a result, it presented an opportunity to include the students in deciding content for the classes, and for me to be creative. I designed the semester's curriculum with input from the students at the beginning of each term, asking them what they felt they already knew and what they wanted to focus on in the coming weeks in terms of topics, language, and discussions.

As an educator who has been teaching for nearly 15 years, I feel comfortable trying new things in the classroom and have been interested in more democratic and inclusive pedagogies for a while now. Particularly in the context of ESOL for adults seeking safety, I felt that Dogme could be useful for students within a complex context that might not be addressed in mainstream textbooks. More generally, with any classroom, I feel that allowing students to collaborate on the content of their education can be beneficial for motivation, engagement, and language development. As a teacher, whilst I love lesson planning, I also enjoy creatively responding to learner-driven content and seeing where the class takes us.

As well as allowing for emergent language or topics at any point in the lessons, I built into each class a check-in activity at the beginning of each lesson called 'rose and thorn' where people were invited to share one positive thing in their week and one struggle. I always joined in with the activity, usually as a model at first, then at the end as students got used to the activity. This section of the class lasted from between 5 to 40 minutes, depending on the day, so it necessitated flexibility with the remainder of my lesson plan as I didn't force the activity to extend, nor restrict it if it was 'flowing'.

I later used 'rose, thorn, and bud' (bud being something they were looking forward to which might stimulate positive thoughts about the future, in line with good practice on psychological well-being for refugee learners). I stressed that sharing with the class was optional, so students could share only a rose if they didn't want to talk about difficult things in their lives, or only a thorn if they couldn't think of anything positive that week; though I did encourage (not insist) people to think of a bud even if they didn't want to talk about their current week.

People shared things from "I visited a nice museum" to "I am worried about my family in my home country", as well as citing our English lessons as their rose. One example of how language – and cultural knowledge – emerged was when a student said she had gone to Liverpool for Eurovision with her "girlfriend" at which her classmate laughed and teased, "But you have a husband". Some people did not understand the joke, so I clarified "girl, space, friend", and then explained that in the US they say "girlfriend" for female friends but, in the UK, it refers to a romantic relationship. The same student then said that British people always ask her when she says "friend" if it is a boyfriend and asked why. I laughed and said maybe they're just "nosy". She asked what nosy meant so, when the others also couldn't offer a definition, I taught the word, which led to a discussion about times people had been nosy with them both in the UK and in their home countries.

In another lesson, my "thorn" was that I had a pinched nerve in my neck. None of the students knew what this was, so I drew a spine on the whiteboard to explain. Someone then asked about names for some other bones, so we ended up eliciting vocabulary for the rest of the skeleton. In order to reinforce this new vocabulary, in the break I printed off the lyrics to the song "Dem Bones" and after the break, we listened to it and did a gap fill with some of the new vocab.

From such conversations, we could focus on vocabulary or grammar points relating to what students were sharing. Moreover, not only did this activity grant students time to 'warm up' their English-speaking vocabulary before launching into the planned portion of the lesson – especially if they hadn't used English since the previous lesson – but also let me know how people were feeling that day. Thinking about trauma-informed teaching, this could also inform how I facilitated the remainder of the lesson in terms of responding to students' mental and emotional states that day. Consequently, the activity served numerous functions.

At the end of the academic year, four students approached me to tell me: "We like your class the best. It's funny and we always know we will get interesting information. We go to another class, but it is very boring." When I asked why, they said: "The textbook is good, but it is exercise one, exercise two... The teachers don't have contact with us." When I asked what they meant by "contact", they replied: "We knew you cared about our lives." I believe that making space for the conversations that emerged during the rose and thorn activity (amongst other moments in class) contributed to my students saying they felt I "cared about their lives".

From this experience, regardless of the context (whether it be an ESOL classroom or another ELT context) I will try to use this activity as I feel it built classroom community, as well as allowing space for students to talk about what they wanted to on any given day (which might vary from what they'd previously asked to study). As an experienced teacher, it did not stress me out having to respond to emergent grammar questions or adapt my lesson plan according to how long students engaged with the activity, however, I admit it might have had I tried this approach fifteen years ago. With that said, I think part of this was due to not having access to models or support, so I appreciate and am grateful to be part of a collection like this to share practices with other educators.

A NOTE FROM SCOTT:

> *Ally's situation, which allowed her to dispense with a coursebook, and instead set up activities (like the lovely 'rose, thorn and bud' idea) that generated learner output to which she was able to respond at the point of need, was not only appropriate to the needs and wishes of the very diverse group of learners, but is, of course, pure Dogme.*

> *Ally also makes the important point that she may not have been able to apply such a responsive approach as a novice teacher, requiring, as it does, the ability to think on one's feet, adapt one's lesson plan, and respond authoritatively to language issues as they arise naturally in real-time talk. But then she wonders whether this was partly due to not having had such an approach modelled to her in her initial training.*

*Hence I was heartened to read, recently, in a report on an initial training program at a university in the US, that the trainee teachers are encouraged to 'teach off your students, not at them.'*

*They make the point that novice teachers 'often overprepare, sometimes scripting out what they intend to say and do, without consideration for how their learners may experience and/ or respond to their instruction.' Clearly, this is not what is happening in Ally's classes!*

# 50

# MEDIATING EMERGENT LANGUAGE WITH BEGINNERS

### SAM SHEPHERD

## UK | ADULTS | A1

It was the middle of March and the beginning of Ramadan, and I was teaching beginners. Beginning students in any setting can be a challenging level to teach, and not, you might think, the first place you would run a lesson based on Dogme.

This group of students, learning English in a community centre in Bradford, UK, were what we might loosely call "false beginners." The students were all migrants who had settled in the UK from India and Pakistan. They used Urdu as a lingua franca within the class, although other languages included Punjabi, Gujarati, and Pashto, none of which I shared with the students. Their language abilities were varied. One of the students had never written in any language, while others had some literacy in another script but only a little in English. And yet they had lived in the UK for years; in many cases with children who spoke English as a first language. They had learned to communicate surprisingly well with a small range of English picked up over the years, but had never attended even a conversation class.

I had set out to teach a lesson on likes and dislikes, starting with a simple activity on the board to refresh some work we'd done in the previous lesson on spelling: days of the week with the vowels gapped out. Today, however, was also the second day of Ramadan, the holy month during which Muslims fast. As usual, I opened the lesson with a conversation:

"Hello, Ramadan Kareem, how are you?"

"Tired."

I paused, quizzical. The student who said this was reliably engaged in the lessons, despite having an informal business making samosas.

"Why?"

"Early wake-up."

There was a general murmur of agreement.

"Oh yes, too tired."

"No eat, Ramadan."

The need for appropriate language was presenting itself here, language that linked to all of the students' lives. It was a Dogme moment where I could embrace it as a learning opportunity or I could close down the conversation and move into my prepared lesson.

In the last lesson, we had been talking about vowel sounds, so I wrote the word "Ramadan" without the vowels and asked the students to suggest the correct sound.

"Tell me about Ramadan. What do you do?"

"Early, Wake up."

"You mean: *We wake up early*."

"I wake up at 5.00."

Gasps of either awe or admiration, I couldn't tell.

"Why?"

"I make chapati."

"Just chapati?"

"No no," offered another student, "make samosa."

"I make samosa."

"Yes, I make samosa."

"Roti," offered another student, from India, "make roti, like chapati."

The previous student jumped in here brandishing a pronoun,

"No, no, I make roti."

Over the next 30 or so minutes we elicited various food types, and some activities focussed on Ramadan, usually by me asking questions to keep the conversation going and to provide a frame for some of the students' ideas.

"What about in the day?"

"Fast. No eating."

"You mean: *We fast. We don't eat.*"

This second required a little more work; some drilling and sharing, but we got there, and as a surprising side moment, a student asked,

"Fast, like quick?"

Homonyms are an unexpected phenomenon with students at this level, but there it was, also acting as an example of the surprising presence of language, rather than the absence of language that beginning learners must cope with.

The students compared when they did different things, on what days, and why. For some, even complex sentences with "because" emerged, as well as a conversation about different practices surrounding Eid. Sometimes I focussed on language form, but just as frequently we let the language go. Plurals, for instance, were abandoned in favour of a focus on verbs, because the thrust of the conversation was around activities rather than things.

Ultimately what we ended up with was a collection of language relevant to the students' needs and lives, which enabled real conversation in English around a shared experience. What was needed now was some means of capturing that language – not just in my photos of the board, which I used the following week to revisit the language, but for students to work on their literacy skills. I asked them to write simple sentences, reminding them to use the relevant pronouns. For one student I asked her to tell me some of the things she wanted to write and carefully wrote them out for her in her workbook. She then used those short sentences to practise writing and letter formation.

Dogme here was exactly the right call. The students at the end were able to say and write statements that had genuine meaning for them. The written sentences along with the photos of the board provided a basis for revisiting the language in the next lesson, as well as, in the form of a simple typed text, a short simple reading activity compiled from the different sentences students had written in the class. International coursebooks are often not appropriate for students whose literacy and culture are far removed from the target readers. There is, thankfully, a wonderful community of teachers sharing resources, but despite this, appropriate materials are not always easy to find. Rich, communicative experiences like this, however, are always interesting – and perfect for Dogme moments.

A NOTE FROM SCOTT:

*Some key takeaways from Sam's narrative:*

1. *A Dogme approach, focusing on emergent language IS possible with beginners, even in contexts where there is no language shared between the teacher and the students apart from English;*
2. *(Selective) scaffolding is the means by which the learners' predominantly lexical utterances are 'grammaticised' by the teacher – and maybe by one or two fellow students;*
3. *Capturing the emergent, grammaticized language in written form is a tool that facilitates the learners' appropriation of the language (but different learners will notice and appropriate different things);*
4. *Contextualizing the emergent language (literally, putting it into a text) for reviewing purposes further optimizes the chances of it being appropriated.*

# 51

# DOGME AS AN UNWINDING TOOL
## BRUNO SOUSA

## BRAZIL | TEENS | B2

This was a group of exam preparation students aiming for Cambridge B2 (formerly FCE). There were ten teenagers in this group, although only six of those attended the lesson on this day. As in any exam preparation course, we usually focused on strategies and language development so they could pass the exam.

This is an elective course at a private school in São Paulo, Brazil. The language courses in the main curriculum tend to focus on English for academic purposes, mostly dedicated to translation and comprehension of a variety of reading genres which may be profitable when students get to university. As someone who teaches both required and elective courses (focusing on General English and Exam Prep classes), I dabble in both worlds.

Learners were overwhelmed with finals during the week I decided to deliver a lesson using Dogme. We had already finished and consolidated strategies and content related to B2 Exams, so I decided to do something different in which students would be able to both express themselves on a topic of their choosing and learn language that would be relevant to their lives and that might be used in the speaking and writing papers of the exam. Using Dogme, therefore, seemed to be a perfect match for my aims in the lesson.

Knowing they had just been through five hours in a row of exams and tests, I asked them how they felt, to which they replied they were absolutely exhausted. Acknowledging their feelings, I told them we would do something different that day and showed them a photo on the interactive whiteboard (IWB) of a famous Brazilian singer. My expectation that they would talk about music took a one-eighty degree turn: they started talking about some gossip related to that person which had happened the week prior. I honestly did not know anything about the piece of news they mentioned so it took me by surprise. What I thought would be a lesson in which we would talk about music wound up becoming a lesson in which learners talked about gossip and rumors.

Having established that the lesson would revolve around gossip and rumors, the control freak in me felt there should be a disclaimer stating that students were not to talk about their peers and classmates. However, I was not able to say a word, knowing that it would surely have the opposite effect.

They were then split into two trios and talked about different rumors about celebrities that had been going on in Brazil. Each trio tackled a different celebrity or topic altogether. They would call me whenever they needed an expression or word to express some idea, but they would also supply each other with words they knew.

For instance, in one of the groups, a student explained what "to throw shade" meant to a classmate who could not express his own idea in English. Other samples of language provided by the learners included "to spill the beans", "to hear through the grapevine", "scoop" and others I did not expect they would know. A few I provided them with were "tabloid", "someone's ears must be burning", "malice", and the difference between "to make a scene" and "scandal", which, surprisingly, were misunderstood by learners, as the word escândalo may be a false cognate in Portuguese.

One hour into the lesson, I drew attention from the whole group to the board, where I had written the most relevant instances of vocabulary. Once these words were checked or clarified, we dealt with pronunciation, mostly in terms of prominence and connected speech. We also did a quick review of modals in the past, focusing especially on should, could, and must as in "He shouldn't have drunk beer before driving". This stage took around fifteen minutes as I had already been tackling these issues during the monitoring of groups.

In order to practice what they had just seen, I decided to do a back-to-the-board activity. Learners were split into three different pairs. In each pair, a student would face the board while the other faced the opposite wall. Then a famous rumor was shown on the IWB and the student facing the board had to tell their peer what the rumor was about so that their peer could find it out. After they discovered the gossip, they gave their opinion about it. This was done to promote both fluency and practice of the new vocabulary which they had come up with during the lesson. By the end of the lesson, learners could use the new lexis somewhat accurately.

This was a successful lesson from my point of view. My main aim, honestly, was to deliver a lesson students could both enjoy and forget a bit about their hectic schedule. Yet, I needed to make sure it was a profitable lesson in terms of language development. Not only did they enjoy the lesson, but they were also able to learn new vocabulary which I had not expected prior to this class.

Insofar as it was not a one-hundred-percent Dogme lesson, there were moments in which Dogme elements were successfully used and implemented. The focus was on the learners and what they wanted to say. This was a very interesting conclusion as it showed we can use Dogme in a myriad of contexts, including exam preparation courses, as the language they learned is suitable for B2, and even C1 exams. In fact, students noted that they wanted to use the lesson's vocabulary in their exams, such as "hear through the grapevine", "malice" and the use of modals in the past in different situations.

A NOTE FROM SCOTT:

*It's so often the case that the teacher's expectations about the direction of a lesson can take 'a one-eighty degree turn', as in the case of this lesson. It's fundamental to a Dogme approach to respect this, and, where possible, to 'go with the flow'.*

*In your case, Bruno, going with the flow led to a highly productive and very interactive lesson and, as you say, a welcome respite from the exam-focused timetable. Not all teachers, of course, are prepared to follow the learners' lead like this: there are risks involved.*

*It helps a lot to have particular routines or activity types you can fall back on, like your 'back-to-the-board' activity – a great way of reviewing and recycling the language that had emerged during the more conversational stage of the lesson.*

*Having a set of reliable routines like this one is what distinguishes expert from novice teachers, and Dogme teachers from more bookbound ones.*

# 52

# A SCHOOL MAGAZINE

### CHARLIE TAYLOR

## TAIWAN I TEENS I B2 – C1

This was a grade 11 class at a senior high school in Taiwan. There were eight students in the class representing varying proficiencies, with the average falling in the B2/C1 range. It was an elective English class, so the students who were there wanted to be there and had a positive attitude towards the language.

The purpose of the course, as laid out by the school administration, was to improve students' four skills in English. How to achieve this specifically was left entirely to me. Since there was no required textbook, I took the opportunity to design a curriculum in concert with the students. During the first class, I proposed several overarching frameworks that could provide a basic structure for the course. The one we ended up settling on was to collaboratively create an online English-language magazine over the course of the school year. The magazine would serve as a travel guide for tourists who were visiting our local county. It would feature information about sites, events, accommodation, food, and so forth.

The students would all contribute articles, and each also signed up for one additional job, ranging from editor-in-chief, to art director, photographer, section head, web designer, or social media team. All decisions concerning the magazine were made democratically and were discussed in class or in the class messaging app, which provided ample opportunities for lively, unscripted interactions in English, both during class time and outside of it.

I was well aware how important it is for students to have a keen interest in the subject matter. It is a rare happy coincidence when this criterion is satisfied by materials created for mass consumption by writers who do not personally know the users, and I noticed early in my teaching career that I could achieve a much higher success rate when students and I developed the curriculum together, allowing lesson plans to emerge organically in class.

The editor-in-chief (a student who had been elected to the position by her peers), called the meeting to order, read out the agenda, and asked if anybody would like to add to the agenda.

**Progress Reports**

Each student reported what they were working on and shared any problems they had encountered. Student A was having difficulty coming up with a third source for an article he was working on about a scenic lookout (each article had to have quotes from at least three people, which meant conducting at least three interviews). Student A had already spoken to a member of the county government, as well as a visitor who gave his impression. Student B said he had made contact with a professor of geology at the local university who could provide some information about the rock formations that were the central attraction of the site in question. Contact information was exchanged.

## Article Pitches

Since it was our goal to publish a new article every week, it was necessary for each of the eight students to complete one article every eight weeks. Some articles were time sensitive, like those covering special events, so we had rolling deadlines that were planned out months in advance. Every eight weeks or so, we would have a pitch meeting, where every student proposed new article ideas. The students then discussed the merits of the various ideas, and finally voted on which articles should make it to press. The students then chose which article they each wanted to write.

## Collaborative Editing

The final draft for the upcoming week's article was shown on the big screen—the latest installment in a series of reviews of local brunch spots. (All the writing was done in a shared Google Drive to make editing and sharing easier.) The students then read the article and made suggestions, beginning with the general, getting ever more specific, and finally zeroing in on spelling and punctuation. By the end of the class, the article was "print ready".

Journalism is a great tool for practicing writing. Sentence patterns and vocabulary are simpler than those typically used for academic papers, making it a good stepping stone. It also allows for classroom discussions about topics that will be critical in students' future academic careers like attribution, avoiding plagiarism, critical thinking, and maintaining objectivity.

This project created some structure for the class, but allowed enough leeway for students to write about things that genuinely interested them. Instead of every student having to write a paragraph based on the same prompt, they could choose whether they wanted to write about restaurants or bicycle races, temple festivals or backpacker hostels. Knowing that their work would be shared with (and provide a valuable service to) people outside the classroom also helped to motivate them beyond what grades alone could have achieved.

This particular project proved so successful in getting students to write and talk, and the students became so invested in the website, that it was later handed off to the next generation of that particular course the following year, with the seniors training the incoming students on the roles they had filled, making sure that their "baby" was left in good hands. This mentoring provided even more opportunities for unscripted discussions.

A NOTE FROM LUKE:

> One of the great things about this lesson account is that it forms part of a longer sequence of lessons across a whole school year.

> It's a great example of how student-generated content, and the language it generates, can be structured and extended over time.

> The magazine provides some of the entry-level benefits of a course book, like being able to look back over past work, and looking ahead to the next task.

> But unlike a coursebook, it is driven by the students' own interests, and has a real-world function – both of which make the magazine project additionally motivating and purposeful.

> Charlie was working without a coursebook, but it's possible to imagine a smaller-scale version of this magazine running along-side one.

# 53

# A TRIP TO VENICE

RACHEL TSATERI

## GREECE | ADULT | B2 – C1

This was a one-to-one online class with a Spanish male in his 30s. The student, who we will call Enrique, was at a high intermediate level with strong motivation. He was taking this class because he enjoys having an English-speaking conversation partner and finds language learning a stimulating experience. Furthermore, he was considering moving abroad in the near future, so being a proficient English speaker would make his life easier.

I am a freelance teacher and I have been teaching online since the pandemic. I sometimes use a coursebook, but I mostly generate my own materials based on what students need to work on.

Also, I should mention that I have already taught Dogme lessons in the past. However positive the experience, Dogme wasn't a desirable option when working in language schools, as teachers are usually expected to cover all the coursebook units by the end of the course. Dogme moments were very frequent in my lessons, though. Now that I am working for myself, Dogme is back on the table!

At the beginning of our lessons, Enrique and I always talked about our weekends. One day, he said that he had recently taken a trip to Venice. He sounded very pleased and refreshed and kept talking about the experience. Although I had already planned a lesson, I soon realised I wouldn't need it for a number of reasons. Firstly, anyone who has ever been to Venice knows that there is so much to talk about! Secondly, I realized there would be lots of useful language to feed in after listening to Enrique. Last but not least, I wanted to make sure I didn't rush him, that I listened with interest, and interacted with him meaningfully rather than just focusing on form. Conversation is, after all, the heart of Dogme!

During the first half of the lesson, we had an engaging conversation. I asked several referential and content questions to keep the conversation going. I asked him what he enjoyed the most and least, so he could share both the highlights and lowlights of his trip. Enrique talked about the beauty of the city, the prices, and the tasty dishes he tried. Then, I asked him what tips he would give travelers who visit Venice for the first time.

As many students do even at the advanced level, Enrique over-relied on certain adjectives, such as "amazing" or "beautiful." He also used some idiomatic phrases such as "perfect for pictures", "like a dream", etc. I praised Enrique for the collocations he used, such as "peaceful atmosphere".

Next, I thought of using one of my favourite techniques for giving feedback on emergent language. I drew a line on the whiteboard and divided it into two columns. I wrote what he said in the first column and what could be said in the second column. This suggests that the first utterance can get the message across just fine, but the second utterance is something a more advanced user of the language would say. So, this technique aims at upgrading the student's language use. Here are some examples of my reformulations:

| *What you said:* | *What you could say:* |
|---|---|
| – We flew at 7 pm from Barcelona. | – We caught an evening flight from Barcelona. |
| – We arrived at 9. | – We landed in Venice at 9. |
| – It is perfect for pictures. | – It is so picturesque / such a picturesque city. |
| – It is beautiful, like fake. | – It is magical, surreal, dreamlike, unique, one of a kind. |
| – It is so expensive. | – It is ridiculously expensive. |
| – The views were great. | – The views were spectacular, breath-taking. |

We also focused on pronunciation by doing a little modeling and drilling. Word stress is something that Enrique often struggles with, so I recorded the words and used syllable circles to help him produce them correctly. I paired these two to remind him the -able suffix does not sound like /eɪbl/. It is a weak (unstressed) syllable that is pronounced /əbl/. Here are some examples:

oOoo
Inevitable
Ooo
Fashionable

I also reminded Enrique he can order the events by using language such as: *First, After that, Next, Finally, On Friday evening, On Saturday afternoon,* etc.

To wrap up, I asked him if he was up for a challenge. I would give him two minutes to summarise his trip to Venice using some of the language I had provided. He agreed, so I gave him some time to prepare and he then introduced his spoken summary. I felt this was a good task for both accuracy and fluency. He also recorded himself so that he could listen again and reflect on his performance.

Enrique was quite happy by the end of the lesson. His motivation was strong from start to finish. He said that he enjoyed talking to me about this travel experience. He noticed new language that helped him raise his language level in a "non-traditional way," as he put it, meaning with typical grammar and vocabulary activities. When he gave his 2-minute summary of his trip he was already speaking more fluently and this visibly increased his confidence. Overall, a truly memorable lesson!

This merely confirmed my belief that Enrique would benefit from Dogme. I will keep planning lessons; however, when he comes to class excited about something that he has experienced, I will give him the floor and help him upgrade his use of language.

A NOTE FROM LUKE:

> This is a really clear, detailed account of how a teacher can manage conversation and emergent language during a lesson.
>
> First the opportunity: the student wants to talk about his trip to Venice. Second the conversation: the teacher asks questions to keep it going, and introduces a little task – coming up with tips for first-time visitors. It's the kind of task you would find in a coursebook, but here it's perfectly matched to the energy of the lesson – reminding us that we can use familiar strategies in new and responsive ways.
>
> Third, the feedback: the 'What you said' / 'What you could say' rubric is beautifully simple and constructive. This leads to familiar teaching procedures, modeling and drilling pronunciation, but applied to the learner's own language production, not abstract model words.
>
> The lesson ends with another mini-task to recycle some of the upgraded language, recorded for further self-study. Throughout the lesson there's a very appealing blend of freedom – allowing the student to talk – and control: managing the outputs and stages of the lesson.

# 54

# A WEEKEND IN "DESTINATION UNKNOWN"

## KATA UJVAROSI

### ITALY I ADULTS I B1

This was originally a class of eight adults I started working with to experiment with English for the global world back in 2022. They had juggled skills, but everyone reached at least B1 CEFR level in two skill areas. In this class, all were present and very enthusiastic about their lessons. For most of them, the weekly class was a unique opportunity to use English, living in a non-native English-speaking environment in Italy and Hungary. The learners were between 25 and 50 years old; some were university students, but most of them had busy lives and families.

Our 1.5-year-running course, which also included my DELTA Module 2 studies, fostered a strong sense of community. It was a skills-based course that benefitted from task-based learning and the Dogme approach, where we focused on coping strategies and discovering learner and learning potentials, such as unlearning and re-learning familiar concepts and language in a highly practical way. These helped learners become more independent and autonomous speakers. My role mainly involved reacting to problem areas and addressing them with tasks drawn from the learners' contexts in international communication.

In 2022, I was feeling that reactive teaching would work better than ready-to-use, one-size-fits-all prescribed content. So, I started creating adventure and discovery lessons for my learners, which were a series of situational contexts from which the emerging language served as input and was meant to create learning opportunities for intake. As Dogme stands for a conversation-driven, materials-light, emergent language-focused approach, this seemed to be the best choice for my context.

The only tools I was ready to use in my Destination Unknown lesson[1] were my Jamboard, which was designated for the group, and Google Earth. Learners knew that they were going to travel somewhere different and unexpected. I divided the learners into two groups for more interactions and uptakes, and I chose the "I'm feeling lucky" option on Google Earth, which initiated the journey. My learners were eagerly waiting for where they would land. I told them that wherever they go, they have two tasks:

**TASK 1**:
Plan a weekend, including finding accommodation, meals, and leisure that is sensibly based on their real budgets and interests. Write a postcard that states where they are and what can be seen.

**TASK 2:**
Find the way home, considering various reasonable options.

---

1. Meddings, L., & Thornbury, S. (2009). Teaching unplugged: Dogme in English language teaching. Delta Publishing.

Prompts on the initial Jamboard

Learners prepared their drafts in breakout rooms, posted pictures on Jamboard, and wrote their postcards. They got organized, set up tasks, and started working quickly. There were four in each group having conversations and asking for help when they were stuck, which prompted error correction on the spot. They were engaged and excitedly discovered their destinations: Denmark and Canada. In order to complete the tasks, they needed authentic tools, such as booking.com for accommodation hunting, museum websites, and Tripadvisor for restaurant reviews, among others.

Learners work on Jamboard

The students were fully immersed in global language use in contexts and situations where they wanted to communicate successfully. In addition, the learners' age range, interests, and nationalities (Italian and Hungarian) enlivened the atmosphere of curiosity.

The travel experiences varied. Some learners tried to work out low-budget options in Canada and suggested renting a car and staying at a campsite. They eventually decided who was driving their converted VW Microbus after taking the train on a scenic route along the Rouge River. They were up to moon viewing and searching for gold and convinced one another that they were not afraid of bears. As for souvenirs, some opted for maple syrup, while some were learning about it for the first time.

The Denmark group planned to visit a natural historical museum and a castle and were ready to stay in tents in the Thorseng Nature Resort while still paying thousands of euros and getting fed by local curiosities like Danish open-faced sandwich, the Smørrebrød (this is when the teacher learns something new too) and the highlight of the trip – seeing the Little Mermaid in Copenhagen.

Dealing solely with emerging language, they could rely on peers and develop better ideas or more correct language just by following hints, activating existing resources, and building on their shared learning opportunity.

In the round-off, we discussed which holiday they would really go for. I highlighted common errors that came in different shapes: spelling and pronunciation that could cause misunderstanding or confusion (e.g. Iceland-island); lexical accuracy to avoid errors becoming fossilized in collocations (e.g. make photos/take photos) and verb phrases (e.g. hear/listen to something, come back/go back, come back at home); the use of pronouns (I and Cosimo) and articles (I especially liked trip by Sara, visit Toronto zoo); and the possessive structure (Sara trip/trip by Sara).

Due to time constraints, some tasks were left for homework and the next class. The learners' homework was to plan the way back and to keep working in their groups.

After these classes, learners made the following comments:

"I am proud of my progress in speaking."

"I created a good empathy despite joining the group late."

"I really appreciate my teacher because she was always helpful, especially when there was the division in small groups and she monitored the conversations between the students."

"I got on well with the other students because we were all happy to learn, interact and socialise thanks to our teacher."

"I can speak the English language more easily."

"I liked that the materials and tasks were easy to understand and relate to everyday life."

A NOTE FROM SCOTT:

*This lesson integrates freely available digital tools in a way that is both consistent with the Dogme principle that encourages learners to share texts of their own finding, but also reflects the 'real-life' processes by which information (in this case, about travel) is accessed online. And what really stands out is the way the lesson becomes a collaborative experience, with learners working together in groups, and then coming together at the end to share and discuss what they have discovered, while opportunities to home in on specific language issues are not neglected.*

*This lesson also demonstrates how closely aligned Dogme is with the philosophy behind task-based language teaching, i.e. that learning is motivated and facilitated by the need to do things with language. It's hardly surprising that the learners were so appreciative!*

# 55

# DARING TO GO WITH THE FLOW
## ZAINAB UNDRE

## UK | ADULTS | B1

The class included six pre-intermediate, multilingual adult students. This is usually a male-dominated class with some strong personalities. However, only one student attended this three-hour class on a Friday – Emir, a gentle and thoughtful young man.

As usual, he was already present when I walked in. After a polite greeting, we usually make small talk as the other students walk in and I arrange my resources. On this occasion, I kept glancing at the clock as twenty minutes had passed and nobody else had turned up. He quietly told me: "Some of the boys 'may' have gone to Edinburgh on a social trip."

At this point, I was in a dilemma. I could continue with my planned lesson, knowing that it wouldn't be ideal as most of my activities required collaborative work. Alternatively, I could think on my feet and change the plan entirely. I decided to give him the choice between doing what I had planned and continuing with our topic or doing something creative. He expressed that he wanted to practice speaking with me and improve his English. As he is usually a shy student, I wanted to grasp this opportunity to get to know him better. So, I said: "Tell me about yourself." His eyes lit up when he said: "I love movies and cinema." I decided to open a discussion about films.

During the discussion, subconsciously my mind was rushing in different directions. I felt that I should have a language focus because I didn't want this to become an aimless discussion. I also felt a little apprehensive about entering conversations which may lead to clarifying language and grammatical structures that I had not prepared; this is a tool that I rely on in my teacher toolkit. As my subconscious was obsessing over how to teach, he began opening up and became more animated. He pulled my attention back to what he was expressing. My thoughts on what I was going to teach were interrupted when he passionately continued speaking about his love of films: "Sometimes teacher, I watch films again and again in one night."

Putting aside my reservations, I decided to focus on allowing him to speak to his heart's content. During this interaction, he was regularly pausing and waiting for my confirmation and asking: "Is this OK, did I say it right?" Eventually, he ended up describing his favourite movies, series and even recommended his favourite Turkish movies. During this activity, occasionally I would interject and upgrade his grammar.  In addition, I would board any language that could be analysed and extended and then used as sentence frames: "When I watch horror films, I feel scared", "I am very keen on films which make me think, I am not a fan of horror films," and adverbs of frequency for precision: "I usually watch films on my laptop", "I hardly ever go to the cinema."

Eventually, I felt that we had exhausted the topic of films. At this point, I took a moment to think about what to do next. I had no slides prepared, no paper resources, and nothing to guide me. Then I remembered that I could be the teaching resource itself. I recalled an activity that I had observed during my CELTA practice which I had never had the opportunity to do. I drew an outline of a figure and said to Emir: "You've told me all about yourself. Now it's my turn." I split the board into two with the outline of a figure in the middle. I wrote Zainab inside the outline. I told him that this is his exclusive chance to ask me questions about me. As he came up with questions, I corrected his grammar and we focussed on different question forms: past and present tense questions, open and closed questions. Then I answered his questions and boarded my answers on the other side of the board. After that, we swapped roles. I asked him the same questions and he responded using the emergent language.

At the end of the lesson, I asked for his feedback. I was conscious that I hadn't used any of my prepared materials and was doubting whether the lesson would have met his expectations and my usual standards. However, he was smiling and kept thanking me for giving him a chance to speak so much and for correcting his mistakes. He said he really enjoyed the lesson and reminded me again to watch that Turkish movie he suggested. This lesson helped me to strengthen my rapport with him and make him feel heard and valued.

I took some time to reflect on my initial fears. Being an organised person, I am used to having prepared lessons and this has always given me confidence as a teacher. However, on this occasion, I was totally out of my comfort zone. I realised that I do have the experience and knowledge to think creatively on the spot and select useful chunks of language, and that I should trust myself and my instincts more. Although Dogme moments do seep into my everyday teaching, as they are inevitable in responsive teaching, this was the first time I had taught for three hours without any prepared materials.

This realisation gave me the courage to let go a little and not be so consumed by the quantity of coverage and doing an activity purely because I've prepared it. I also learnt that by giving students the choice and ownership over the content of the lesson, they are likely to be more invested. This is the first time I had seen Emir express himself so willingly. As a result of this experience, I have started to provide less prepared slides and just enough structure for students to allow them to generate their own examples. Now, I ask students to tell me what they are interested in and give them more choice and freedom to come up with topics.

A NOTE FROM SCOTT:

> This is a textbook account of how, by being compelled to step outside her 'comfort zone', a teacher took an enormous stride in terms of her own personal development.
>
> There are so many things here that are worth highlighting: Zainab's relatively short experience, her professionalism in not resigning her responsibility to deal with just a single student; her own interior monologue as to how to cope with the unexpected situation, and her consequent willingness to give the student the floor; her ability to retrieve an appropriate activity out of her initial training experience; and the lessons learned from reflecting on the experience, the most salient being her learning "to think creatively on the spot" and to trust her instincts more.
>
> This account also serves to remind me that, for many teachers, Dogme is not merely a method or an approach, but an invitation to experiment, to take risks with their current practice and thereby develop as a truly adaptive professional.

# 56

# TEACHING AWAY FROM THE TEST
## CHRISTOPHER WALKER

## POLAND | TEENS | B2 – C1

This was a group of ten teenagers preparing for the C1 Advanced exam. The students were diligent, bright, creative, and highly motivated. Of the ten, half attended the same school and would turn up en masse, usually a few minutes late and with takeaway coffees.

In my 15 years teaching at International House Bielsko-Biala, I've always been attracted to approaches that put the student front and center. Coursebooks can never do that – they're simply too generalised. Try to satisfy everyone, and you satisfy no one, as the saying goes. Whenever an opportunity arises, I like to break free of the textbook. This lesson was one such opportunity, and I'm glad that I had Dogme to provide me with the foundation for what follows.

As usual, some of my students arrived slightly late, but this time many of them seemed more disgruntled than usual. It turned out that they went to the same school and had fallen foul of a teacher who'd realized the class had failed to complete the requisite number of tests. The result? Test after test for the next two weeks.

Obviously, whatever I had wanted to do during the lesson had just gone out of the window. We began to discuss their problems at school instead. The other students contributed too, given that these issues seem universal across the education system. To avoid this just becoming a prolonged exchange of complaints and insults, we nominated a student to keep track of the main issues on the whiteboard – this gave the discussion a semblance of structure.

Complaining about school is one of the principal hobbies for Polish teenagers, and we could have gone on all day if not for the fact that the C1 Advanced exam itself was fast approaching. Fortunately, one of the more curious students finally said, "What good does it do to complain?"

This question turned the dynamic of the lesson on its head. We had already listened to a long list of complaints, and the note-taker must have been getting tired. But now we started to look at each point in turn, thinking about what it meant for the students, and what action might improve, if not solve the problem. For instance, the students agreed that the way they were graded was wrong. They would be tested on new material immediately after encountering it, and the grades would be recorded on their personal records. "But surely," said one, "we should have some time to let the ideas settle? If we make mistakes, can't we learn from them first before we're tested?"

We proceeded through each of the issues on the board, thinking about why they were unfair or unreasonable and suggesting alternative approaches the school might adopt. I listened, and made notes on areas of language that I thought were either worth sharing later because of their brilliance, or because a tweak to the structure was required; and I kept silent, not wanting to tell the students that this was the most worthwhile practice that they'd ever had. But we didn't stop there. The students were buzzing with ideas, and with just over twenty minutes of the lesson left, I wanted to capitalize on the atmosphere in class. I asked them, "Who would you go to if you wanted to change some of these problems?"

The first answer was that it fell to the principal or head teacher to fix such problems, but this immediately seemed like a dead-end.

"Is there anyone at your school you think would take your side?" was the next question. It took a moment of reflection for the answer to become clear, but when it did, we found ourselves propelled into a short writing task.

On their own, each student took one of the problems from the board and wrote a letter about it to their chosen champion; again, I monitored their work, remaining outside of it for the most part. When I saw examples of particularly good polite language, I invited the student to copy it onto the board as something for others to follow, and soon the board was covered with highly useful and appropriate structures. My hope was that, by sharing them in this manner, my students will have committed these structures to memory, ready to recall them on the day of the exam.

When they had finished – the letters were relatively brief, so as not to exhaust their audience – the students exchanged their notes. Reading each other's work, their task was simple: to check if the argument was convincing, and if it was conveyed politely enough to guarantee that their representative – their messenger – would remain on their side.

And that's when we ran out of time – sadly. The students departed, but not without first sharing many words of thanks. I hadn't done anything special though, so I felt decidedly awkward. They had done all the work; all I had done was to use the tenets of Dogme to make sure it happened. I think they were glad that they finally got to say what was on their mind, and I was glad to have been able to help them do it in English.

We hadn't even strayed too far from the core skills that the students needed to develop in facing the C1 Advanced exam, either – which suggests that if you keep the exam format in mind, anything that happens in the classroom can be turned in that direction, subtly and appropriately. In fact, students can satisfy their own preferences without costing them a good grade on their certificate.

A NOTE FROM LUKE:

*The need to teach to the test is one of the main reasons educators say it's hard to 'do Dogme' and unplug. Like it or not, the exam syllabus often dominates our teaching lives.*

*Of course, this means that it also dominates our students' lives. Here, a bunch of sparky, hard-working teenagers rock up to an English lesson in a bad mood specifically caused by too much testing at their high school.*

*First, the students are allowed to vent, and one of them is tasked with making notes to help shape this phase of the lesson. But the lesson pivots on another student's question: what's the use of complaining? This shifts the focus to solutions.*

*Finally, the class 'buzzing with ideas', they write letters to real-life people about their test-related problems – while (perhaps unconsciously) practising for their own English language exam.*

*Christopher gives the credit to the energy in the room: 'We found ourselves propelled into a short writing task.' But the teacher's role here is vital: noticing, listening, and shaping activity that makes the lesson meaningful and productive.*

# 57

# ASKING QUESTIONS OF AI
## MARINA YESIPENKO

## UKRAINE | ADULTS | B1 – C1

This online class includes 6 young women of Ukrainian descent (25-30 years old) with a variety of occupations ranging from psychologists to lawyers to IT specialists. The group has recently started B2 level and is primarily using a lexical syllabus to develop their collocational knowledge and feel for appropriacy. The participants are relatively autonomous, eager to explore and evaluate pieces of language they come across and to put the language into use at the earliest opportunity.

The idea for the lesson "Can AI replace a teacher?", though seemingly outrageous, was to get B2 students involved in a 60-minute lesson with minimal intervention from the teacher. This meant that the main source of reference was their peers and ChatGPT[1]. As an outcome, the students assessed whether ChatGPT was a good substitute for a teacher or not and evaluated their experiences and quality of the AI-generated language input.

My lesson was grounded in the following Dogme principles: learning

---

1.  OpenAI. (n.d.). *ChatGPT*. https://openai.com/chatgpt

through dialogue and interactivity, engaging and relevant content, scaffolding, eliciting and expanding on emergent language, as well as critically assessing created materials and the outcomes of the lesson[2]. These points closely matched the needs of my group, while the learners also showed signs of being "weary of traditional communicative course books" (ibid). In this lesson, emergent language is uncovered rather than explicitly taught via ChatGPT with minimal assistance from the teacher. The materials are created and searched for by the learners, and they had the opportunity to create texts with ChatGPT, including video. Once generated, the text was explored and critically evaluated in terms of content and useful language.

At the outset, learners were introduced to the topic and provided with access to ChatGPT. After brainstorming how AI could enhance their lives and reviewing a list of professions, learners searched for a YouTube video on the same topic and compared their own ideas with the perspectives in the video. At this stage, they needed functional language for brainstorming and listing items. Students compiled their own lists and referred to ChatGPT for suggestions (Figure 1). The best and most useful samples were added with the teacher helping students to clarify the meaning and drill the most difficult areas. For example, one YouTube video dealt with the controversial idea of ChatGPT being used for giving relationship advice.[3] Learners discussed this idea using the functional language elicited for agreeing and disagreeing (Figure 2). In the same vein, they brainstormed their suggestions, then added more items from ChatGPT followed by teacher drilling and meaning clarification.

2.  Meddings, L., & Thornbury, S. (2017). *Teaching unplugged: Dogme in English language teaching.* Delta Publishing.
3.  7 ChatGPT prompts to improve your everyday life. (2022, November 22). *YouTube.* https://www.youtube.com/watch?v=ON9XPDE-2NA&t=1s

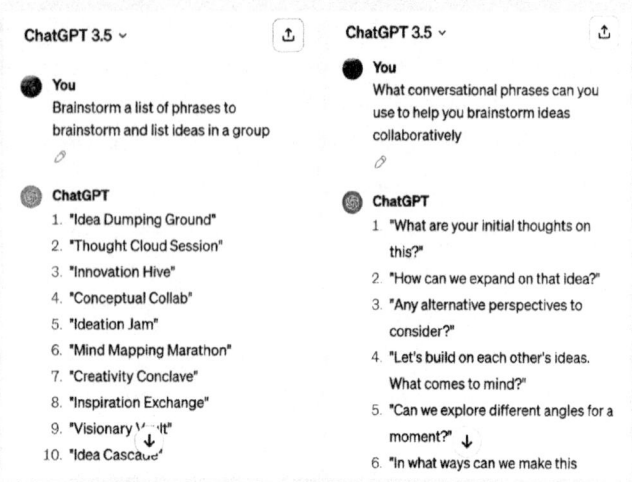

1. Functional language for brainstorming and listing

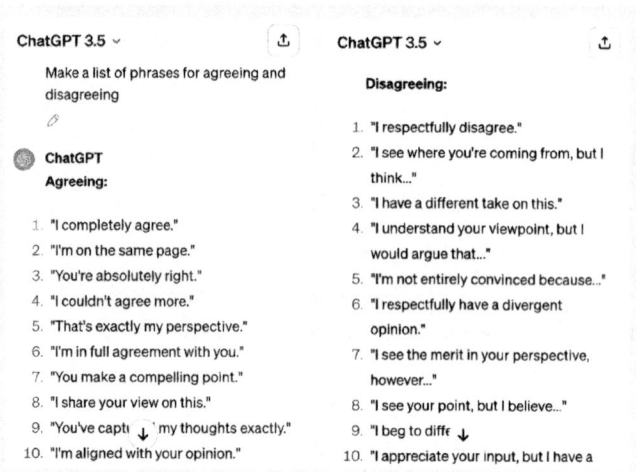

2. Functional language for agreeing and disagreeing

Next, learners agreed on a sample relationship situation ("My boyfriend does not give me enough attention") and used ChatGPT to generate a text with the seven bits of advice on the topic. This led them to discuss the tips critically and arrive at the conclusion that ChatGPT might be of limited use as a relationship advisor. Additionally, they explored the text for interesting collocations on relationships and for structures related to giving advice (Figure 3). At home, they wrote their own improved and humanised set of tips on this topic.

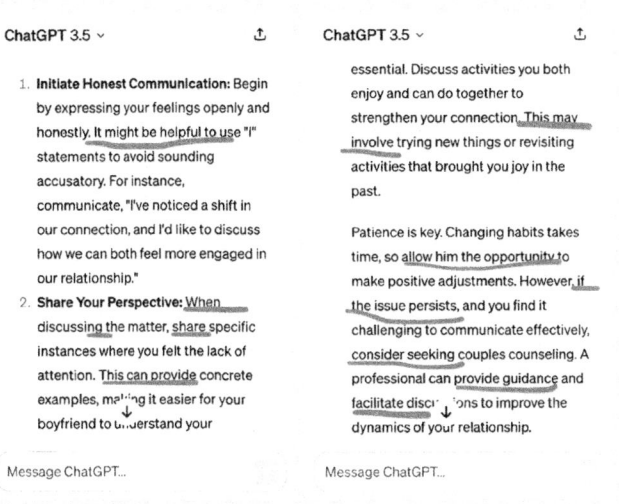

3. Mining AI text for useful language chunks

For reflection, students shared their impressions of dealing with an "AI-teacher", labeling it as a "weird but interesting" experience. One of the main concerns was the fact that AI needed clear instructions on how to do a task, which led to a few unsuccessful attempts before students could get an appropriate outcome. Yet it prompted them to critically assess the AI-generated output and come up with the evaluation skills to gauge the efficiency of their own language production in the classroom. Later on in this course, students also focused on the use of functional language and language for giving advice, as well as listing and brainstorming.

A note from Luke:

*I'm intrigued by the dialogue between human collaboration and machine learning here.*

*At heart, Dogme is about communication. In the 2000s we thought of this chiefly in terms of face-to-face conversation; in the 2010s messaging services became part of everyday life and we could chat remotely; in 2025, people increasingly interact with ChatGPT to generate solutions and suggestions.*

*But while conversation between people can arise spontaneously, has layers of emotional nuance, and leads in unexpected directions, ChatGPT is both explicitly 'cued' and largely transactional – a way to find an answer to a problem.*

*And while ChatGPT can collate multiple sources in an instant, it also tends to homogenize. Which of the options for agreeing and disagreeing in Marina's appendices are most useful? Which are most appropriate in different contexts? Are any of the phrases in Figure 1 as useful as the word 'brainstorm'?*

*We and our students still need to be critical. Seeing AI-generated content as raw material, rather than an end product, is one way to do this.*

# 58

# ONE LONG FREE CONVERSATION
## ROSLYN YOUNG

## FRANCE | ADULTS | A1 – A2

This class of about 35 French-speaking students met over two weekends in 2014, for 6 hours a day, so 24 hours in all. The specific lesson described took place towards the end of the course. Except for some introductory work on pronunciation, the class work for the course was designed around a sustained free conversation between the students, lasting for the whole course. In the lesson described, as the result of a sentence made by a student, the class was introduced to the present perfect progressive form which was new for them.

The students all had at least 5 years of studying English involving exercises and dialogues, but they had little or no experience in speaking spontaneously; they came to these weekends specifically to learn to speak. Once they understood how they could work together, they had a long free conversation for the remaining twenty-two or so hours over the four days.

The students were told in French the rules they were expected to follow:

1. This is a conversation. You can take it wherever you like. You are responsible for the content, the teacher is responsible for

making sure that everything is corrected before the conversation goes further.

2. Every sentence must be true.

This last rule is necessary to ensure that the conversation does not drift off into flights of imagination where no one, sometimes not even the speaker, really knows exactly what is being referred to.

The focus of my work is always on speaking since overwhelmingly, this is what my students want to learn to do. I never use a textbook or any materials or exercises, but I do use tools. Since immediate feedback is essential for learning[1], and I know that learning takes place essentially because of the feedback they receive, I have four tools that allow me to correct any error a sentence might contain when it is first spoken. They consist of 1) a phonemic chart for the sounds, 2) functional vocabulary charts for grammar problems, 3) a symbolic verb tense layout on a table for mistakes in the use of tenses, and 4) a spelling chart that allows me to show students both the spelling and the exact pronunciation of any word we might need during the class.

The course itself started with a couple of hours of intensive work on pronunciation, followed by the beginning of the conversation which carried on until the lesson I will describe. At any point, I only have to spread out my hands in a welcoming gesture and wait for a speaker to continue the conversation.

---

1.   Dehaene, S. (2021). *How we learn: The new science of education and the brain.* Penguin.

As a result of a mistake made by Ben, the current speaker in the conversation, I needed to introduce a new verb structure, a difficult one for French speakers, the present perfect progressive. This was done, not by giving rules or an explanation, but by using the verb tense layout on the table as follows:

**Teacher**: Somebody please make a short sentence using this one (*pointing to the present simple box*) or this one (*pointing to the present progressive box*).

**Student**: I drive a Ford.

**Teacher**: Now put it here (*past tense box*). Begin with "I started …"

**Student**: I started driving a Ford in 2010.

**Teacher**: Now you can move it here. (*present perfect progressive box*)

**Student**: I have been driving a Ford since 2010. (*I have to show the student whether he should choose "for" or "since" in his sentence*)

**Teacher**: Voilà!

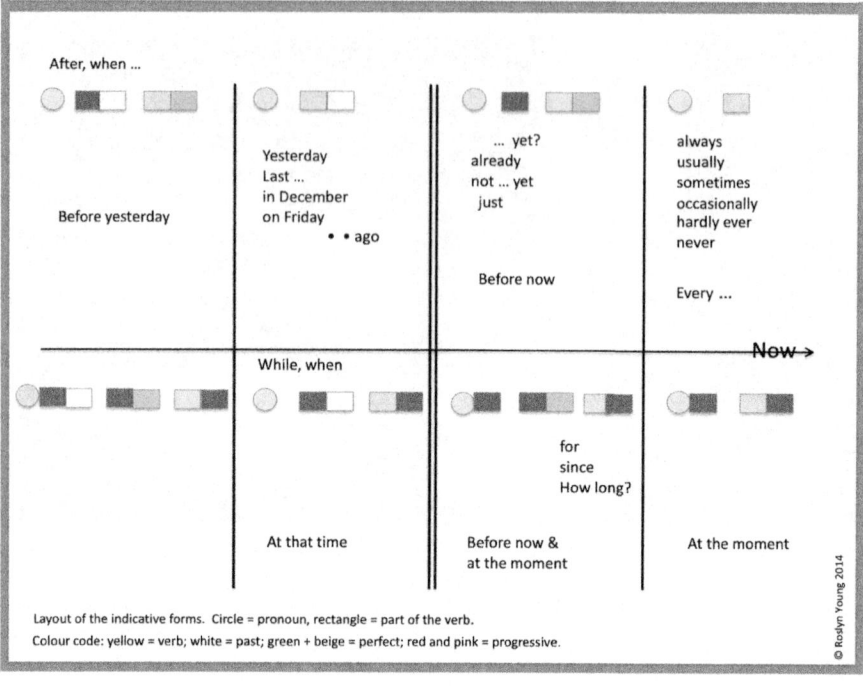

Layout of the indicative forms.  Circle = pronoun, rectangle = part of the verb.
Colour code: yellow = verb; white = past; green + beige = perfect; red and pink = progressive.

© Roslyn Young 2014

Other examples followed, always working from an initial sentence proposed by a student. Soon I didn't have to indicate the way to think through the problem; they could take the three steps by themselves. I'm learning to skate. I started learning to skate three months ago. I've been learning to skate for three months. Trigger words usually found with this verb form were introduced, in particular, How long...?

Now we could go back to the conversation. Interruptions for grammar points like this can be surprisingly long. It's not uncommon for a clarification to take twenty minutes or so, after which the conversation picks up again from where it was before the interruption.

The class[2] began with me waiting until Ben felt he could relaunch the conversation using this new item, the present perfect progressive. I was confident that he would be able to do this.

_____

2.  A video of this class is available on YouTube at https://rb.gy/eu8zug

**Ben**: Nancy, where do you work?

**Nancy**: At the moment, I'm working at home.

**Ben**: How long have you been working at home?

**Nancy**: I've been working from home since I … since I … I've been learning a new job.

**Teacher**: I suggest she use, "since I decided to change jobs" which Nancy can't hold in her mind, but the class has it and gives it to her.

**Students**: I decided to change jobs.

**Nancy**: I've been working from home since I decided to change jobs.

**Aude**: When did you decide to change jobs?

**Students**: Jobs? Jobs? (Several students don't understand the use of the plural for this word.)

**Teacher**: How many jobs?

**Students**: One.

**Teacher**: The old job and … the new job.

**Students**: Ah!

**Aude**: When did you decide to change jobs?

**Nancy**: I made the decision at the beginning of the year.

The students, like almost all my students, love to talk about themselves, be listened to, and listen to stories from other people's lives. In this case, for example, it turned out that Nancy was a veterinary surgeon, but became allergic to the products she was using and had to leave the profession.

Since I never use any other methodology now, my practice didn't change because of this experience, it had already changed years before. I can say from experience that students learn much better when they talk about things that really mean something to them, and what could have more meaning than their own lives?

A NOTE FROM SCOTT:

*Although she doesn't actually name it, Roslyn's lesson draws heavily on the principles and practices associated with the Silent Way, a method developed by Caleb Gattegno (who himself was a mathematician) in the 1950s.*

*Roslyn's description demonstrates how the Silent Way procedures merge fluidly with the principles of Dogme, specifically the importance of students talking 'about things that really mean something to them'.*

*The teacher's role is not to put words into the learners' mouths, but, instead, to uncover the learners' meanings and to prompt them, in a non-assertive way, towards greater precision. In this way, it is assumed that learners will develop their own 'inner criteria' (to use Gattegno's term) and an intuitive 'feel' for the language.*

*I particularly like the idea of the whole course being one 'long, free conversation': that is a very Dogme idea!*

# COLLABORATING WITH EDUCATIONAL LEADERS SINCE 2012

## STEVEN HERDER

The International Teacher Development Institute (iTDi) was originally conceived as a commercial business *for teachers by teachers*. What started as a wholesome pursuit of financial success, eventually revealed to us the true meaning of the riches we would acquire – building, nurturing, and appreciating long-term relationships with some of the best professionals in the EFL and ESL worlds. As Chuck Sandy, one of our co-founders and a passionate, well-known EFL teacher, often said,

> *"Whatever the problem, community is the answer."*

This iTDi online community[1] has weathered several ups and downs over the past 12 years, but as they say, "whatever doesn't kill us, makes us stronger...". iTDi started as a limited liability company (LLC), with six directors covering business, finance, sales & marketing, and education, as well as 29 teacher investors, hoping to make a profit and earn dividends. Unfortunately, our main product was not sought after as our business plan boasted, and within two years we were faced with closing down as a commercial business or morphing into something else. We knew we had

---

1.  https://www.itdi.pro/community/

something beyond just a great reputation; we had established countless warm and meaningful relationships with teachers all around the world. Luckily, we discovered something called a *social enterprise*, and that's what we became.

> *"A social enterprise is an operator in the social economy whose main objective is to have a social impact rather than make a profit for their owners or shareholders."*

Our efforts were empowering teachers, but how does this relate to Dogme in Practice? Well... one of our founders was Scott Thornbury, who graciously accepted the role of Academic Director for iTDi. This was such a generous move on his part. The other directors were just a small group of teachers who had a good idea. Scott was the only one of us who had an international reputation that might have been ruined through association with another online start-up company that never got traction. How we originally connected with Scott is a story worth reading.

As part of my distance learning MA TESL/TEFL from the University of Birmingham, I was required to purchase and read MANY books. Having graduated through distance learning in 2009, while juggling a full-time job and two young children, I was thrilled to receive a distinction. I can now confess that I only managed to read one book cover to cover – every single word – and that was *How to Teach Grammar* by Scott Thornbury.[2]

Furthermore, I still clearly remember at the end of the last page, I said out loud to myself, "OK, Thornbury, teach me some more!"

---

2.   Thornbury, S. (1999). *How to teach grammar*. Longman.

A few months later, having found out that Scott had never been to Japan, I decided to reach out directly and ask if he would consider coming here as a headliner for a conference and tour that I wanted to organize around him. He said he would love to visit Japan, and so a small but mighty conference called *MASH Equinox* was born.

It was a magical time in 2010, starting in Tokyo and finishing 10 days later in Sapporo. Scott gave about six different talks multiple times and made hundreds of new friends on that trip. He was so much more than an author and academic; he was kind, genuine, funny, and passionate about education AND people. He was the real deal and a joy to hang out with.

Since that initial connection, Scott has been a friend, a role model, and a supporter of iTDi. For the past 14 years, we have been thrilled to work with Scott on several groundbreaking webinars and successful live courses, all receiving rave reviews and growing our iTDi community. To illustrate Scott's effectiveness as a teacher trainer, we currently have a waiting list of over 300 teachers around the world wanting to be told whenever he does a new online course with iTDi. Back to iTDi...

iTDi certainly had traction in the early days. We held a live launch online from the 2012 Brazil TESOL conference. We held a series of free global webinars with up to 700 teachers pre-registering for workshops led by internationally known teachers such as Penny Ur, John Fanselow, Barbara Sakamoto, and Scott Thornbury. We also set out to tell the world about iTDi. For example, we sponsored a booth at Thai TESOL in 2013 and sent an iTDi team to Indonesia for a series of iTDi days the following year.

We also innovated beyond our original TESOL Certificate product to introduce month-long Advanced Skills courses beginning in 2014. These courses were led by a long list of passionate teachers and trainers, including Vicki Hollett, Scott Thornbury, Penny Ur, Jill Hadfield, John Fanselow, Caroline Linse, Shelly Terrell, Jason R. Levine, Katherine Bilsborough, Curtis Kelly, Marc Helgesen, Joseph Shaules, Pete Sharma, Stephen Krashen, Luke Meddings, Steven Herder, Philip Kerr, Chuck Sandy, Juan Uribe, Patrice Palmer, Susan Hillyard, Kate Cory-Wright, Dorothy Zemach, Katy Simpson, Paul Raine, Heike Philp, and Marcos Benevides.

I first met Luke Meddings when he graciously agreed to do an Advanced Skills course with iTDi in 2015. I remember we were very excited to have the "other half" of the Dogme Duo. Luke did not disappoint. We were thrilled that 30 teachers from 20 different countries quickly signed up for his course, *Learning Space: A Guide to Teaching Unplugged*. It is already 10 years ago, but I clearly remember being in awe of his presentation style and discussion skills. I swear we spent the most engaging hour together and he didn't get past two or three slides in his PowerPoint – Now that's going unplugged in true fashion!

Looking back, this is a phenomenal group of educators, many of whom offered multiple iterations of their 4-6 week online courses, with some of these courses still available now as *Advanced Skills Self Study* courses on the iTDi website. Little did we know in 2012, the depth of our learning potential, nor the breadth of learning opportunities available online. It goes without saying,

*"Anything I can do, we can do better."*

A special shoutout does need to go to Dorothy Zemach, our reigning Queen of Advanced Skills courses, who has offered her 'Self-Publishing for ELT Professionals' a record eight editions, guiding over 100 teachers in everything one needs to know to publish a book online or for print sales.

Almost 900 words into this chapter and I cannot write another word without telling you all the one singular secret to iTDi's survival, our reputation, and our continued GRIT and RESILIENCE as a social enterprise.

She is Barbara (Hoskins) Sakamoto, an internationally acclaimed team member of the super successful Oxford University Press young learners series *Let's Go*.[3] Barb joined iTDi as a director just minutes after we began to get organized and has grown to become the behind-the-scenes de facto leader of our organization.

It is safe to say that anyone who has dealt with iTDi in the past 12 years has had helpful and detailed interactions with Barb. She is the G.O.A.T. supporter of EFL teachers worldwide. I could tell you stories that would bring a tear to your eye but would embarrass Barb because her generosity and philanthropy remain a private commitment she has to give back to her teaching community.

The endless hours she puts into iTDi have guaranteed her a special place in EFL heaven someday. When we lost our financial director, Barb took

---

3.  Hoskins Sakamoto, B. (2018). *Let's go, 5th edition* [Textbook series]. Oxford University Press.

over. When we lost our website guru, Barb began a new career in IT. When we began publishing, the little graphic designer dying to get out and spread her wings appeared and got to work. Barb simply knows how to get things done!

*"Barbara Sakamoto is quite simply the heart and soul of iTDi."*

Without her, iTDi would be a distant memory. Her commitment to excellence and community is beyond description. I first met her through her blog, Teaching Village, which has a byline I've heard her say countless times,

*"We're better when we work together."*

As for iTDi these days, life carries on, people's priorities change, and subsequently, our original team of 6 directors has been reduced to just Barbara Sakamoto and myself (with Scott Thornbury still on call as Academic Director).

We also have Philip Shigeo Brown as the Director of our *TESOL Certificate* and *Chief of Social Media*. Phil has become one of the greatest mentors I've ever met. If you ever want to hear some incredible testimonials, search *What do YOU want out of TESOL/TEFL Certificate?* on YouTube.[4]

Another innovative course began in 2021 called *Great Minds in Language Education* (GMILE). The premise of the course was to study a seminal book together. Again, we not only read important books, but we got some very experienced mentors to lead these courses including Scott Thornbury, Kevin Ryan, Steven Herder, and Penny Ur.

As our community grew, teachers gained valuable experiences and increased their confidence, which led to another opportunity to support

---

4.  https://shorturl.at/zV3Rn

teachers. In 2017, we published *Small Changes in Teaching Big Results in Learning* by John Fanselow. Then we got serious and added iTDi Publishing to our website. Since then, we have published *101 EFL Activities for Teaching University Students* (2022) by Hall Houston and *Re-Envisioning EFL Education in Asia* (2023), edited by Theron Muller, John Adamson, myself, and Philip Shigeo Brown.

And this brings us to our current book project, *Dogme in Practice*. It is a testament to iTDi that our call for submissions, in collaboration with Scott Thornbury and Luke Meddings, received a large number of manuscripts from teachers in 30 different countries. This book will share nearly 60 teacher reflections on using Dogme ELT in their classrooms. It is bound to be an invaluable source of ideas and inspiration for many teachers.

Personally speaking, Dogme gave me license to riff (judiciously and with intention) in the classroom. My own contribution to the *Dogme in Practice* book is based on a blog post I wrote in 2009 called *Spontaneous Learning Opportunity Windows* (S.L.O.W. moments), where I realized that the more I allowed myself to see these little gems, the more they appeared. Reading Scott's approach to teaching opened my mind to discovering S.L.O.W. moments in my own teaching journey.

Scott Thornbury and Luke Meddings created the Dogme approach to teaching, and like so many other teachers have told me, it has given form and meaning to what many of us recognize as our best teaching moments in the classroom.

We knew when magic was happening with our students, but we just didn't know what to call it at the time. Thank you, Scott and Luke, for all you have contributed to the Dogme ELT movement.

Steven Herder
Co-Founder
International Teacher Development Institute

# THE WRAP-UP
## LUKE MEDDINGS & SCOTT THORNBURY

Our introduction to this book quoted a question we know well from training contexts: 'What is a Dogme lesson actually like?' This question can reflect uncertainty about what the approach looks like in practice, before a teacher has tried it out. Another query we often encounter, and one that reflects lingering uncertainty *after* trying it out, is this: 'Was that lesson really Dogme?' We found ourselves asking the same question as we read teacher submissions from around the world for this book.

We didn't use a checklist to decide which were most suitable. But we didn't just go on instinct either. Like teachers trying out the approach, we were able to refer back to the three principles outlined in *Teaching Unplugged* for orientation. That allowed us to split the single yes/no question around authenticity – 'Is it Dogme?' – into three more prag-matic, open questions:

- To what extent is the lesson conversation-driven?
- To what extent is it materials-light?
- To what extent is there a focus on emergent language?

Revisiting Dogme through the lens of other people's teaching gave us the chance to reflect further on these principles, and on the nature of the approach they help to define.

## Three Principles

From the start, and as it developed organically from online teacher conversation, Dogme ELT embraced the non-linearity of attention and language needs: what are students interested in right now, and what language do they need to talk about it?

Embracing this, we chose not to offer teachers a set of step-by-step instructions or sequential 'how to' guide in *Teaching Unplugged*. Instead, we used our three principles to mark out a space in which teachers could experiment and grow – the kind of experimentation and growth encountered in this book.

We articulated these principles carefully, to avoid being overly prescriptive. Thus lessons are conversation-*driven*, not 'conversation only'; they are materials-*light*, not 'materials-free'; and they are *focused on* emergent language, not 'restricted' to it.

If we were framing the same principles now, we might define the first as 'interaction-driven': after all, as noted in the introduction, conversation has been transformed by messaging platforms – WhatsApp was launched just a few weeks before *Teaching Unplugged*, in early 2009.

Today's conversation is not just made up of words spoken face-to-face and in real-time: it is fingertip text, it is emoji, it is image, audio, and video. This multimodal interaction is another way to communicate our thoughts, feelings, and interests to one another. And there still isn't much room for that in lessons overcrowded with digital content, pre-determined language exponents, and preset learning outcomes.

It's important to remember that the three principles create the conditions for Dogme in combination, not in isolation.

After all, one could use a very short text to introduce and exemplify a pre-determined set of language exponents: this is an activity that would be materials-light, but it wouldn't be driven by conversation or focused on emergent language.

One could allow a conversation to develop spontaneously, but avoid drawing attention to form: this part of the lesson would be conversation-driven, but opportunities to focus on emergent language would be missed. In other words, the three principles need to work in harmony with each other.

**The Nature of the Approach**

Is it a strength, or a weakness, that Dogme isn't a 10-point plan, a process to follow?

To some, the variety of settings described in these accounts might indicate strength – a kind of plasticity in the framework approach which means it can be applied in all sorts of contexts, countries, class types, and so on.

To others, that malleable quality might suggest something shapeless and indefinable.

But Dogme is by definition a responsive approach to teaching. Because the conditions for its use differ, so will the precise nature of the response. This non-doctrinaire, tensile quality is key to its adaptability in context.

It is of course possible to stretch it too far: then the principles start to fray, and the lesson stops resonating with the overall approach. We encountered some examples of this as we read through the accounts.

### Conversation-Rich – The Importance of Flow

Accounts of lessons based on the *Silent Way* – often proceeding rather slowly, and under close teacher control – didn't fit the remit of the book, or reflect the more fluid, collaborative style of Dogme.

One benefit of interaction-rich lesson phases is to prepare students for the free flow of English outside the classroom. The teacher doesn't give up control, but instead becomes a participant and facilitator, helping to draw less talkative students into the conversation, and so on. This role is at odds with the self-effacing, even robotic, nature of the teacher in some so-called humanistic methodologies, such as the Silent Way or Community Language Learning.

### Materials-Light – Making Room for the Learners

Reducing the amount of pre-prepared materials doesn't just mean published content, physical or digital. It also relates to teacher-generated material – the kind of material typically compiled in a personal materials bank. But this can be as out of date as the coursebook. And we should be wary of filling the space vacated by coursebook content with our own passion projects.

There is room for sharing things we care about, in small amounts, but the aim should be to model a learning space in which students can do the same. Dogme decentres the teacher along with the materials, leaving the students at the heart of things.

### Emergent Language – Watch Out for 'Grammar Gravity'

While language emerging from classroom interaction is unpredictable, it also generates plenty of language that relates naturally to the syllabus – words and forms that have already been 'covered', or soon will be. Drawing parallels with the syllabus is sensible and helpful, but this is not the only reason to focus on emergent language.

Coursebook materials are designed to exemplify items from the grammar syllabus, and this helps shape our attention from our initial training on. So it's not surprising if we pick up on grammar exponents like verb forms, even when they may not be the most relevant language to address in the moment.

This can happen almost unconsciously, even if we are trying to do something different. 'A conditional,' we say to ourselves, 'Now I can really get to work!' It's as if a focus on grammar, rather than the wider field of language being produced, and its expressive potential, validates our practice. This phenomenon might be termed 'grammar gravity': it pulls classroom interaction away from words and meaning and towards form for its own sake. Of course, it may be helpful to model that conditional, but we need to be aware of the pull of grammar gravity, think twice, and keep an open mind. Lexis, intonation, and register can be just as important in the moment.

Questions like this can resolve themselves over time when teachers reflect deeply on their practice. We always get a second chance in the classroom, and we can refine our work as we go along. But we typically teach alone, so it can also be useful to watch other teachers at work – observing colleagues, and inviting them to observe us. Reading accounts of other teachers' practice, as shared in this book, can also provide inspiration.

**Dogme in the Real World**

As noted above, Dogme focuses on what students are interested in right now, the language they are already using to express it, and the help they need to do this more effectively.

To be alive to these possibilities requires us to be flexible and spontaneous. It demands a pedagogy that is dynamic, not linear. And this represents a challenge in most teaching contexts. 'Is there time to set the plan aside?', we wonder. 'And how do I get back on track if I do?'

Even if we feel an instinctive sympathy with the idea of unplugging, we feel the pressure of the exam-focused curriculum. Often expressed as a local or national concern ('We have so much testing here'), this is better understood as an international issue.

Test-focused education is top-down and delivery-led – however sensitively managed by teachers, it serves a system and is authoritarian at heart. Dogme in contrast is bottom-up, needs-led, and fundamentally collaborative. It's part of a different, more progressive educational tradition.

So what gives? We could pretend the test-driven orthodoxy doesn't exist and strike out alone, but that won't get our students (or us) very far.

We could give up and say it's impossible to find space for more organic classroom practice, but that won't get our students very far either! The most compelling accounts in this book are driven not by an abstract desire to experiment, but by an urgent need to find new ways to motivate and empower the students. Think of the Egyptian children leaping at the chance to use all the English at their disposal (Chapter 8, *An Off-Grid Lesson Lights Up the Room*), or the Polish teenagers worn out by test prep who wind up buzzing with ideas about how things could be changed (Chapter 56, *Teaching Away From the Test*), or the stand-by teacher in Vietnam looking for ways to engage a class of 45 teens at short notice (Chapter 35, *An "On-the-Spot" Lesson*).

This book confirms that Dogme is more than a nice idea – it's a practical solution to a real-world problem. When teachers open up their lessons to the learners, it's to address areas like motivation, relevance, and real-world usefulness that aren't always served, and indeed are sometimes undermined, by the coursebook-based curriculum.

If Dogme is a practical solution to a real-world problem, we need to think beyond 'moments' in the classroom, or 'experimental practice' on training courses, and consider how it can be applied more consistently within the prevailing orthodoxy.

To do this, Dogme needs to be in dialogue with the orthodoxy: how can we foster responsive, student-led teaching on initial training courses? We need to be in dialogue with our colleagues: why is this a viable alternative that motivates us as well as our students? And, as reflective practitioners, we need to be in dialogue with ourselves. Dogme becomes an option when teachers ask meaningful questions of their own work: 'How can we do this better? How can I be more responsive to my students' needs?'

This brings us back to Dogme as a space for experimentation and growth: there are guidelines, but there's no one-size-fits-all. We were struck by the number of contributors who use borrowed or self-derived rubrics to help anchor and orientate their Dogme practice – see Chapters 6 (Clayton), 8 (Dajani), 21 (Hasper), 42 (Roland), and 53 (Tsateri). If our three principles also constitute a rubric, it's not the only one.

Reflection is central to an approach focused on the students and their context, as the accounts in this book amply demonstrate. There's plenty of room for experiment, individual strategies, and context-based solutions in the Dogme space.

# AUTHOR BIOS

**Bruno Albuquerque**
bruno.albuquerque.elt@gmail.com

ELT professional who works as a teacher and teacher educator, materials writer and editor, writer, and speaker. Holds the ECPE, CELTA, DELTA, and TTT, and he is currently taking an MA in ELT with the University of Chichester with a focus on teacher education and assessment.

*1: Scaffolding the Under-30 Bucket List*
Brazil | Adults | A1

**Zarafshan, Syeda Aslam**
aslamzarafshan@gmail.com

I am a dynamic ESL/EAP instructor and teacher trainer. I taught at the American University in Cairo and King Abdulaziz University's English Language Institute in Jeddah. I specialize in creating inclusive curricula that resonate with multicultural audiences, fostering academic success, and managing diverse teaching styles. Currently, I am pursuing an MEd in Second Language Education at the University of Ottawa.

*2: A Rainy Day in Jeddah*
Saudi Arabia | Adults | A1 – A2

**Brad Barker**

brad_barker_10@hotmail.com

Brad Barker teaches at the Center for Foreign Language Education and Research (FLER) at Rikkyo University in Tokyo, Japan. His main research interests are spontaneity and improvisation in the language classroom, Dogme ELT, emergent language, and the negotiated syllabus.

*3: Teeth*
Japan | Adults | B1 – C2

**Peter Brereton**

pbrereton@icu.ac.jp

Peter Brereton is an English for Liberal Arts Instructor at International Christian University in Tokyo and a freelance teacher trainer. He has been involved in English language teaching since 2005 and has worked in a range of teaching contexts in France, Spain, Australia, Ireland, and, for the past decade, Japan.

*4: Dogme in Critical Thinking: Working with Emergent Beliefs*
Japan | Adults | B1 – B2

**Alexandra Jane Burke**

alexburke.barrierfreelearning@gmail.com

Alexandra Burke teaches English at several universities in Japan. She is one of the editors of *Barrier Free Instruction in Japan: Recommendations for Teachers at All Levels of Schooling* (Candlin & Mynard ePublishing 2024). Burke received the 2024 JALT mid-career scholar award (research). Her goal is that all students will feel welcome in education.

*5: Getting Students Into the Zone*
Japan | Adults | B1

**Jamie Clayton**
jamie.clayton@rmit.edu.vn

Jamie Clayton is a Senior Educator at RMIT Vietnam. He has taught English since 2011, in Spain, England, and predominantly in Saigon. These days he is primarily involved in developing language assessments, but still very much enjoys teaching.

*6: A Love Story*
Vietnam | Adults | A2 – B2

**Fernanda Cwiertnia**
fernanda.englishteacher.br@gmail.com

Fernanda is a freelance English teacher from Brazil, holding both the Cambridge C2 Proficiency and CELTA certificates. Passionate about language development, she has been guiding students and educators worldwide since 2012, with a focus on language awareness, writing refinement, and meaningful preparation for Cambridge exams (C1 and C2 levels).

*7: Grammar at the Point of Need for Exam Preparation*
Brazil | Adults | C1 – C2

**Hassan Dajani**
dajanihn@gmail.com

My life has been always blessed and fueled by an unwavering passion for continuous learning. During college, I tutored Calculus to first and second-year engineering students, driven by a keen desire to elevate underrepresented individuals to a higher level of expertise.

*8: An Off-Grid Lesson Lights Up the Room*
Egypt | Young Learners | A1

**María José Dearmas**

mdearmas467@gmail.com

María José Dearmas has been an ELT teacher for 20 years. She has recently obtained her DELTA. Her professional interest is developing lessons where emergent language is tackled right on the spot, and where differentiated instruction and active learning are fully visible.

**Jacqueline Douglas**

jacquelinetheteacher@hotmail.com

Jacqueline Douglas is a freelance teacher and trainer with 25 years of experience on five continents. She's a materials writer, a Cambridge CELTA and DELTA tutor, and a regular speaker at conferences including IATEFL. When not in the classroom, she enjoys life in her South Cambridgeshire village.

**Jeremiah Dutch**

jeremiahdutch@gmail.com

Originally from the US state of New Hampshire, Jeremiah Dutch has lived in Japan for over 25 years. Currently, he teaches at Rikkyo University in Tokyo and lives in Yokohama with his wife and two daughters. He enjoys reading, writing, running, and following baseball.

**Jenny Galligan**

galliganjenny@gmail.com

Jenny has been teaching for 8 years in the south of Spain. A teacher and DOS, she is particularly interested in the confines of the language classroom within a traditional language school and how these boundaries can be manipulated and exploited in order to deliver learner-centered classes.

**Dylan Gates**

britishenglishcoach@gmail.com

Dylan Gates is a teacher educator, business English trainer, and Dogme advocate. He's interested in using an 'unplugged' approach with adult professionals as he feels they benefit more from participating in instructional conversations than attending teacher-led lessons. When he trains teachers, he always reminds them that 'learners are the best resource'.

**Paolo Ghidini**

paologhidini84@gmail.com

A late learner of English (well into adulthood, through traveling), I have been teaching in contexts as diverse as Kazakhstan, Tunisia, and currently Sri Lanka. I am an avid reader of everything that advocates for progressive education and believe that teachers can contribute to making the world a better place.

**Maria Glazunova**

mariaglazunova.english@gmail.com

Maria Glazunova is a Cambridge-certified ESL teacher, author, and speaker from Ukraine. She has been teaching for 12+ years. After online Dogme training with Scott Thornbury, she now helps tech professionals build confidence with advanced English communication skills.

**Carol Goodey**

carol.goodey@glasgow.ac.uk

Carol started in ELT in 2006 as an Adult Literacies and ESOL Worker in Scotland. She has also worked in more formal ELT contexts. She has an MSc in TESOL from the University of Stirling and an EdD from the University of Glasgow, where she now works as an Associate Tutor.

**Viltė Gridasova-Rusevičienė**

info@kalbaspalva.lt

MA English Language and Education, Cambridge DELTA. Secondary/business college language teacher. Language/Public Speaking teacher (Lithuanian Academy of Music and Theatre, since 2015), corporate trainer since 2000. Lives in Vilnius, Lithuania. A passionate learner, teacher, and painter. Her "Telling Stories with Watercolour" workshops are about to appear.

**Nick Hamilton**

Nick Hamilton works as a teacher and teacher trainer at International House London. When he's not working, he practices Wing Chun and Tai Chi, enjoys reading and playing guitar, and walks in the countryside of West Somerset where he comes from originally.

20: *A Personal Anecdote*
UK | Adults | A2 – C1

**Anna Hasper**
anna@teachertrain.org

Anna is an experienced teacher and trainer. She worked in ELT in New Zealand and Australia before moving to the Middle East. She is a CELTA tutor and assessor and has written various teacher development courses. She is passionate about anything related to IELTS and making better learning happen.

21: *Strategising for IELTS*
New Zealand | Adults | B1 – B2

**Steven Herder**
steven.herder@gmail.com

Steven Herder is a professor at Kyoto Notre Dame Women's University in Japan. He has been teaching EFL since 1989 and continues to enjoy spending time with young people. From 2025, he teaches about women and leadership in a Women's Career Development program.He shares his teaching philosophy and research at https://jarinefl.word press.com

22: *Windows Into Interactive Teaching*
Japan | Teens | A1 – B1

**Peter Holly**

pdholly@gmail.com

Peter Holly has taught, trained, and managed overseas all his life since leaving university. He has had full-time assignments in Sudan, Hungary, Bahrain, and the UAE – working with the British Council, Ministries of Education, and several ELT publishers. Now ELT freelancing in Hungary, he has joined the Green Action ELT steering committee.

23: *Sustainable ELT*
Hungary | Adults | A2 – C2

**Jancileidi Hübner**

jancihubner@gmail.com

Jancileidi Hübner is a Brazilian teacher and teacher educator. She holds a Master of Linguistic Studies and has taught English in a variety of contexts for around 22 years. Her interests are focused on the development of pre-service and in-service English teachers and the uses of technology in ELT.

24: *Magicking Grammar Out of Student Talk*
Brazil | Teens | B2 – C1

**Ruth Iida**

ruthiep43@gmail.com

Originally from a small New England town in the U.S., I'm now a long-time private English language school owner in the countryside of Japan. My MS in TESOL is from Temple University, Tokyo. Although I enjoy language learners of all ages, my special passion is for teaching children.

25: *Circle Time*
Japan | Young learners & Teens | A1 – B2

**Henry Jones**

Originally from the UK, I've been living in Colombia since 2015. I've taught English in a variety of contexts but now I mostly teach IELTS preparation online.

*26: Talking Through Tricky Times*
Colombia | Adults | B2

**Dani Kabbani**
dani.kabbani@ihlondon.com

I've spent just over a decade teaching English. Initially, I taught at private language schools and corporate settings in Indonesia. After gaining my Delta certification in 2020, I've been working at IH London where I've learnt an invaluable amount from a team of passionate and experienced teachers in a collaborative atmosphere where innovative ideas are shared and there is a focus on learner-centric approaches.

*27: A Harry Potter Moment*
UK | Adults | B2

**Elena Kapshutar**
elena.kapshutar@gmail.com

Cambridge Delta-qualified teacher of English, German, and French with 15+ years of experience, CELTA and Delta M1, M3 trainer, PhD, speaking and writing examiner for Cambridge A2-C2, and published language assessment writer and editor.

*28: A Teacher Training Lens on Dogme*
Russia | Adults | C1 – C2

### Khanh-Duc Kuttig

Khanh-Duc Kuttig, a doctoral student at the Heidelberg University of Education, has an MA in TESOL and works with pre-service teachers in Germany. She is involved in IATEFL's Teacher Training and Education SIG, TESOL's Teacher Educator Interest Section, and is Chair of TESOL's Professional Development Professional Council.

29: *Teacher Trainees Empowered by Dogme*
Germany | Adults | B2 – C1

### Anastasiia Lollo
anastasiya.lollo@gmail.com

I worked in Russia for over 15 years, teaching English in different settings and providing teacher training. Two years ago, my family moved to Serbia, and I transitioned to freelancing. Now, I specialize in teaching English for Specific Purposes, particularly in IT and finance, and offer consultations to fellow educators.

30: *Collaborative Puzzle Solving*
Russia | Adults | B1

### Clariana Lucas
clarianalucas@gmail.com

With almost 20 years of experience, Clariana's passion for language learning has taken her from Brazil to Italy. Inspired by Paulo Freire, she finds Dogme the perfect approach for creating engaging classrooms that respect diverse learner backgrounds. She fosters teacher communities, empowering instructors and students as their own best resources.

31: *Finding a New Rhythm*
Italy | Teens | B2 – C1

**Anna Lyons**

I've been an English teacher for five years – working in Spain and the UK. After doing the DELTA course I started working at International House London where I currently teach exam and general English courses. I love helping people learn and learning so much from my students in turn.

32: *Cooking Up an Impromptu Lesson*
UK | Adults | C1

**Liz McFarland**
emcfarlandes@gmail.com

Degree in Linguistics and TESOL and Trinity CertTESOL. Currently doing my DipTESOL at Oxford House, Barcelona; my research is focused on teacher attitudes towards dealing with emergent language, peer collaboration in PD, and developing techniques for dealing with emergent language and teacher listening time.

33: *Plugged In: Music is Magic*
Spain | Adults | A2 – B1

**Stella Muntian**
mrs.stella.muntian@gmail.com

Originally from Ukraine, I have been teaching students of different ages for more than 30 years in a Dogme-like way without realizing it. Over the years, many students have become close friends and even relatives. I earned my CELTA at the IH in London, which made it possible to develop my professional skills. Dogme rocks my world!

34: *My Lovely Neighbours*
UK | Adults | B1

**Phuoc Dieu Hang Nguyen**

hang.nguyen25101989@gmail.com

Hang Nguyen is currently an English teacher at a high school in a small town in Phu Yen, Vietnam. She has worked as a teacher for 8+ years and obtained her master's degree in TESOL at a university in Viet Nam. She is interested in English teaching and learning methods, particularly new methods to involve her students of all levels in English language learning.

**Sandra Guadalupe Ojeda**

ojeda.sandra@uader.edu.ar

Sandra Ojeda holds an M.A. in TEFL and she has specialised in ICT, Teaching Practice, Research, Inclusive Education, and Sexuality Comprehensive Education. She is an educator at Universidad Autónoma de Entre Ríos and I.S.P.I 4020 in Argentina. She is an active member of the ELT community as a writer and presenter.

**Chris Ożóg**

ozog.chris@gmail.com

My three years at International House Costa Rica—a private language school—were among the happiest of my career. I gained invaluable experience, advancing as a CELTA and IHCYLT tutor, IH LAC trainer, and IELTS examiner.

**Sinalie Rithma Perera**

srithmaperera@gmail.com

I'm an educator with a passion for teaching and always looking to add a fun twist to class. Holding a Cambridge CELTA and a BA (Hons.) in English and TESOL from Coventry University, I've embarked on adventurous teaching journeys at the British Council and Avinya Foundation in Sri Lanka.

*38: Building Blocks with Beginners*
Sri Lanka | Young Adults | Pre-A1 – A1

**Vida Rahpeima**

1996vida@gmail.com

I'm Vida Rahpeima, an English educator with 8 years of experience. I started teaching at 16. I hold a B.A. in English Teaching. Two years ago, I did my CELTA, and I recently passed my Delta Module One with merit, deepening my expertise. I'm passionate about guiding students in language learning journeys.

*39: Next-Level Motivation for Teenagers*
Iran | Teens | B1

**Mahdi Ramezani**

mramezani@isans.ca

Mahdi Ramezani is a university instructor, teacher trainer, and ESL/EAL educator with a keen interest in research areas including SLA, TBLT, and LOA. He designs dynamic lessons to enhance language proficiency and cultural awareness.

*40: Talking Without Limits*
Canada | Adults | B1 – B2

**Débora Rocha**

neirosrocha@gmail.com

Debora Rocha, a Brazilian educator, was educated in Film Production at UCLA and holds a CELTA certification. With a background in language schools, she now thrives as a freelance online teacher, blending her expertise in education and film to create engaging learning experiences. She currently works as a private teacher and educational content creator.

41: *Life Lessons for 1–1*
Brazil | Adults | A2 – B1

**Chris Roland**

chris.roland@gmail.com

Chris Roland is a freelance teacher, trainer, and methodology writer based in Seville, where he has lived, on and off, since 2000. His other teaching posts have included Damascus, Barcelona, and Cádiz. He considers himself a 4x4 all-terrain teacher covering young learners, teenagers and adult classes.

42: *Harnessing the Communication*
Spain | Young learners | A1 – A2

**Valeria Russo**

valeriarussoistruzione@gmail.com

Valeria Russo holds a PhD in English Language. She is an adjunct teacher of English for Tourism Science at the University of Calabria and was an English Instructor in Higher Education for 3 years. She is currently teaching English at Vocational High School for mechanics.

43: *Critical Thinking for Trainee Mechanics*
Italy | Teens | A1 – B1

**Kevin Ryan**

tokyokevin@me.com

Kevin has taught in Chicago, Barcelona, Nanjing, and Tokyo. Recently retired, now "emeritus", he teaches part-time at a large university in Tokyo. Tech, cycling, and learning Japanese continue to challenge him.

**Nadine Saassouh**

nadinesaassouh@gmail.com

I'm a Lebanese EFL teacher, passionate about teaching and learning. Throughout my career, I've taken on various roles, from teaching English to leading curriculum development as Head of the English Department. I successfully defended my M2 thesis, where I studied the impact of Dogme ELT on enhancing 11th graders' speaking efficacy.

**Barbara Sakamoto**

Barbara Hoskins Sakamoto is co-author of the bestselling *Let's Go* series, and course director of the International Teacher Development Institute (www.itdi.pro). She is an English Language Specialist with the U.S. State Department and has conducted teacher training workshops in Asia, Europe, the Americas, and online.

**Maria Sampio**
be.trainer.sampio@gmail.com

Having taught business English for over 17 years, Maria is a Cambridge-certified teacher, coach, and blogger with profound hands-on experience in business. Currently, in Alicante, Spain, she is pursuing her Master's degree at NILE and has successfully completed the Instructional Leadership program at the Harvard Graduate School of Education.

47: *There is No Such Thing as a Bad Question*
Spain | Adults | B2 – C2

**Saeid Sarabi Asl**
s.sarabi.tnb@gmail.com

I am an ESL/EAP teacher and teacher trainer based in Toronto with 16 years of experience. I hold a Master's and Ph.D. in TEFL and have published research papers, but my true passion is conducting action research to help current and prospective teachers enhance their teaching skills.

48: *I Wonder Why...*
Canada | Adults | B2 – C1

**Ally Victoria Shepherd**
allyvictoria.shepherd@yahoo.com

Ally Shepherd is a teacher, trainer, and researcher with a PhD in Education Policy from the University of Wisconsin-Madison, USA. She is from the North of England but is often found elsewhere having taught in Europe, S.E. Asia, and North America.

49: *Teaching With the Students*
UK | Adults | B1 – C2

**Sam Shepherd**

smshphrd@gmail.com

Sam Shepherd is an ESOL teacher working in Bradford in the UK, teaching students who have come to live permanently in the UK. At the time of writing, he is finishing a PhD looking at an emergent, responsive curriculum in ESOL on principles drawn from Dogme and from participatory pedagogy.

50: *Mediating Emergent Language with Beginners*
UK | Adults | A1

**Bruno Sousa**

bgsousa87@hotmail.com

Bruno Sousa is a teacher and teacher trainer based in Brazil. He has worked in EFL since 2010. He holds the Delta, CELTA, Train the Trainer, TKT CLIL, and CPE qualifications. His interests, currently, revolve around bi/multilingualism, ideology in ELT, and teacher training.

51: *Dogme as an Unwinding Tool*
Brazil | Teens | B2

**Charlie Taylor**

15cgt1@queensu.ca

Charlie Taylor is currently a graduate student in the English and American Studies department at the University of Graz. He taught English at high schools and universities in Taiwan for seven years, and he has published over thirty articles on second language acquisition and English teaching.

52: *A School Magazine*
Taiwan | Teens | B2 – C1

**Rachel Tsateri**

racheltsateri.elt@gmail.com

Rachel is a freelance teacher, teacher educator, and ELT blogger from Athens, Greece. You might know her from her blog, *The TEFL Zone*. She has taught students of over 50 nationalities, in 6 countries and online. She is currently an assistant tutor on DELTA Module 2 courses.

*53: A Trip to Venice*
Greece | Adults | B2 – C1

**Kata Ujvarosi**

uklanguage@yahoo.com

Kata Ujvarosi (DELTA, IH TT, BA in Education, IH CAM, CELTA) is a freelance EFL teacher and teacher trainer collaborating with learners and schools globally, including IH Budapest. She is particularly interested in helping learners communicate in an international context while fostering positive self-efficacy to facilitate learning and make teaching programmes more learner-centered.

*54: A Weekend in "Destination Unknown"*
Italy | Adults | B1

**Zainab Undre**

zainab.undre@ihlondon.com

I am currently in my first year of teaching as an English language teacher at International House London and a former primary school teacher.

*55: Daring to Go With the Flow*
UK | Adults | B1

**Christopher Walker**

closelyobserved@gmail.com

Christopher Walker is the Director of Studies at International House Bielsko-Biala, where he has taught for 15 years. Though now focused on administration, he still enjoys classroom teaching. Outside of work, he writes fiction and teaching-related nonfiction.

**Marina Yesipenko**

yoroshiimm@gmail.com

Marina Yesipenko holds an MA in TESOL and Applied Linguistics, along with DELTA, IHCYLT, CELTA, and NILE certifications. A teacher and trainer for nearly 20 years, her interests include linguistics, teaching methodology, language acquisition, cognitive science, social semiotics, and multimodality.

**Roslyn Young**

roslyn.young@orange.fr

Roslyn Young has over 50 years of experience teaching foreign languages. She taught English and sometimes French at the Centre de Linguistique Appliquée in Besançon, France. Together with other members of that team, she has been using the approach she describes for intermediate and advanced students for many years.

# PRODUCTION TEAM

**Scott Thornbury** – Executive Editor, Author, Chapter Commentary
**Luke Meddings** – Executive Editor, Author, Chapter Commentary
**Steven Herder** – Project Coordinator, Chapter Editor, Author
**Barbara Sakamoto** – Project Manager, Cover Design, Author
**Jerry Talandis Jr.** – Layout Editor, Vellum Specialist
**Cynthia Quinn** – Chapter Editor

Printed in Great Britain
by Amazon

60484902R00188